Kunstsammlungen Chemnitz **MUSEUM GUNZENHAUSER**

Kunstsammlungen Chemnitz

Prestel Museum Guide

MUSEUM GUNZENHAUSER

PRESTEL
Munich · Berlin · London · New York

ACKNOWLEDGEMENTS

envia Mitteldeutsche Energie AG

E.ON – Ruhrgas AG

Erdgas Südsachsen GmbH

Stadtwerke Chemnitz AG

Thüga AG

Yvonne Wagner

Dr Johannes Krimphove

Freistaat Sachsen

Stadt Chemnitz

THE CITY AND THE COLLECTOR

Chemnitz, the city of art, is prosperous once more. Over the years, this metropolis of industry has attracted attention with its artistic treasures and created a profile of its own. Temporarily known as Karl-Marx-Stadt, Chemnitz has rediscovered itself: its citizens gather at the exhibition openings of the Kunstsammlungen Chemnitz, at the opera, at Kulturkaufhaus Tietz, at the Henry van de Velde Museum and, in future, at the Museum Gunzenhauser. The civic pride of the city is evident in its museums.

THE GROWTH OF A CITY OF ART

The Chemnitz citizens' keen interest in art has its origin in their business acumen, which came to the fore in the nineteenth century. Today Chemnitz still owns one of the greatest German collections of textiles, in which artistic expression and both economic and technological proficiency have formed a close connection in an area characteristic of the recent history of the city. It is this link between economic activity and artistic interest that characterises the city.

Chemnitz is admittedly not a princely seat. It was not the rulers of the house of Wettin who gave the stimulus to art and culture in the city. Another result of its past is that even today, Chemnitz can claim no cultural institution of note supported by the Free State of Saxony. This will change with the planned extension project for the Chemnitz museum landscape, when, in 2011, the State Museum of Archaeology moves to Chemnitz and opens its portals as the House of Archaeology in the former Schocken department store.

Chemnitz has relied on other kinds of help, and enjoyed these in rich measure. It comes from sources both within and without the city. The museum tradition in Chemnitz goes back to the Kunsthütte, the art society founded in the mid-nineteenth century. With more than 1,100 members, the Friends of the Kunstsammlungen Chemnitz today still represent a significant potential within the community. The revitalisation of the Villa Esche on the Kassberg – to name another example of committed citizen participation – would have been unthinkable without the Chemnitz Van de Velde Society.

This outstanding cultural commitment of the citizens of Chemnitz has attracted attention and aroused admiration far beyond the city, and thus brought supporters onto the scene who are providing a new impetus to Chemnitz as a city of art. It was a momentous occasion when, in 2002, the art collector Hartmut Koch donated the entire graphic work of Wolfgang Mattheuer to the city. As a result, the first comprehensive retrospective was held of the work of this important postwar German artist, who died in 2004. The Museum already owned the second largest collection of the great Chemnitz Expressionist Karl Schmidt-Rottluff. It sounds like a fairy tale when one learns that a Düsseldorf couple,

Gisela and Dr Wolfgang Flügge, who were art collectors, reading about the Kunstsammlungen Chemnitz in an art periodical, donated their valuable collection of modern art to the museum. Karl Otto Götz, an important painter of German *Art Informel* and a leading teacher at the Düsseldorf Academy, whose parents came from Saxony, gave Chemnitz 120 graphic works, a large glass window and a metal relief. Thus, step by step, with many further donated and acquired works of art, the Chemnitz collection of art treasures grew into what it is today.

And now Dr Alfred Gunzenhauser.

CHEMNITZ AS A SHOWCASE OF CLASSICAL MODERNISM

With Gunzenhauser, not only is Chemnitz honoured as a city of art, but his collection exerts its influence throughout the state of Saxony. With important parts of the collection consisting of works by Otto Dix and Conrad Felixmüller, artists are returning to Saxony whose work is closely linked with our state. Together with the further pieces in this collection, the home of Karl Schmidt-Rottluff is now finally becoming the Mecca of Expressionism and Classical Modernism in Germany. The Museum Gunzenhauser is a new highlight of the Chemnitz museum world, but it is perceived as a part of the Kunstsammlungen Chemnitz, not only because of the close connection in personal and organisational terms, but above all because the collections complement each other and, taken together, form a consistent whole.

If one were to describe in somewhat simplified fashion the main thematic focus of the art museums of Saxony, one might say that the Dresden museums, with their Old Masters and impressive works from the Romantic period, are our 'documentation centre of the history of painting', extending far back into the past; Leipzig represents contemporary art; and Chemnitz is the showcase of Classical Modernism. Chemnitz is the 'City of Modernism', as the city's marketing slogan has it, for after all, it was here that modern art came into being, on the breeding ground of the scientific and technical modernism of the industrial revolution.

This internal differentiation of the museum landscape of Saxony does not exclude the fact that all the art museums are intent on documentation of the visual arts in all their multiplicity. But it is precisely the historically determined emphases of the various collectors that are valuable to our state. In Saxony we can count ourselves fortunate to have achieved success in depicting the whole range of artistic creativity with such specific focal points.

At the same time, this broad museum landscape reflects the passionate interest that Saxony has brought to art from time immemorial. Perhaps the main regional focus corresponds to some extent to the character of each part of the population. While the Wettin rulers were concerned with grandiose art that would surpass all others in competition with the European royal courts, the citizens of Leipzig and Chemnitz preferred an art that had some connection with their lives, that was realistic rather than escapist. And so it was that enthusiastic art collectors like Elector Friedrich August II and Alfred Gunzenhauser shaped the museum landscape of Saxony, in similar and yet fundamentally different ways.

CAN THE COLLECTOR REPLACE THE STATE?

As these two Saxon examples show, art has always inspired a passion for collecting. At first it was the princes who, not infrequently out of a love of display, but often out of pure passion, became collectors of art. Today it is the private collectors who, since the days of Wilhelm von Humboldt, have helped modern art towards its breakthrough. For these friends of art, collecting does not only mean personal preoccupation with the work of art; rather, the private collection should also become part of public and cultural life, in accordance with the motto "Museum usui publico patens" which is written over the entrance to the Japanese Palace in Dresden.

Collectors know how to value art, and at the same time they are aware that art enjoys high status in the culture of the society in which they live. 'Collecting art is a passion which cannot be entirely explained,' says the noted German art collector Frieder Burda, evaluating the enthusiasm that he has recently expressed in a museum open to the public. I believe that every genuine art collector manifests this passion, which is directed not just at oneself, but also always at the external influence of art.

Alfred Gunzenhauser too possesses this passion – and a particular kind of eccentricity which is sometimes found in art collectors, and is part of their charm. This is wonderfully described by his friend, the museum director Herwig Guratzsch, in a catalogue entry for the first presentation of the Gunzenhauser Collection in Leipzig in 1998. Here Herwig Guratzsch allows the gallery owner Gunzenhauser to meet the collector Gunzenhauser, and brings to life the creation of the collection out of this almost schizophrenic situation.

Such a passion for art is not to be expected on the part of the state. Admittedly the constitution of Saxony elevates the conservation and support of culture to a national objective, and this for good reasons. Art is culture, and culture, together with economic competence, is the life-blood of a society. But the thought of a state that develops passions with reference to art is ominous – as we have learnt at the latest since the National Socialists persecuted modern art as 'degenerate'.

But art is also unthinkable without the state. The collector cannot always achieve what he wants in isolation. Here the state can help. Not out of compassion, not out of social need, but in order to supplement the work of the collector and thus to fulfil its public duty. But it is not only our constitution, but also our common sense that makes the conservation and support of culture into a public duty. This is why the state must help the art collector.

A FUNCTIONAL ALLIANCE FOR THE GOOD OF ALL

We support public museums as places of an 'ethics of remembrance' and the preservation of our cultural traditions, as places of culture and the human characterisation of posterity. But it is not the state alone that should decide what is brought into these museums. We do not need state art, any more than state supervision of culture. For this reason I believe it to be right to restrain the state and its museums from the active collection of art. Nevertheless they should open themselves up to the private collector, the art collector who takes part with passion and expertise in current developments in the art world, and helps to decide what later ends up being preserved in the museums.
So I see a significant difference between art museums and galleries of contemporary art. Our contemporary museums must open themselves up to collectors for the care of current art, and profit from them. As long as there are art collectors who do justice to their role, the museums will open their exhibition galleries to them, for the benefit of all those interested in art.

This relationship in the best sense has now been established and put into motion between the private collector Gunzenhauser and Chemnitz, the city of art. I congratulate the city of Chemnitz and its citizens, I congratulate the art lovers of the Free State of Saxony, and I thank the art collector Alfred Gunzenhauser and say to him: You have rendered a great service to the culture of our state.

Georg Milbradt
Prime Minister of the Free State of Saxony

A SUITABLE HISTORIC BUILDING

Chemnitz is one of the liveliest centres of art and culture among Germany's industrial cities. The imposing Wilhelmine museum building on Theaterplatz, which today houses the Kunstsammlungen Chemnitz, was opened in 1909. But this 'Manchester of Saxony' has also repeatedly attracted attention in the realm of avant-garde culture. The Norwegian Edvard Munch, for example, by no means an established artist at the time, lived and worked here in 1905. The weeks he spent in Chemnitz at the invitation of Herbert Esche, an outstanding entrepreneur, were to prove of great consequence for art history. After costly refurbishment the villa built for the textile industrialist and connoisseur by Henry van de Velde was re-opened to the public several years ago.

The former Chemnitz Sparkasse bank building is situated on Falkeplatz, halfway between the Villa Esche and Theaterplatz. It was built in 1930 in the style of the New Objectivity to designs by the chief city architect, Fred Otto. Since 2005 its elegant travertine façade, the curved glass of the entrance and stairwell, and the well-lit interior spaces have been restored according to historical preservation principles with the help of the Ostdeutsche Sparkassenstiftung im Freistaat Sachsen (East German Savings Bank Foundation in the Free State of Saxony).

The Ostdeutscher Sparkassenverband (East German Savings Bank Association), Ostdeutsche Sparkassenstiftung (East German Savings Bank Foundation) and Sparkasse Chemnitz (Chemnitz Savings Bank) are particularly proud of the fact that the historic Chemnitz bank building is to house in future the Gunzenhauser Collection. Over the past four decades Dr Alfred Gunzenhauser has assembled one of the most important private collections, primarily of the art of German Expressionism. Among the more than 2,400 works can be found important paintings by artists of the *Brücke* group, including Karl Schmidt-Rottluff, who was born near Chemnitz, and of the *Blauer Reiter* group, as well as works by Otto Dix, Conrad Felixmüller, Willi Baumeister and Gerhard Altenbourg.

The generosity of Dr Alfred Gunzenhauser in allowing his treasures to be permanently displayed in Chemnitz will permit the city to reclaim its position as an important site of Classical Modernism in Germany. It is a proud tradition which was interrupted by the 'Degenerate Art' operation of 1937. The Gunzenhauser Collection in Chemnitz promises not only an encounter with an exquisite art collection in a historically appropriate building. This opening of a new art museum in East Germany is the most important for many years; it is also a tribute to the exemplary work of the Kunstsammlungen Chemnitz under their General Director Ingrid Mössinger, which has already attracted international attention. And, of course, it is a tribute to the lively art scene of a city which never faltered even during the days of the German Democratic Republic,

thanks to the nationally respected gallery "oben" and the *Clara Mosch* artists' group.
The catalogue presents the exceptional collection of an exceptional collector, which will now be on permanent display in an exceptional city. It documents an important chapter of international art history, to which an essential contribution has been made in Chemnitz and Saxony.

Claus Friedrich Holtmann
Chairman of the Board
Ostdeutsche Sparkassenstiftung
Executive President
Ostdeutscher Sparkassenverband

Reiner Grimm
Chairman of the Board
Sparkasse Chemnitz

A NEW MUSEUM FOR CHEMNITZ

Chemnitz is the third largest city in the new German Länder. Among its chief attractions is one of the most extensive historical districts in Europe to have been preserved until the present day. It dates back to the Gründerzeit, the period of German industrial expansion in the early 1870s, and the Jugendstil (Art Nouveau) period, recalling an era in the city's history that was marked by successful enterprise and flourishing culture. Chemnitz's period architecture is a link to that great past. Energy and a passion for innovation have long been outstanding characteristics of the city, its economy and its citizens. They have been successfully reborn in the past decade in the city's remarkable structural transformation.

Since the 1990s, the Kunstsammlungen Chemnitz have worked together with other cultural institutions to establish the public perception of the city as a place of art and culture. In the tradition of the patronage of wealthy local industrialists in the first half of the twentieth century, the aim now is to present Chemnitz as a city of Modernism, where artists of international renown such as Edvard Munch, and *Brücke* members Karl Schmidt-Rottluff, Ernst Ludwig Kirchner and Erich Heckel, not to mention Max Klinger and Otto Dix, have made their mark. In future, with the help of the important collection of the Munich gallery owner Dr Alfred Gunzenhauser, this venture will gain added weight. When searching for a suitable permanent exhibition space for his collection, Dr Gunzenhauser always considered it important that it should be displayed in a building of its own. Chemnitz was able to provide this in the form of the Sparkasse building by the architect Fred Otto.

After more than seventy years of continuous use as the banking headquarters of the Chemnitzer Sparkasse, the building was converted in the autumn of 2003 for use as an art museum. The exterior of the building, protected since 1995 as a historic monument, was renovated and cleaned in accordance with conservation principles, and the interior was restructured. Of the expert proposals submitted, that of the renowned firm of Staab Architekten Berlin BDA emerged as victor in February 2004. The experienced museum architect Volker Staab rebuilt the former Sparkasse building by the Chemnitz city architect Fred Otto, incorporating sensitive but clear alterations.

For any city, a new museum building is a particular challenge. The success of this enterprise is the result of the co-operation over many years by several participants and the considerable financial effort of private and public sponsors and the local authority. To all, I extend my cordial thanks.

First of all I would like to thank Dr. Alfred Gunzenhauser for agreeing to donate his extensive collection to the city of Chemnitz in the form of an endowment, thus making it accessible to a wider public.

Without the historic Sparkasse building on Falkeplatz and the financial support of the Ostdeutsche Sparkassenstiftung and the Sparkasse Chemnitz, the collector's wish for a dedicated house for his art collection could not have been fulfilled. My cordial thanks go to Claus Friedrich Holtmann, Executive President of the Ostdeutsche Sparkassenverband, Reiner Grimm, Chairman of the Sparkasse Chemnitz, and Friedrich Wilhelm von Rauch, Managing Director of the Ostdeutsche Sparkassenstiftung.

Ingrid Mössinger, who has demonstrated her outstanding ability as General Director of the Kunstsammlungen Chemnitz, will be responsible for the management of the museum in future. I am greatly obliged to her for acting as intermediary between collector and city. My predecessor in the office of Mayor, Dr Peter Seifert, deserves praise for his implementation of this ambitious undertaking.

I am delighted with the result, which represents an architectural highlight of our city to add to the Henry van de Velde Villa and many other protected buildings. My heartfelt thanks go to the architect Volker Staab, to his colleagues, and also to Petra Wesseler, head of the building projects department, and her fellow-workers. I also owe a debt of thanks to Maximilian Müllner, member of the foundation board, for his liaison between the collector, the project manager and the city during the entire building phase.

The city councillors have lent their support and goodwill to one of the most ambitious post-reunification projects in Chemnitz. For this I am very grateful. I hope that many of the city's residents and visitors from near and far will share our pleasure in this fine new building.

Barbara Ludwig
Lord Mayor of the City of Chemnitz

A WONDERFUL HOME

It has truly not been easy for me to part with the pictures in my collection, which I have gathered over the decades and which have been the central focus of my interests for a lifetime. In some cases, I have had to fight for years before actually gaining possession of them. I have literally lived with my artworks. Daily they have looked at me from all available walls, while their numbers increased to the extent that in the end only a fraction of the collection could be displayed. At this point, at the latest, one must ask oneself: sell or donate? Since I am not only a collector, but first and foremost an art lover, bound to my paintings not only by the pride of possession, but above all by my love for them, it was my urgent wish to keep the collection together and to find a suitable place for its display.

For example, I found unbearable the notion that my collection of 290 works by Otto Dix, gathered over a period of decades, might be torn apart. Of all the offers that I received for my collection from museums and cities, Chemnitz was not at first the most obvious choice, but ultimately it was the most appealing. The charming museum director, Ingrid Mössinger, succeeded in her gentle but purposeful manner in convincing me that Chemnitz was the right place and she the right person to care for the collection in the best possible way. Dr Peter Seifert, Mayor of the City of Chemnitz from 1993 to 2006, impressed me with his personal involvement and his interest in my collection. Thanks to the generous support of Carl Friedrich Holtmann, Executive President of the Ostdeutscher Sparkassenverband, as well as of the Chairman of the Sparkasse Chemnitz, Reiner Grimm, it has been possible to convert the Sparkasse bank building of 1930 on the Falkeplatz, which is under a protection order, into an aesthetically attractive museum for my collection. The building and the foundation have been 'married' and they complement each other wonderfully. I am convinced that my works will be seen to their best advantage and presented in the best possible way in these newly created spaces.

Dr Peter Seifert's successor, Barbara Ludwig, has welcomed my collection to Chemnitz with the same interest as her predecessor, which gives me further confidence in the worthy future of my artworks. An excellent curator, Thomas Friedrich, whom in the meantime I have learnt to appreciate highly, has been appointed for the house. My special thanks go to my adviser and friend, Maximilian Müllner, who has selflessly supported me over the years through all the negotiations and in the realisation of the building project.

An important aspect of the happy period of my collecting is the fact that I was able to acquire so many wonderful friends in the process: Willi Baumeister, Gerhard Altenbourg, Karl Fred Dahmen, Bernard Schultze, Horst Antes, Johannes Grützke, Heinz Rabbow, Reiner Wagner, Felix Weinold, Herwig and Gudrun Guratzsch, and Ilse Holzinger, who unfortunately passed away a few months ago – to name but a few.

I am very grateful to a number of people for contributing to this successful project to provide a fitting home for my life's work. This makes the separation a pleasant one – and the thought that in future, as it is hoped, many thousands of people will see the pictures, and experience a little happiness in doing so, is a great source of joy to me.

Dr Alfred Gunzenhauser

KUNSTSAMMLUNGEN CHEMNITZ – MUSEUM GUNZENHAUSER

On the occasion of the exhibition "German Painting of the 20th Century – A Private Collector's View" at the Museum der bildenden Künste in Leipzig in 1998, people wondered about the identity of the mysterious collector who was able to gather paintings from Corinth to Hödicke. As soon as the secret was disclosed, many a museum director's silent longings came to the surface. But it was only when it became clear that such a comprehensive collection would require a building of its own that the unique opportunity arose to acquire one of the most important German collections for Chemnitz. The first visit to the city in broad sunshine by Dr Alfred Gunzenhauser was an auspicious start to my contact with him. It was thus a moment of glory for a museum director when I was entrusted with the care of such precious works of art, and what is more, in a beautiful building specially converted for the purpose.
So I express my warm thanks to Dr Alfred Gunzenhauser for having decided in favour of Chemnitz. In future, he will be able to enjoy his life's work from the apartment installed for him in the museum building.

His path begins on the third floor of the museum, where the work of Otto Dix, born in Gera, is displayed. Here we have the largest Dix collection worldwide in a public museum. Out of the total stock of 290 works, a selection of some 100 paintings, watercolours, gouaches, drawings and prints are to be seen, including a group, little known until now, of early paintings from the period between 1910 and 1914, when Dix was a student at the Königliche Kunstgewerbeschule (Royal College of Applied Arts) in Dresden. Also of importance are the gouaches from the years of the First World War and above all the central works of the 1920s, which depict the society of the Weimar Republic in all its facets. In addition there are little-known landscapes by Otto Dix from the Second World War period, as well as impressive later works. The presentation of the Dix Collection is complemented by selected works by his friend and fellow artist Conrad Felixmüller.
On the second floor, a further important focus of attention is formed by the works of Alexej von Jawlensky. Only Wiesbaden, where Jawlensky lived from 1921, owns a marginally more comprehensive collection than the Museum Gunzenhauser. It is of particular interest for tomorrow's visitors that Jawlensky is represented here by outstanding examples of all the phases of his work, including above all the famous icon-like paintings of his late period. All the works in the collection of Dr Alfred Gunzenhauser have been authenticated by the Alexej von Jawlensky Archive and are listed in the catalogue raisonné of his works.

With 40 paintings by Alexei von Jawlensky and twelve important paintings by Gabriele Münter, the *Blauer Reiter* group is now superbly represented in Chemnitz, while the Kunstsammlungen Chemnitz already possess one of the largest collections in the world of works by Karl Schmidt-Rottluff of the *Brücke* group.

Since the Kunstsammlungen Chemnitz were deprived by the National Socialists of four paintings by Ernst Ludwig Kirchner, the five paintings by Kirchner from the Gunzenhauser collection are particularly highly valued. As was recalled by the exhibition "Ernst Ludwig Kirchner – The German Journey 1925/1926" in Chemnitz in 2007, the artist spent his childhood and youth in the city, and his parents remained in Chemnitz to the end of their days. Thus there is a close connection between the Kirchner family and the city.

As a further enrichment and extension of works by the *Brücke* group of artists in the collection, Karl Schmidt-Rottluff, Erich Heckel and Hermann Max Pechstein are represented here with one painting each. One of the most important German artists of the twentieth century, Max Beckmann, is represented by four paintings. In addition, four fine examples are displayed here of the paintings of Christian Rohlfs, popular with many visitors for their flaming colours.

I am delighted that the Gunzenhauser collection includes paintings by the Dresden-born painter Paula Modersohn-Becker. With Gabriele Münter, she is among the few women artists of her generation to gain worldwide fame. Modersohn-Becker's work was considered 'degenerate' and thus removed from the museums during the period of National Socialism, and I take pride in the fact that in the Gunzenhauser collection we now have the largest stock of Modersohn-Becker paintings in the eastern Länder.

The works of Lovis Corinth are in great demand worldwide, as the Kunstsammlungen Chemnitz on the Theaterplatz have been in a position to appreciate from the number of loan requests for their only Corinth oil painting, a flower still-life. It is all the more gratifying that it is the Gunzenhauser collection that can boast two magnificent pictures of 1916, an important self-portrait and a portrait of the artist's mother-in-law.

On the two lower floors, we are witnesses to Dr Alfred Gunzenhauser's interest not only in Classical Modernism, but also in the classic works of the postwar period. These include as many as 16 paintings by Willi Baumeister. Chemnitz can consider itself fortunate as a result to be the location with the largest Baumeister collection in the eastern Länder. Baumeister's artistic thought influenced countless artists. At the same time his work is part of a global form of expression which created a sensation with its slogan 'Abstraction as a world language'. In addition, for years Willi Baumeister had strong links to the Kunstakademie (Art Academy) in Stuttgart, so that in the case of this artist a pleasing connection is created with the collector's region of origin, Baden-Württemberg.

An invaluable enrichment, from far beyond the region, is supplied by the ten paintings by an artist born in Moscow, but who worked all his life in Paris: Serge Poliakoff. In the context of the wide-ranging Carlfriedrich Claus exhibition of

2005 in the Kunstsammlungen Chemnitz, his bond with Fritz Winter became clear. The two artists were linked by mutual appreciation and exchanged works with each other. It is thus a particular gift that after the losses of his works under the National Socialist regime, Fritz Winter will be represented by eight paintings in the new Museum Gunzenhauser.

Outstanding artists of postwar abstraction are displayed with paintings by Emil Schumacher, Bernard Schultze, Ernst Wilhelm Nay, Fred Thieler, who was born in Königsberg (Kaliningrad), and with pictures by Gerhard Hoehme, from nearby Dessau.

The style of the New Objectivity is demonstrated by artists including Georg Schrimpf and Gustav Wunderwald.

As evidence of the inclination of contemporary artists towards large formats, the former counter-hall of the Sparkasse Chemnitz is transformed into an impressive museum space with monumental paintings by Johannes Grützke, Horst Antes, Karl Horst Hödicke and Rainer Fetting.

At the end of his tour, the donor Dr Alfred Gunzenhauser can look forward to a coffee break in the entrance area of the museum.

My first approaches to the collector go back to 2002. The contact was initiated by Prof. Dr Rainer Beck, who comes from a Stuttgart family of collectors, has taught in Nuremberg and now teaches in Dresden.

I recall with grateful pleasure that it was the then head of the cultural department and present Mayor of Chemnitz, Barbara Ludwig, and also, above all, Dr Peter Seifert, Mayor from 1993 to 2006, who recognised the unique opportunity for Chemnitz and made this ambitious project into their personal goal.

While walking through the city, I was struck by the beautiful former Sparkasse bank building, which seemed positively to be waiting for a new appropriate use. This idea too fell on fruitful ground in an open city with an upper-middle-class past. Apart from the mayors already named, I would therefore like to give especially warm thanks to the following for their generous help over the years, which also made possible the present museum guide: Claus Friedrich Holtmann, Executive President of the Ostdeutscher Sparkassenverband; Reiner Grimm, Chairman of the Sparkasse Chemnitz; and Friedrich Wilhelm von Rauch, Managing Director of the Ostdeutsche Sparkassenstiftung.

The new museum, whose management is the responsibility of the Kunstsammlungen Chemnitz, has been legally designated as a foundation. The board of the foundation consists of the collector and patron Dr Alfred Gunzenhauser; Maximilian Müllner, head of administration at the German Film and Television Academy in Berlin; and the General Director of the Kunstsammlungen Chemnitz. The donor, of course, can never be sufficiently thanked, but Mr Müllner has conducted the running of the foundation and the building process with passion and perseverance in the spirit of the collector, and has thus contributed substantially to the success of the project.

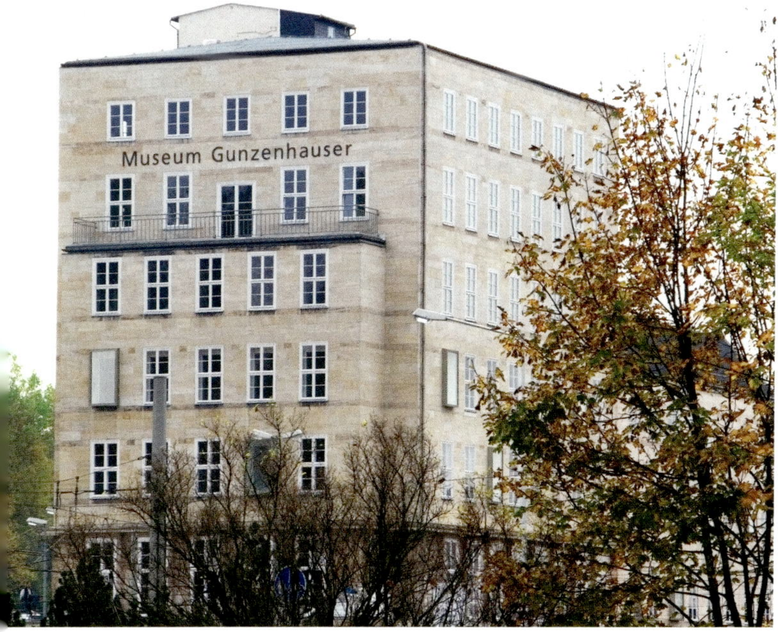

Museum Gunzenhauser, October 2007

I would also like to express warm thanks to the head of the building projects department, Petra Wesseler, who has always been open to all the special issues involved in the conversion of a bank into a museum building.
It was a stroke of luck for the collection to have been able to appoint Thomas Friedrich as the curator in charge of the works of art. He has committed himself to the collection with unparalleled interest, tireless enthusiasm and wide-ranging competence. My special thanks are due to him as well as to all those involved in the setting up of the museum.

Finally, let me once more thank the collector and donor Dr Alfred Gunzenhauser most warmly for allowing the first sparks of hope to blaze into a radiant miracle for Chemnitz.

Ingrid Mössinger
General Director of the Kunstsammlungen Chemnitz

FROM MUNICH TO CHEMNITZ – THE GUNZENHAUSER COLLECTION

When, in the summer of 2003, it became known that the Munich gallery owner Dr Alfred Gunzenhauser was to donate his private collection of twentieth-century German art to Chemnitz, it caused surprise in the German museum world. One of the most important factors in the collector's decision in favour of Chemnitz in Saxony was the dedicated building that the city was able to make available to him, in the form of the historic Sparkasse of 1930. Here architecture and collection form an ideal symbiosis, since the aesthetics of the building's architecture correspond to one of the main focuses of the collection, the New Objectivity movement from the days of the Weimar Republic.

THE BUILDING

In the 1920s, Chemnitz constructed a larger number of attractive buildings than any other town in Saxony except Leipzig. The most important protagonist of the New Architecture in the city was Fred Otto, head of the city's building and planning department from 1925 to 1944. The notable city building projects of that period nearly all bear his signature and still impress today through their intelligent functionality and outstanding design; they include the city baths, built between 1928 and 1935, and the Sparkasse building on Falkeplatz, dating from the same period.

Historic view of Falkeplatz, 1930

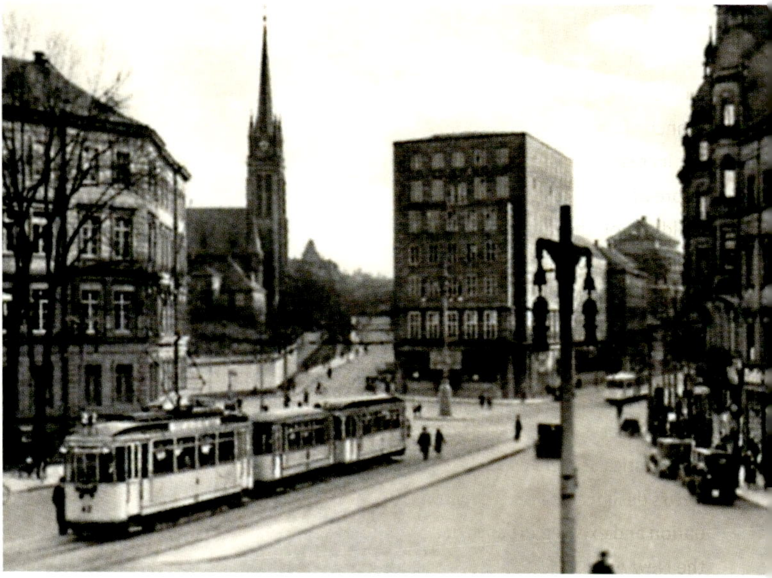

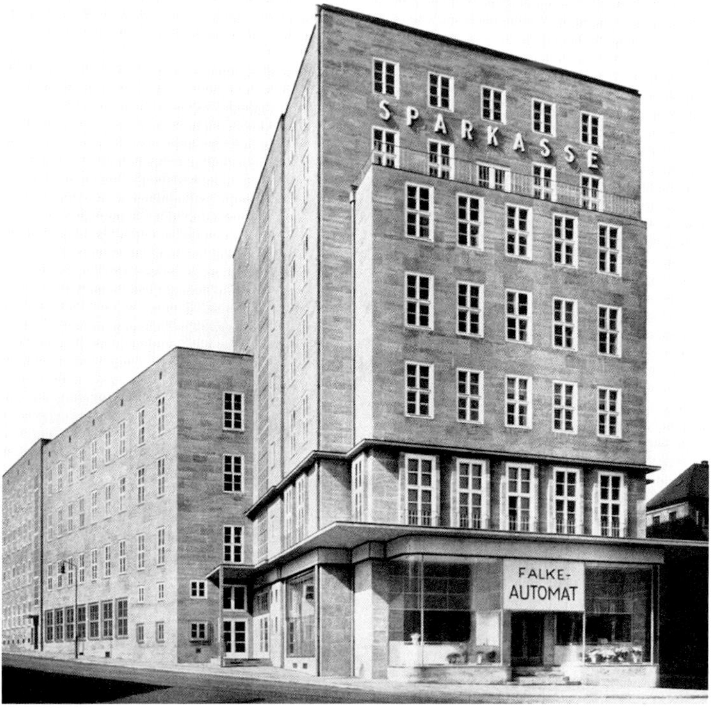

Chemnitz Sparkasse, historic view from Stollberger Strasse, 1930

The Chemnitz Sparkasse was founded on 1 July 1839. During the nineteenth century it was initially located in rented premises in the city centre. As the industrial power of the region grew, during the 1880s it became necessary to set up branch offices; by 1926 eleven branches in total had been opened. The corresponding increase in bank administration in the mid-1920s demanded the building of an impressive central office. Once suitable sites had been acquired and the existing buildings on the site had been demolished, Otto designed the new bank building between 1928 and 1930. One of the first high-rise buildings in modern Chemnitz was erected on one of the busiest squares in Saxony. For the façade, Otto used beige-coloured travertine – a natural stone which fulfilled the design demands for a homogeneous surface and at the same time formed an attractive cladding for the new edifice. In addition, the loose structure of the building masses and the well-considered arrangement and form of the windows ensured that despite the practical, severe cuboid form there was no sense of monotony.

Otto's designs are also characterised by a consideration for the urban planning situation and existing urban structures. Fred Otto created his building in the style of the New Architecture, forming a striking landmark at the intersection of the main

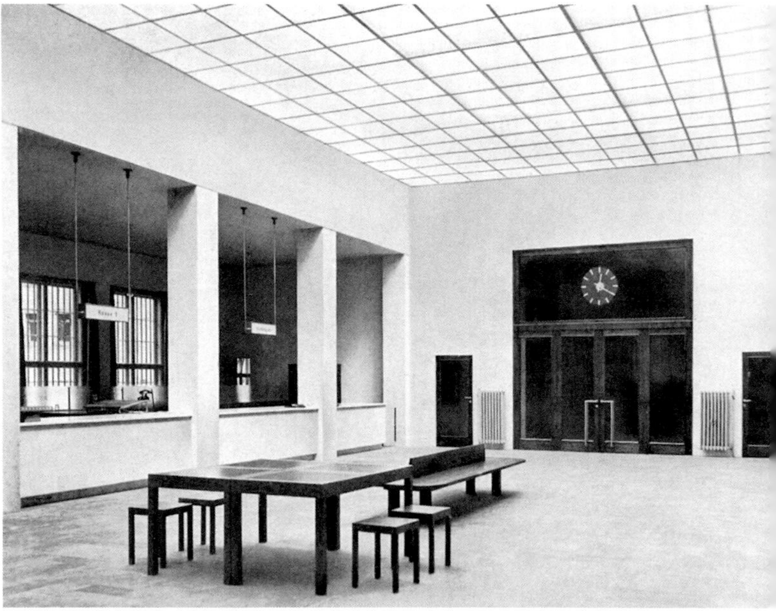

Chemnitz Sparkasse, historic view of the main hall, 1930

roads to Zwickau and Stollberg. The architectural language is simple and precisely defined; Otto has deliberately renounced all decorative elements. The aesthetic effect is based on the balanced proportions and clear structuring of the building in layers of high-grade natural stone. The main hall, which was lit through a glass roof, formed the bustling heart of the building. On the first floor were administration areas and an imposing conference room. At the ground floor level of the high-rise building, to enliven the area, the city's first *Automat* (a self-service restaurant) was installed, the so-called Falke Automat.

The historic bank building was renovated and rebuilt as a modern museum of art by the renowned Staab Architekten Berlin BDA between 2005 and 2007. The presentation of the collection of Dr Alfred Gunzenhauser is organised on the upper floors, around the central light well. By means of a facing placed in front of the outer skin throughout the building, the architect Volker Staab succeeded in creating maximal hanging space and optimal light and climatic conditions for the works of art.

Furthermore the configuration on the ground floor of the building allows the museum a central exhibition hall, lit by daylight, in place of the former main hall of the Sparkasse, while the adjacent areas are used for the display of sculpture and special exhibitions. The four levels of the museum are linked to each other by an important twenty-first century feature introduced by Staab: a cascading staircase which traverses all the floors along the Zwickauer Strasse. Its interior wine-red colouration subtly contrasts with the grey metallic cladding of the outer staircase walls, the pale grey walls and the iridescent anthracite floors of the exhibition halls.

The new purpose of the building is also clearly visible from the outside. Twelve of the outer windows have been transformed into an illuminated showcase, in which historic portrait photographs show the most important artists of the museum's collection. In this way the contents of the building are conveyed to passers-by. A particular attraction in the building is represented by two glazed loggias, which serve as rest areas and permit an extensive exterior view. In the rear area of the building, a small courtyard has been created for two characteristic sculptures by Horst Antes and Eduardo Chillida, serving at the same time as a space where visitors can rest and relax.

THE COLLECTION

Since 1964 Dr Alfred Gunzenhauser has run a gallery in Munich specialising in art of the classical modern period and selected artistic movements since 1945. As he himself relates, his interest in collecting goes back to his childhood. At first he was fascinated by stone fossils which provided evidence of a long-past period in the history of the earth, but during his years as a student in Heidelberg it was the visual arts which increasingly drew him under their spell. As a young student he often travelled to Berlin to gain an overview in its galleries of current art production. It is from this period, too, that the painting stems which represents the beginning of the Gunzenhauser Collection. *Forgotten Coast* by Manfred Bluth fascinated the young collector and marked the start of a passion which continues

Model of the Museum Gunzenhauser, Staab Architekten Berlin BDA

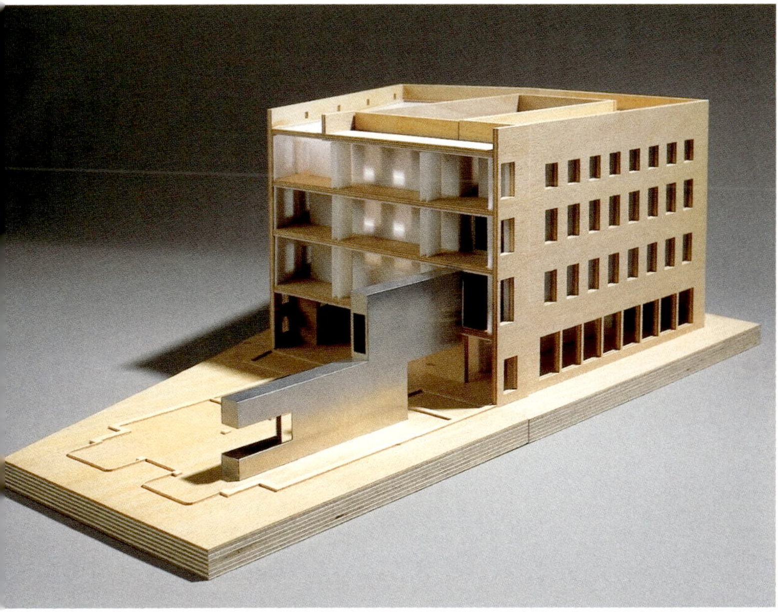

to characterise the life of Dr Alfred Gunzenhauser to this day. In 2003 more than 2,400 works belonging to the foundation served to form the basis for the Museum Gunzenhauser in Chemnitz.
Since then, as a gallery owner and art dealer, he has systematically pursued various art-historical periods and areas. These interests are reflected in the museum collection, whose central components include artworks of the turn of the century around 1900, Expressionism, the New Objectivity as well as representational and non-representational art of the twentieth century.

The prologue to the collection is formed by a comprehensive group of graphic works from the turn of the century, the main focus being on the artists' association *Die Scholle* and works associated with the satirical magazine *Simplicissimus*. German Art Nouveau is represented notably by Franz von Stuck and Carl Strathmann. To these are added a comprehensive range of Expressionist works, guaranteeing the future status of the Kunstsammlungen Chemnitz together with the Museum Gunzenhauser as an important site for the art of German Expressionism. The local roots of the *Brücke* movement are acknowledged by the presence in the collection of works by Ernst Ludwig Kirchner, Erich Heckel and Karl Schmidt-Rottluff, who are linked by their schooldays in Chemnitz. More strongly represented in quantitative terms, however, are Alexej von Jawlensky and Gabriele Münter of the *Blauer Reiter* group; Jawlensky's oeuvre above all is displayed in its entire breadth and inner development. These two groups of Expressionist art are supplemented by the works of various individuals such as Christian Rohlfs, Paula

Manfred Bluth, Forgotten Coast, 1954, tempera on canvas, 67 × 84 cm

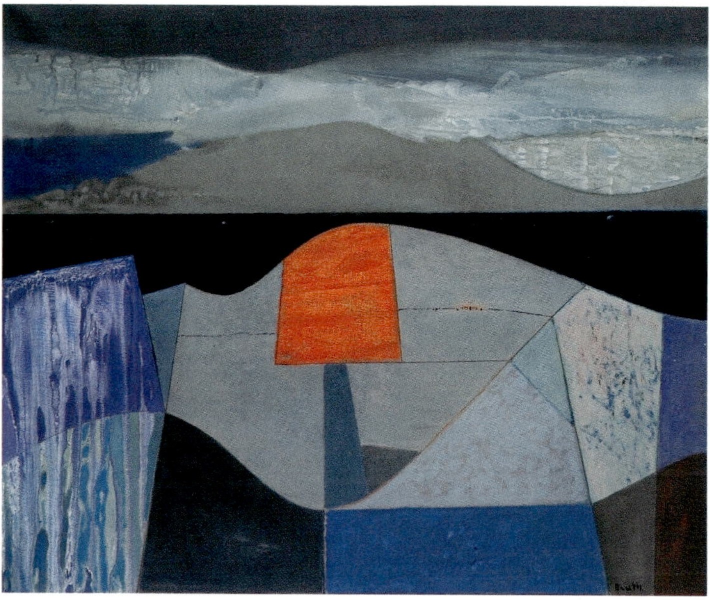

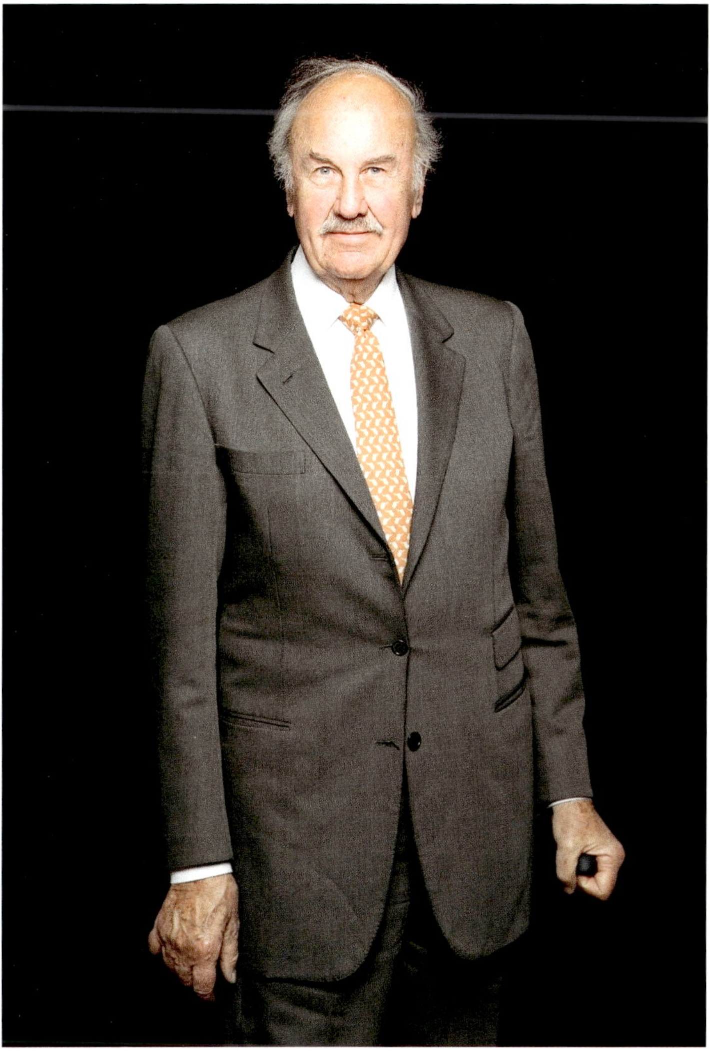

Benjamin Rinner: Art Collector, 2005, C-Print, framed, 73.2 × 52.2 × 6 cm, Kunstsammlungen Chemnitz, Inv. No. 2006-3q

Modersohn-Becker and Helmut Kolle, who each made a special contribution to the avant-garde before and after the First World War. Among these, Helmut Kolle, who died at the early age of 32, should receive a special mention, since he has so far been little known to the wider public. The Museum Gunzenhauser owns nineteen paintings which constitute a representative collection of his work. In the case of Max Beckmann the museum owns a number of interesting paintings from the late 1930s and 1940s, as well as an early landscape.

The art of the Weimar Republic between 1918 and 1933 is reflected by painters such as Karl Hubbuch, Franz Radziwill, Alexander Kanoldt, Georg Schrimpf and Gustav

Wunderwald. Works by these artists had already been displayed in 1925 in the third station of the "Neue Sachlichkeit" exhibition at the Kunstsammlungen Chemnitz on the Theaterplatz. More than eighty years later, their works have become a permanent feature of the museum. Among them are the central figures of their time, Conrad Felixmüller and Otto Dix, who with more than 400 works contribute substantially to the profile of the Museum Gunzenhauser. The core of the museum is the unique collection of 290 works by Otto Dix, beginning with the first self-portrait painted in oil of 1912 and also including early paintings from the period of his studies at the Dresden Academy of Applied Art; important watercolours and gouaches from the First World War period; significant works of the 1920s in all artistic techniques; the great symbolic landscapes from the time of the Inner Emigration; and the pictorially designed lithographic late work. Through the paintings, watercolours, pastels, drawings and graphic prints, it is possible to follow the artist's entire development from his juvenile to his late work. With this unique complex of works, Chemnitz has strengthened its position as one of the foremost museum locations in Germany.
The collection is rounded off by examples of representational and non-representational art before and after World War II. These include works by artists such as Willi Baumeister, Fritz Winter, Ernst Wilhelm Nay, Bernard Schultze and Emil Schumacher, as well as Karl Hofer, Johannes Grützke, Horst Antes, Klaus Fußmann, Karl Horst Hödicke and Rainer Fetting. This group reflects above all the personal interest of the founder and the very individual view of art of a private collector. The open-minded gaze of Dr Alfred Gunzenhauser however was also directed at artists who created their works in the former German Democratic Republic, such as Gerhard Altenbourg, Strawalde, Max Uhlig and Albert Ebert.

The extent of the foundation does not allow the entire collection to be permanently displayed. Rather, it will be the task of thematic, monographic and biographical special exhibitions to open it up to the public. This museum guide therefore meets the need to convey to the interested visitor a representative impression of the paintings, watercolours, drawings and graphic prints of a private art collection which is one of the most important of the second half of the twentieth century in Germany.

Thomas Friedrich
Curator | Kunstsammlungen Chemnitz –
Museum Gunzenhauser

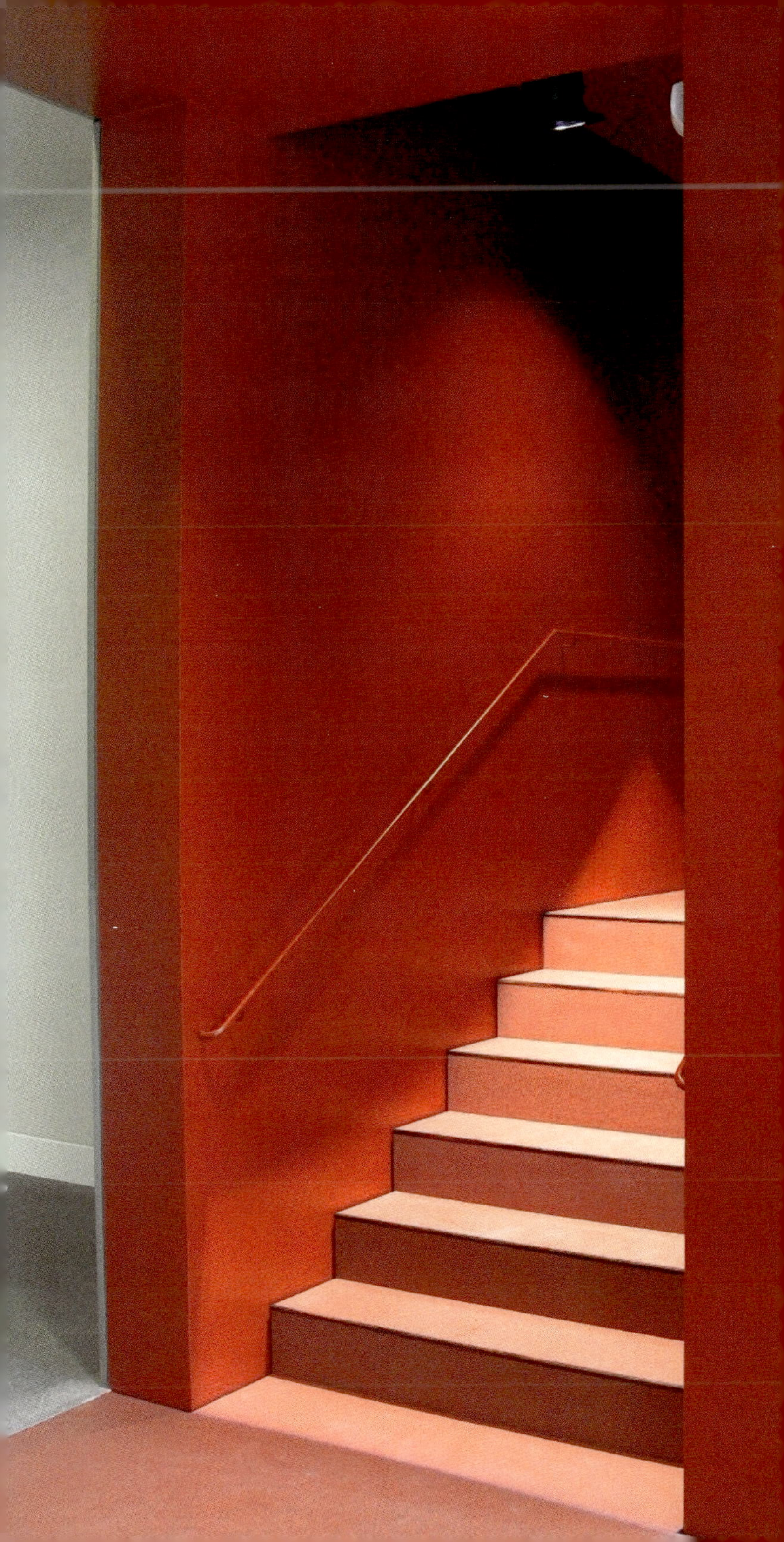

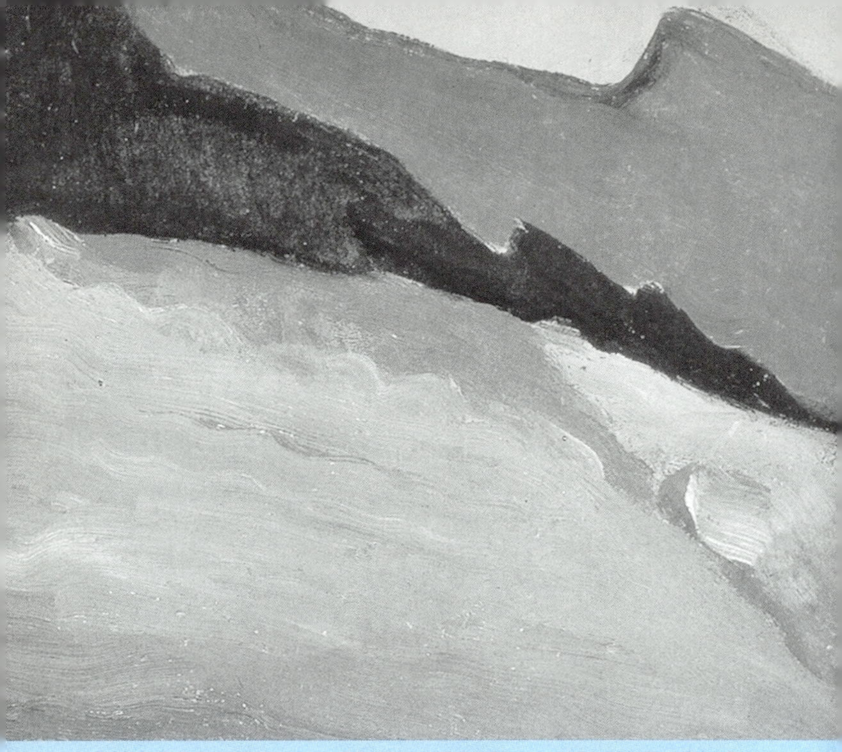

LOVIS CORINTH ERICH HECKEL HELMUT KOLLE
CHRISTIAN ROHLFS
KARL SCHMIDT-ROTTLUFF

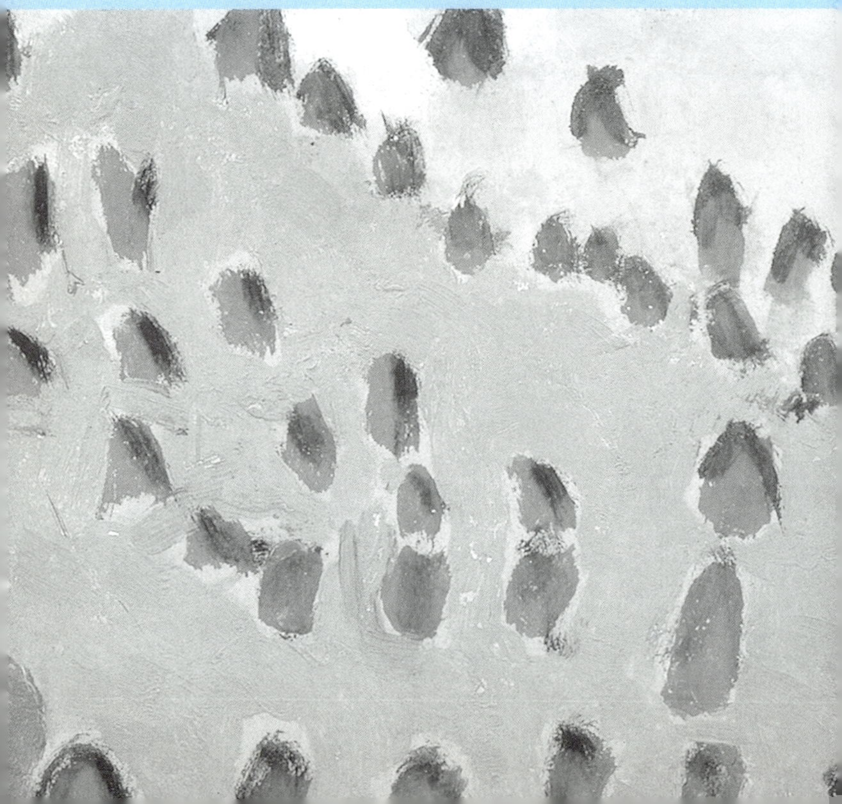

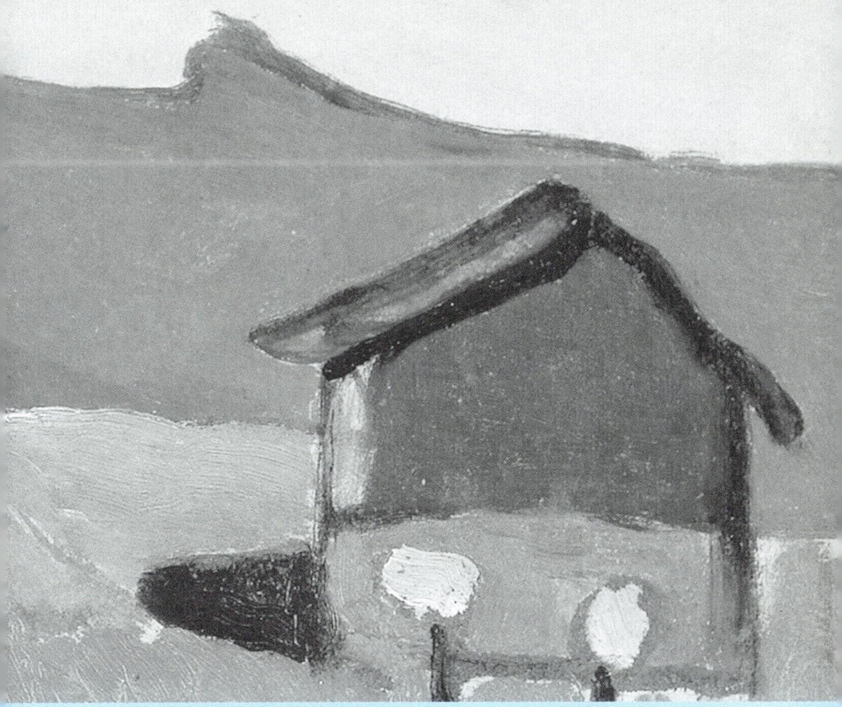

ERNST LUDWIG KIRCHNER GABRIELE MÜNTER
PAULA MODERSOHN-BECKER ALEXEJ VON JAWLENSKY
MAX BECKMANN

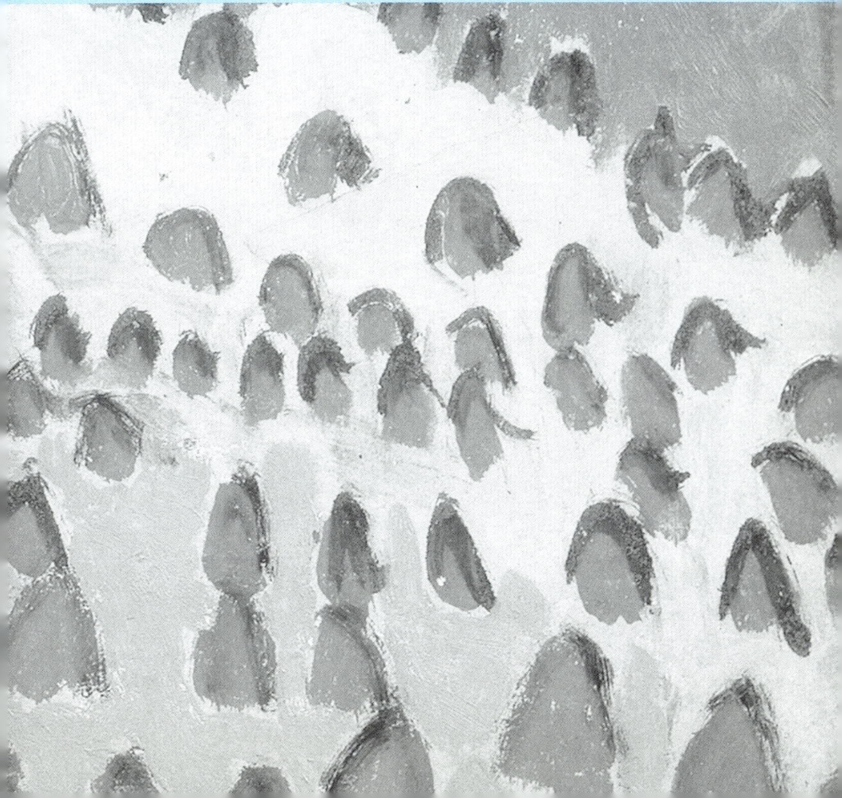

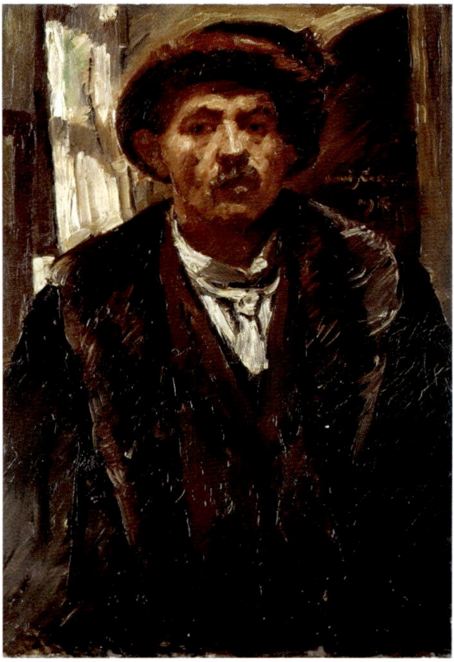

LOVIS CORINTH 1858–1925

Self-Portrait in Fur Coat with Fur Cap, 1916

Oil on canvas, 105 × 75 cm
CR Berend-Corinth 670

Lovis Corinth forms as it were the prelude to as well as the precondition for the avant-garde of classical Modernism, both within the generational structure of the collection, and also with respect to the development of art in the early twentieth century. As a member of the *Berlin Secession* and from 1915 as its president, Corinth had lived in the German capital since 1902. In 1911 the artists of the *Brücke* moved from Dresden to Berlin, and Corinth, who had succeeded Liebermann as the director of the *Secession,* reacted positively to their arrival. As a figure of fatherly authority he was of decisive importance for the generation that followed him. Corinth belongs among the influential representatives of German Impressionism not only because of his spirited history paintings of Biblical themes, in which the paint was applied *impasto* in thick layers.

His late work, represented by the two portraits, is equally important for the budding Expressionist movement. These late paintings are characterised by the free manner in which he handled the paint. This alone forms the subject, while the painter continually succeeds in finding psychologically sensitive, expressive formulations, particularly in the portrait genre. In a manner reminiscent of Rembrandt, he presents himself in 1916 in a winter overcoat. The figure of the painter, filling a full three-quarters of the picture, gains sculptural presence from the light coming from the depth of the space. In this dark composition, built up entirely in brownish tones, the painter's sceptically probing gaze at the axis between the window and the white shirt collar acquires a particular power of expression. Equally brilliant is Corinth's portrait of his mother-in-law. He depicts Hedwig Berend, his "belle-mère", as he tenderly called her, as a stylishly ageing lady in her domestic setting. This painting too achieves its spatial depth from the layering of dark shadows between brightly lit passages. The materiality of the garment which gives the work its name is almost sketched in, and again the stress falls on the brightest part of the image, the woman's face.

Both paintings were exhibited in 1918 at the *Berlin Secession* on the occasion of the painter's sixtieth birthday. In 1937, Corinth's self-portrait suffered the same fate as many other works by the artists gathered together here. It was vilified and seized as 'degenerate art'.

Portrait of Hedwig Berend in Pink Morning Gown, 1916

Oil on canvas, 90 × 70 cm
CR Berend-Corinth 686

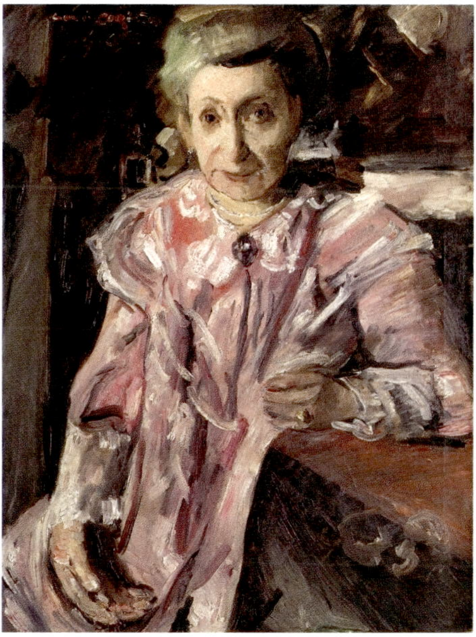

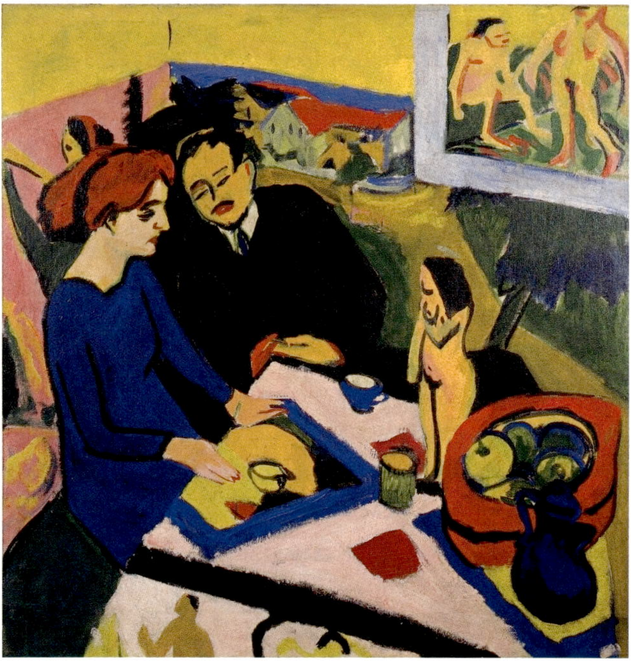

ERNST LUDWIG KIRCHNER 1880–1938

Erich Heckel and Doris in the Studio, 1910/11

Oil on canvas, 120 × 120 cm
Canvas painted on both sides, front
CR Gordon 744v

In 1905 Kirchner, Fritz Bleyl, Erich Heckel and Karl Schmidt-Rottluff together founded the artists' association *Die Brücke*. In the years that followed, up to 1911, when they moved to Berlin, they developed one of the most important versions of German Expressionism. During the early years in Dresden this culminated in joint painting sessions in the studio and near the Moritzburg lakes. The artists maintained a close friendship, which is documented in the painting *Erich Heckel and Doris in the Studio*. Created towards the end of the Dresden period, it shows the characteristic living and working atmosphere of the artists, a lifestyle which has also been preserved in Kirchner's photographs. Heckel is sitting with Kirchner's life-partner Doris Große, known as Dodo, in a corner seat in the studio at a table with a tablecloth printed by himself, on which stands his 1910 carved wooden caryatid, which was presumably used as a shelf support. Typical are the furnishings and decorative items made by the artists themselves: wall hangings, tables, stools, tablecloths etc. Behind the two subjects we can recognise various works by Kirchner.

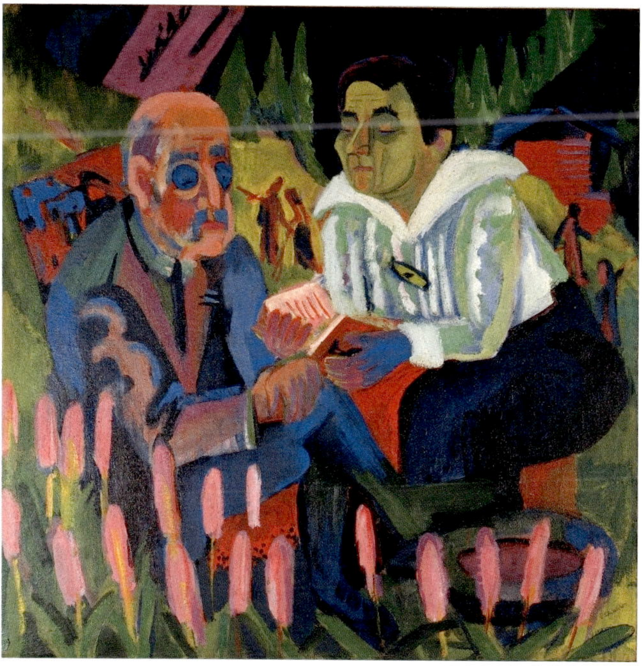

Schiefler Couple, 1923

Oil on canvas, 120 × 120 cm
Canvas painted on
both sides, reverse
CR Gordon 744

Typical of the artist's style around 1911 is the breaking up of the space of the image and the black contour lines which bring together the individual forms and colour surfaces. The depth of the space seems to be two-dimensionally tilted downwards in the painting.

Whilst still in Dresden, Schmidt-Rottluff and Kirchner visited the Hamburg district judge and art collector Dr Gustav Schiefler, who became a lifelong, important patron of the *Brücke* artists. In 1923 Schiefler, together with his wife, stayed with Kirchner in the latter's home in Switzerland, in order to discuss with him the planned catalogue of his prints which was published in two parts in 1926 and 1931. It was during this visit that Kirchner painted a portrait of the couple, using the back of the canvas painted around 1911 with the subject of the Dresden studio. The colour scheme and composition demonstrate the style developed by the artist during the 1920s.

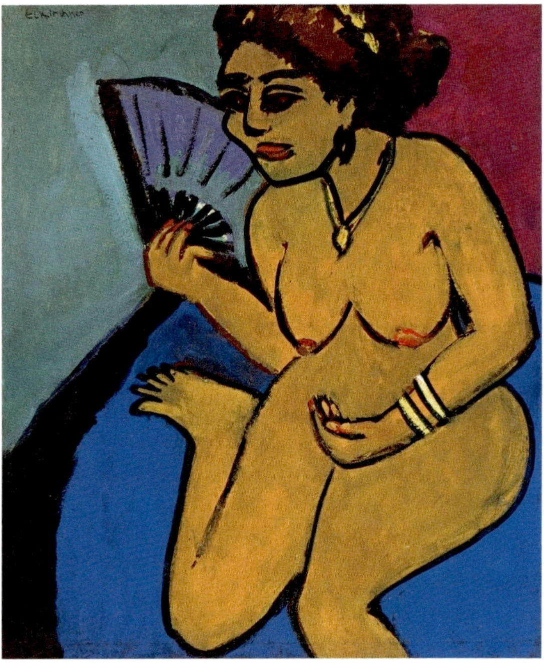

ERNST LUDWIG KIRCHNER 1880–1938

Seated Nude with Fan, 1911

Oil on canvas, 73.7 × 63.3 cm
CR Gordon 915v

The seated nude from the artist's bequest is closely related to the well-known *Female Semi-Nude with Hat* (Cologne) as well as to a further nude portrait of Doris Große from the Buchheim collection. Together they typify the full flowering of Kirchner's painting of female nudes shortly before his move to Berlin. The composition is determined by balanced forms and lines. The harmonious course of the curved line in the contour of the body is characteristic of this period.

In September 1910, in Dresden, Kirchner first encountered the art of Paul Gauguin, whose strongly simplified forms and powerful colours – inspired by primitive art works – had a strong impact on Kirchner's own work, and led to the masterpieces he created around 1910/11.

In October 1911, Kirchner left Dresden and moved into a flat in Durlacher Strasse in the Wilmersdorf district of Berlin. *The City Tower* was one of the first works to be created in his new home and place of work. The *Brücke* artists' move to Berlin prompted the gradual abandonment of their common painting style which was in evidence in around 1909/10. It was replaced by individual forms of representation influenced by the multifarious attractions of the big city during the pre-war years. Kirchner's work underwent a marked development. Following on from his Dresden cityscapes, Kirchner turned his attention to the prosperous German capital. The compositions of his Berlin period are marked by strong verticality and pointedness of forms, while he abandons the strict two-dimensionality of his representation and indicates a third dimension by means of shading and zigzag lines at the contours of the bodies.

The City Tower, 1911
Oil on canvas, 95.7 × 83.7 cm
CR Gordon 210

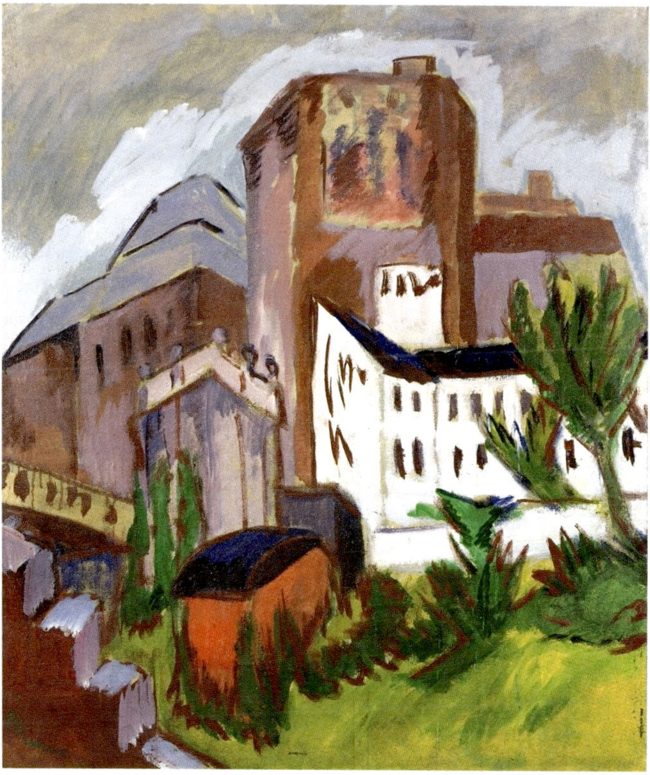

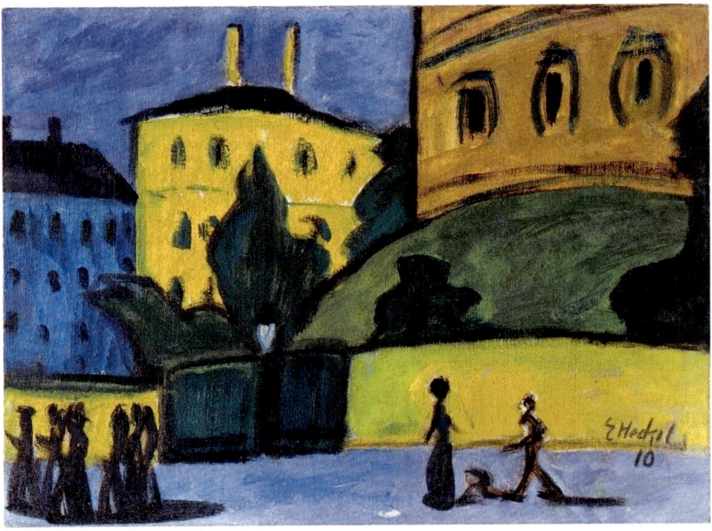

ERICH HECKEL 1883–1970

Dresden Suburb, 1910

Oil on canvas, 48.5 × 68.5 cm
CR Vogt 1910/21

Like Kirchner and Schmidt-Rottluff, Erich Heckel also went to school in Chemnitz before moving to Dresden to study architecture. It was there, in 1905, that he founded the association *Die Brücke* together with the other artists. Apart from Man and his relationship to Nature, the subject of the modern city formed one of their prime interests. This Expressionist 'veduta' comes from Erich Heckel's last year in Dresden before the move to Berlin. It shows the round gasometer in Schweriner Strasse in the Wilsdruffer Vorstadt district. In their cityscapes, Heckel and his fellow-artists of the *Brücke* were concerned not about precise spatial reproduction, but about the psychological perception and painterly realisation of city life. A severely reduced, highly contrasted colour palette and a roughly suggested sculptural quality of the buildings and figures allow Heckel to create this tension-laden nocturnal city scene.

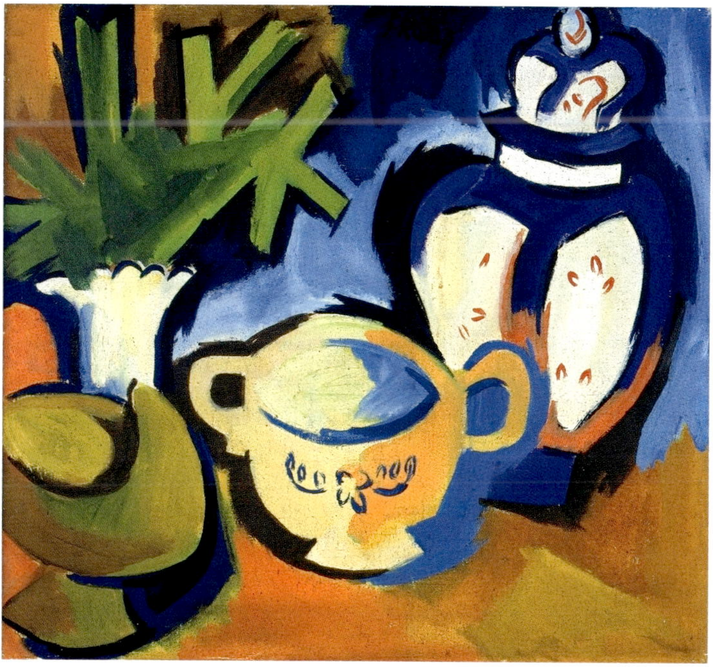

KARL SCHMIDT-ROTTLUFF 1884–1976

Still Life with Lidded Vase, 1921

Oil on canvas, 66 × 71 cm
CR Grohmann p. 292

Together with Erich Heckel and Ernst Ludwig Kirchner, Karl Schmidt-Rottluff was one of the founder members of the artists' association *Die Brücke* (1905–13). Born Karl Schmidt in Rottluff, a suburb of Chemnitz, he is today among the best-known of German Expressionist artists. After Impressionist beginnings he developed a colourful two-dimensional style around 1910. From 1920 he spent several months of every year in Jershöft on the Baltic coast of Pomerania, where many of his works were created. The *Still Life with Lidded Vase* dates from that period. Schmidt-Rottluff groups three objects of varying size in the image in staggered formation on the diagonals; the back of the left half of the image is filled by a vase containing greenery. Stylistically, this still life stands between Schmidt-Rottluff's more mature Expressionist painting before the First World War and the questions of image space and physical volume which preoccupied him above all after his trip to Italy in 1923, and which led to changes in his painting.

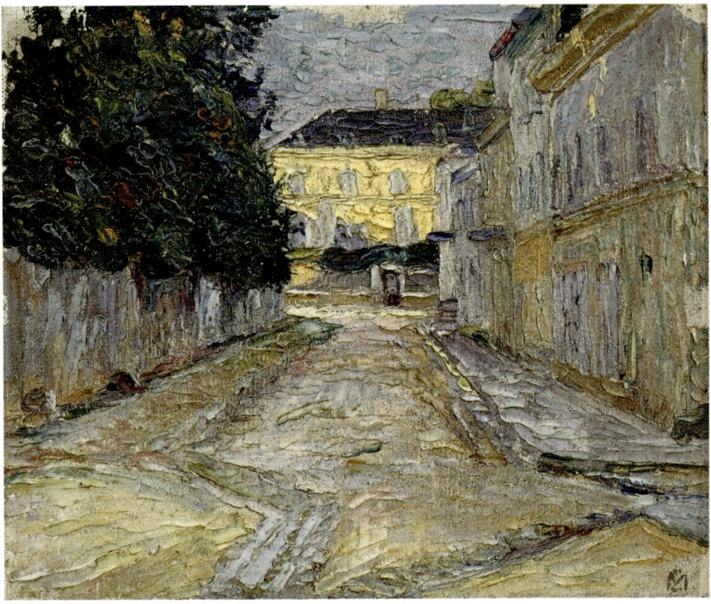

GABRIELE MÜNTER 1877–1962

House in Sèvres, 1906
Oil on hardboard, 21.5 × 26.5 cm

The years between 1901 and 1908 in the life of Gabriele Münter were marked by numerous travels in Germany, France and Italy. Between the summers of 1906 and 1907, for example, she lived with Kandinsky in Sèvres, near Paris. During those years she completed small-format oil studies of the landscapes in which she stayed. In a filigree scraping technique borrowed from Kandinsky, she created urban and park views in the manner of the late Impressionists. The motifs are composed of the fine textures of the paint, which is applied with relief-like *impasto*, and captivate with their harmonious composition. The *House in Sèvres,* for example, depicts the course of a street from a strong central perspective, at the end of which is a yellow-toned mansion, whose entrance is shifted slightly out of the vertical axis of the picture. The palette of these small studies consists of a small number of carefully matched colours.

After years of travel, in 1908 Münter and Kandinsky settled down in the Schwabing district of Munich. Earlier, in late summer, they had discovered for themselves the Bavarian Alpine landscape near Murnau. The clarity and brilliance of the colours – especially during the *foehn* wind – and the harmony of nature inspired them and their friends Alexej von Jawlensky and Marianne von Werefkin to numerous depictions of landscape. In these, Münter soon began to free herself from the detailed spatula technique she had used hitherto. The motifs, now painted with a brush, became more and more simplified and the colours were combined into surfaces of partly unbroken tones. The composition space is abandoned in favour of a two-dimensionality which emphasises the decorative quality of the works. The textures, formerly placed close together, are now united by Münter as larger areas which constitute the motif in themselves.

Landscape with Hut at Sunset, 1908

Oil on cardboard, 33.1 × 40.7 cm

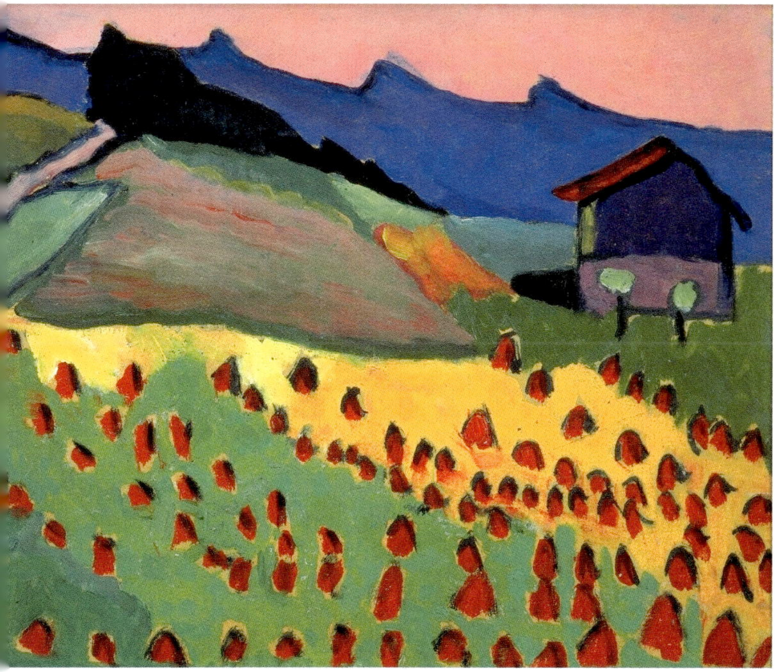

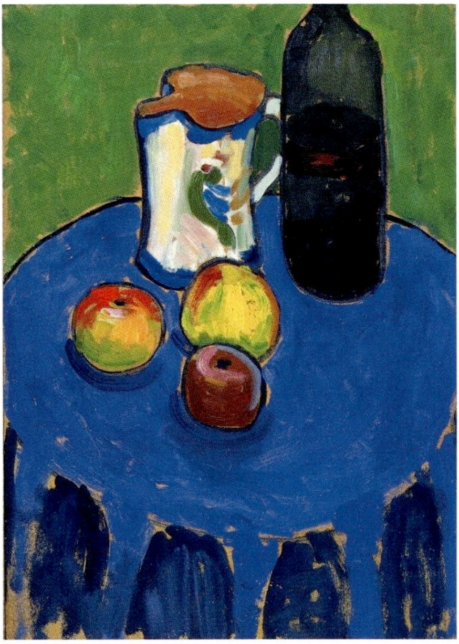

GABRIELE MÜNTER 1877–1962

Apples on Blue, 1908
Oil on cloth-lined board,
52.5 × 39 cm

This luminous still life also arose as a result of the significant impressions of the late summer of 1908 in Murnau. Arrangements of apples on a table inspired Paul Cézanne to countless variations on this theme, which Münter and Kandinsky must certainly have seen during their Paris years. In her formulation of this subject, the painter reduces her ensemble to a few objects, carefully arranged on the surface of the table. The area of the image is so reduced that only a section of the table remains in view. The third dimension is suggested by the downward folding of the table surface. The two levels are separated by a thick black contour line. In terms of colour, the still life is composed of primary and their secondary colours, while areas of light and shadow are only suggested. With the works she created in the second half of 1908, Gabriele Münter moved within a very short time from a late Impressionist approach to the simplification of forms and a free expressive handling of colour.

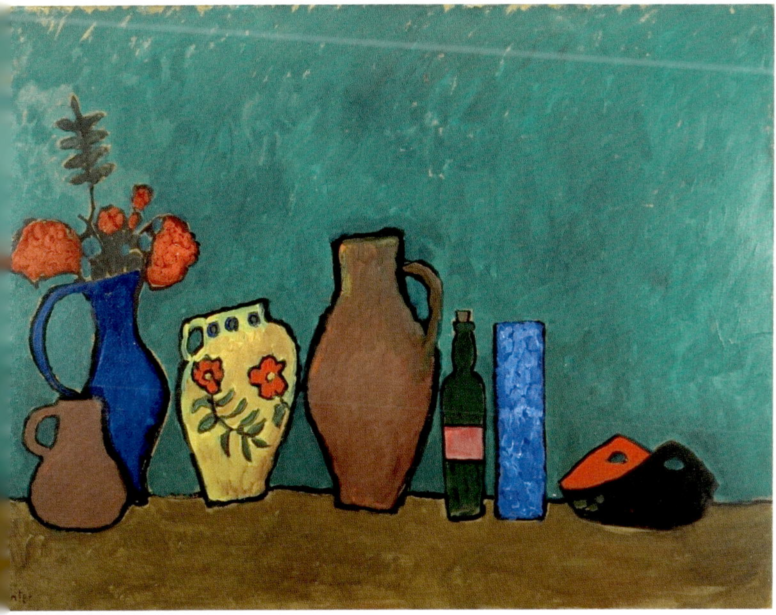

In this still life, seven different ceramic objects are lined up like actors at the front of a stage. The clear composition structures the whole in such a way that it fills the lower left half of the picture's diagonals, whereby the bowl and vases are arranged from right to left in an ascending line of height. They are presented to the observer as if for a factual stocktaking, the artist being concerned primarily with the skilled limitation of individual areas by means of colour. In 1908, Gabriele Münter, following the example of Alexej von Jawlensky, began to separate the areas of colour, mostly by means of black contour lines. As she had already done with the *Apples on Blue*, Münter conveys her subject using a strongly reduced palette; the primary and secondary colours bring out each other's luminous qualities and infuse the whole image in its simplicity with life.

Still Life with Vase, Bottles and Rowan Tree Branches, 1908/09

Oil on cloth-lined board, 74.8 × 103.8 cm

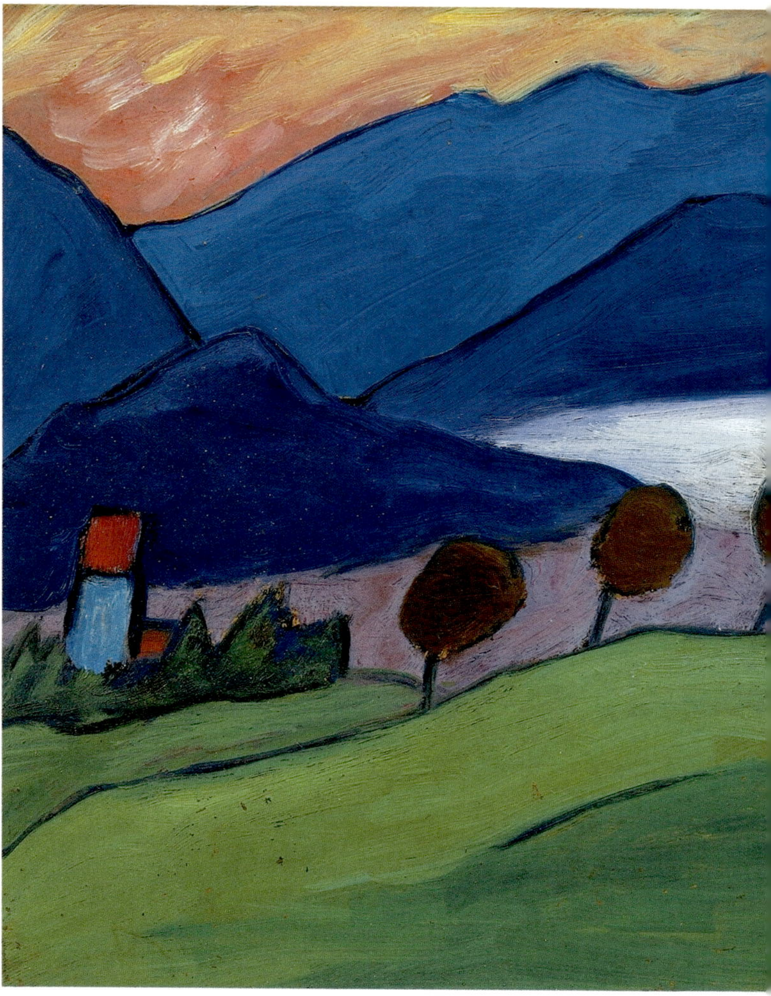

In 1909 Gabriele Münter acquired a house in Murnau which she used as a mountain retreat for many summers and winters up to the outbreak of the First World War. In Munich, in the same year, the Neue Künstlervereinigung München (New Artists' Association of Munich) was founded by the circle of avant-garde artists around Kandinsky and Jawlensky. During this time, Münter, Jawlensky and Kandinsky repeatedly depicted the Murnau mountains. Münter often made nature trips together with Jawlensky, and whilst working with him she further developed her simplifying style. Using only a few colours, she succeeded in recording her impressions of nature in a succinct and precise

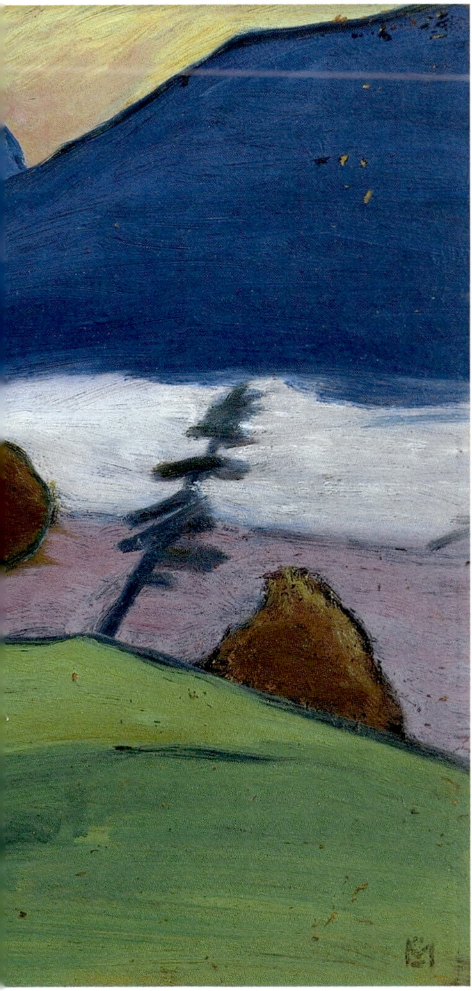

GABRIELE MÜNTER

Staffelsee Landscape with Murnau Marshes and Church, c. 1909

Oil on cloth-lined board, 25.5 × 35.3 cm

way on her small-format sheets of cardboard. She particularly loved recording the deep dark blue of the mountains at sunrise and sunset. It was at this time, too, that Münter's exploration of Bavarian folk art provided her with a new stimulus.

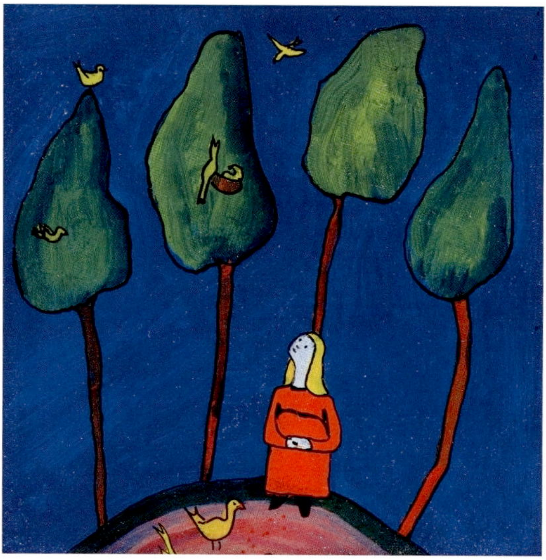

GABRIELE MÜNTER 1877–1962

Song, c. 1917
Reverse-glass painting, 12.5 × 13 cm

Apart from the experience of the Alpine landscape of Murnau, Bavarian reverse-glass painting was a significant influence on the work of Münter and Kandinsky in the years up to 1910. These apparently naïve, popular depictions of saints and the votive images created for various purposes encouraged them in their quest for greater simplicity in the structure of their images and clarity of composition. At first Gabriele Münter copied these small panels, thus quickly acquiring facility in the new style. After learning the technique of painting on the rear side of glass from the Murnau artist Heinrich Rambold, she finally began to work from her own designs.

The *Song* depicts a little girl deeply absorbed in the sight of birds in God's creation. Surprised and fascinated, she gazes toward heaven at the freely flying creatures. In its simple but profound piety the picture seems an impressive paraphrase of the well-known scene from the life of St Francis.

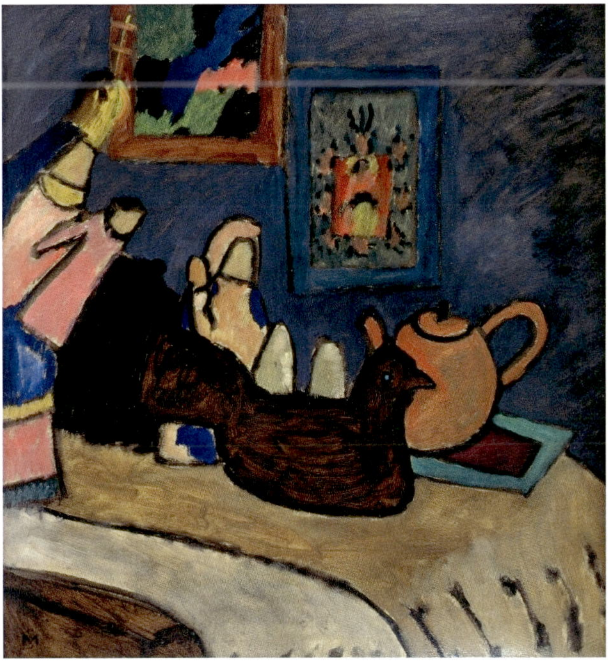

Around 1910 Gabriele Münter attained a high degree of abstraction in her work, as she herself observes in various statements. In the period that followed, she predominantly sought an all-embracing form in her painting technique. She created still lifes in which she repeatedly arranged objects from her personal environment to form impressive compositions. These include religious folk-art objects and reverse-glass paintings from her collection, as can be seen in the *Russian Easter Still Life.* At the left-hand edge of the picture rising up above all else is a Madonna figure with child and a crown with a double cross which Kandinsky had brought from Russia and which is to be found in various works from this period. The high degree of abstraction in Münter's compositions is tangible here too. The Madonna is hardly recognisable as herself any more, but is reduced to her basic forms and colours. The artist treats all the other objects in the same way, so that they receive a reality of their own, marked by an intensely mystical character.

Russian
Easter Still Life, 1912

Oil on cloth-lined board,
73.2 × 69.9 cm

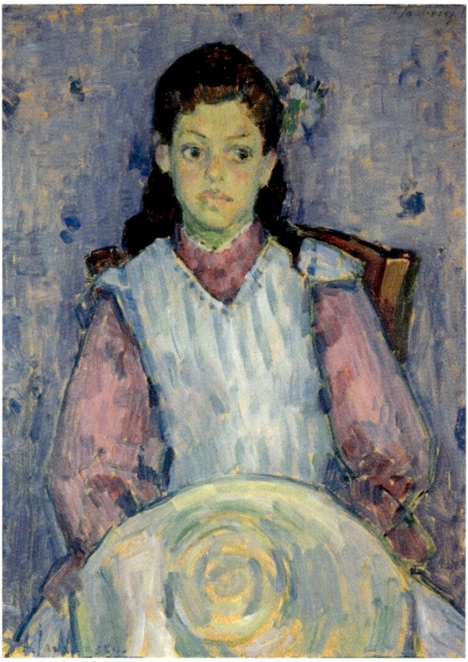

ALEXEJ VON JAWLENSKY 1864–1941

Girl in Pink Dress, 1906
Oil on cloth-lined board,
65.5 × 48 cm
CR Jawlensky 127

After an initial military career, Alexej von Jawlensky, born in Russia, resigned his officer's commission and went to Munich in 1896 with Marianne von Werefkin, where he studied at Anton Ažbe's art school. At the start of the twentieth century he was preoccupied above all with French artists such as Gauguin and the *Fauves*, and in particular he was devoted to the art of Van Gogh. He made an examination of their perception of form and colour as well as their new painting technique, and during those years continued in search of an artistic path of his own. He spent the summer of 1906 in Wasserburg, where he created many portraits of young peasant women. Still dependent on the narrative tradition of the nineteenth century in terms of composition, he carefully matched the delicate pastel tones in a rough Impressionist brush style. In this early work the artist is clearly already striving to go beyond the realistic depiction of nature to portray what is hidden within. Over the years this was to develop into Jawlensky's great artistic theme.

This still life, created in c. 1907, provides evidence of Jawlensky's intensive study of contemporary French art and demonstrates his knowledge of the work of Cézanne and Matisse. He became personally acquainted with the latter in 1905; two years later he visited him in his studio. It was the art of the French Expressionists, the *Fauves*, that Jawlensky studied intensively at that time and that validated his own work. The advanced degree of gathering colours together into larger areas is clearly recognisable. The depth of the picture area is abandoned and the surface of the table, covered with a red cloth, is tilted two-dimensionally. The compositional curve swings harmoniously from the blue-green vessel at the left-hand edge upwards over the white cloth and down again to the smaller ones and the fruit at the lower right corner. The colours are restricted to primary and complementary colours.

Red Table, c. 1907
Oil on cloth-lined board,
59.7 × 66 cm
CR Jawlensky 186

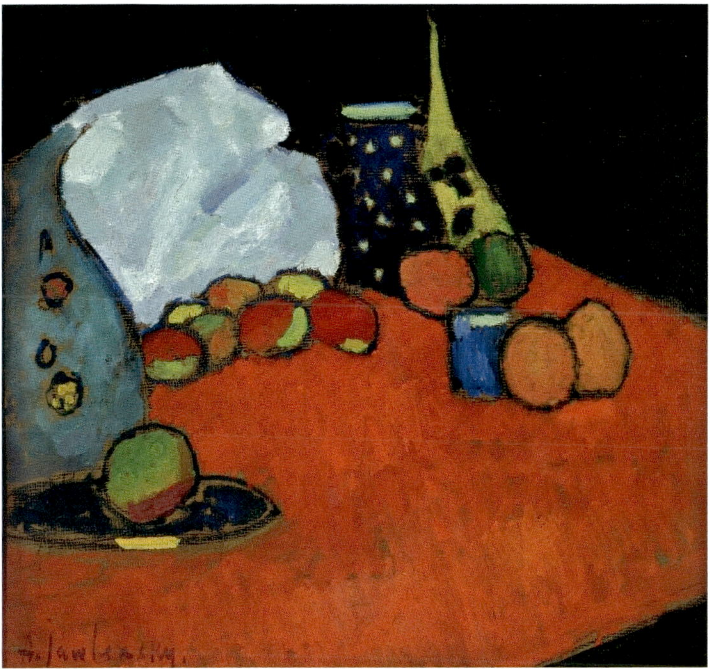

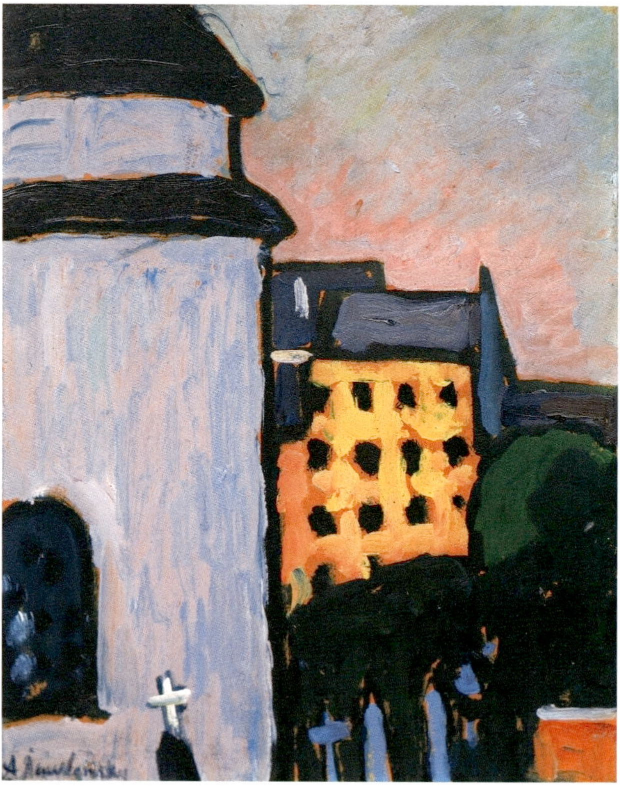

Church – Village Subject in Murnau, 1908/09

Oil on cardboard, 40.8 × 33 cm
CR Jawlensky 275

The years before the founding of the Neue Künstlervereinigung München (New Artists' Association of Munich) brought intensive stimuli for Jawlensky, which were not without influence on his artistic work. Through his Dutch friend, Jan Verkade, he became familiar with the art of the *Pont-Aven* school, above all with the works of Paul Gauguin, and later also with those of the *Nabis*. From 1907/08 one can clearly recognise in Jawlensky's work the enclosure of individual coloured areas by mostly black or dark blue contours. It is the principle of cloisonné, which supports the luminosity of the strongly contrasted inlaid colours, which gives the painting the effect of old stained-glass windows. This was supplemented by the experience of the Staffelsee landscape. On a trip to the Bavarian Alps in the early summer of 1908, Gabriele Münter and Wassily Kandinsky visited Murnau and told Jawlensky and Marianne von Werefkin of their impressions. As early as the autumn of the same year the two couples began their work together; it was marked, particularly for Münter and Jawlensky, by great reciprocal enrichment. Both reproduce in many landscape paintings the special effect of the mountains and the colours of nature at different times of day and year. These works, mostly in small format, glow with expressively heightened colours, proclaiming an intensive experience of nature. The motif of the church at Murnau must be stressed in this context, for it gives evidence of Jawlensky's deeply religious sensibilities. With a graduated palette of subtle nuances and fine brushstrokes he builds up the compact composition from the walls of the houses and the cemetery. A mood of farewell, but also of hope, lies over the twilight scene and guides the gaze beyond the brilliant yellow façade away into the distance.

Landscape – Murnau,
c. 1909
Oil on cloth-lined board,
31 × 41 cm
CR Jawlensky 284

ALEXEJ VON JAWLENSKY 1864–1941

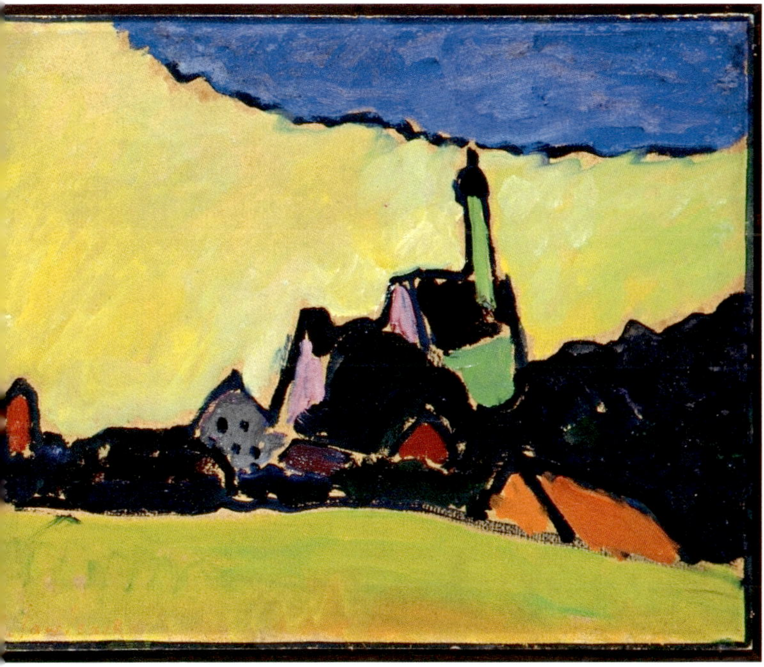

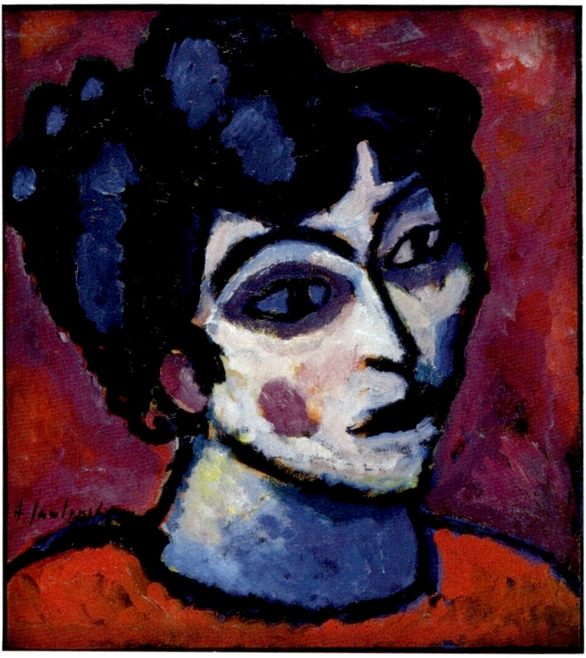

ALEXEJ VON JAWLENSKY 1864–1941

Frenchwoman, 1912
Oil on cloth-lined board,
54 × 49.6 cm
CR Jawlensky 452

1912 was the year of *Der Blaue Reiter* (The Blue Rider). While Kandinsky and Franz Marc worked intensively on the eponymous almanac, Jawlensky concentrated on the further development of his formal techniques. His main theme at this time was the human face, though not in the mimetic sense of a naturalistic depiction of the individual. Throughout his life the artist was intent on looking behind objects, exploring their nature and inner life and expressing them in artistic form. This theme preoccupied him up to his death in 1941 and led him to a series of works with this theme.

The paintings of female heads that he completed before the First World War stand at the beginning of this path. Unlike his portraits of the previous decade, in these works Jawlensky reduces the area of the square medium to the human face and neck. Against a neutral background, the head occupies most of the surface of the painting. This enables the painter to direct the observer's attention entirely onto the face, which thus acquires a profoundly transcendent quality. Instead of the portrayal of a specific individual, Jawlensky is inter-

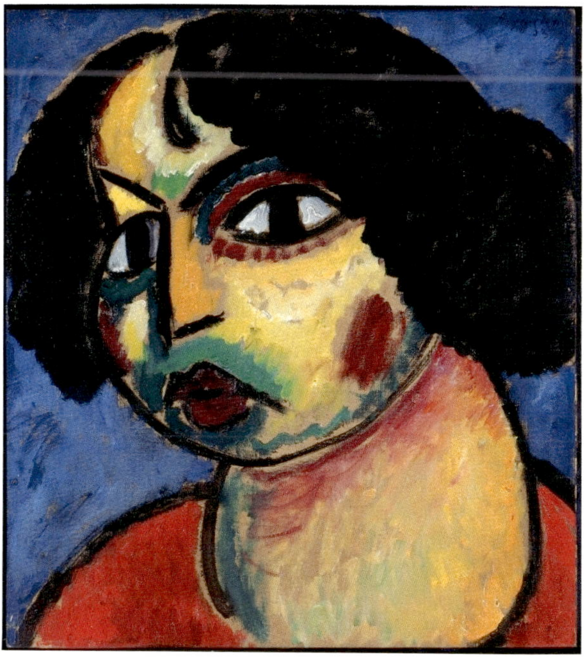

ested in general traits, conditions or moods, which he attempts to express by means of form and colour. The parallels with artistic works from Jawlensky's homeland are no coincidence. Many stylistic characteristics refer to Russian icon painting; in both cases it is a question of an attempt to depict transcendent content.

While the pointed forms of the pale face of the *Frenchwoman* are reminiscent of elegance and reserved nobility, supported by the restrained harmony of red, blue and purple, *Messalina* expresses the exact opposite. The historic figure was the wife of the Roman emperor Claudius and was notorious for her dissolute, depraved lifestyle as well as her unscrupulousness. In his painting of the same name, Jawlensky is concerned with portraying these traits, using violent contrasts of primary colours. Instead of the harsher features of the *Frenchwoman*, there are only soft, sensually flowing lines. The characterisation is further underlined by the form of the mouth, which is similar to that of *La Cocotte* (1912).

Messalina, 1913

Oil on cloth-lined board,
54 × 50 cm
CR Jawlensky 462

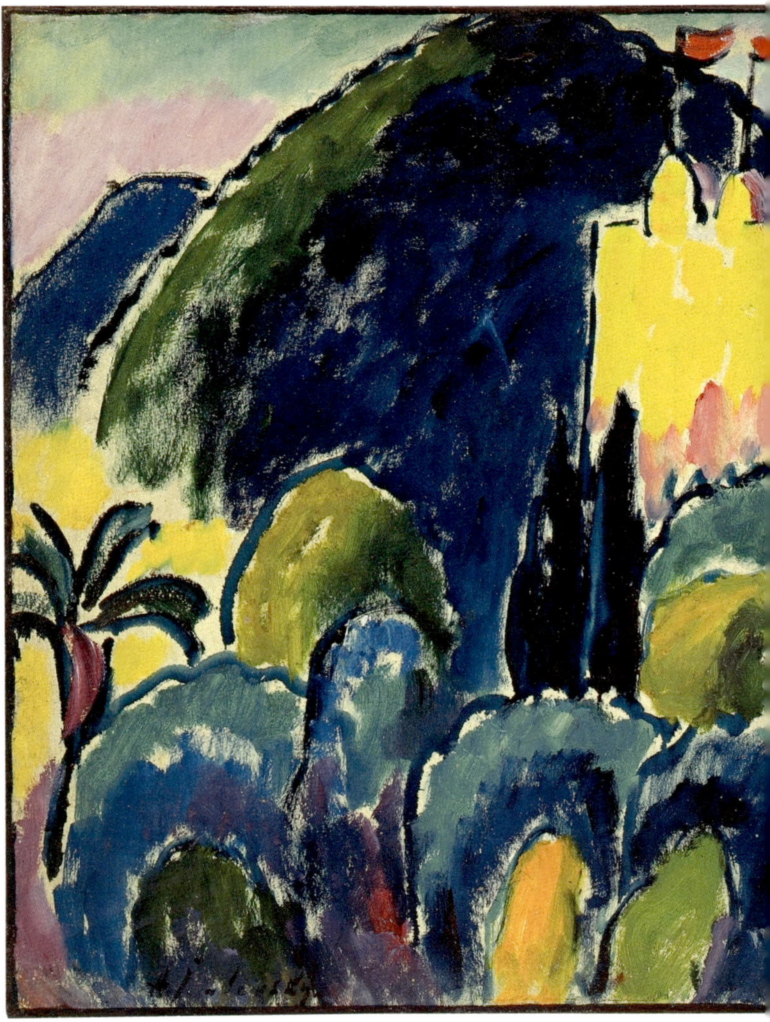

The subject of the yellow house was created by Jawlensky during a stay at a health resort at Bordighera. Shortly before the outbreak of the First World War the artist spent a few carefree weeks in the pleasant climate of the Mediterranean coast. Since the end of the nineteenth century Bordhigera, like San Remo, has been a popular seaside resort in the Italian Riviera. During the mild winter months it was frequented in particular by English, French and Russian visitors.

Paintings have been preserved by Jawlensky which show various motifs of the resort. The artist was stimulated by the view of the rising coastline with its dense vegeta-

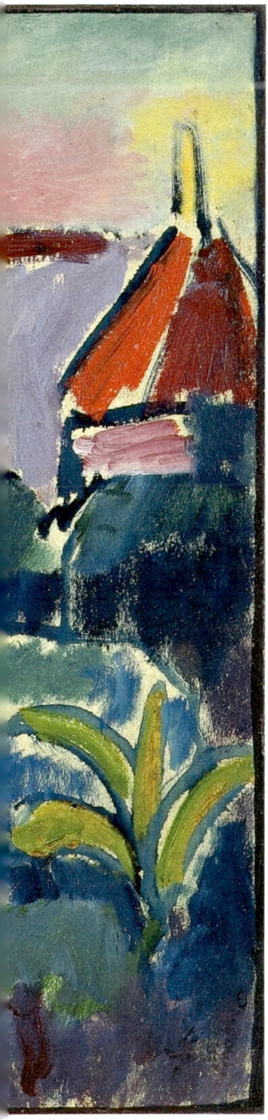

ALEXEJ VON JAWLENSKY 1864–1941

Yellow House –
Bordighera, 1914

Oil on cardboard, 49 × 53 cm
CR Jawlensky 622

tion, with the occasional villa rising out of the woods. In terms of composition, the almost square area of the image is divided by the diagonals into two equal triangles; the primary colours red, blue and yellow form a harmonious com-position, with complementary tones of green and purple. Nothing in this picture gives a hint of what was to happen to the artist and his family a few months later on the outbreak of war. Rather, a light-hearted cheerfulness reigns throughout the painting.

Variation – Spring, c. 1916
Oil on linen-finish paper laid down on cardboard, 36 × 27 cm
CR Jawlensky 763

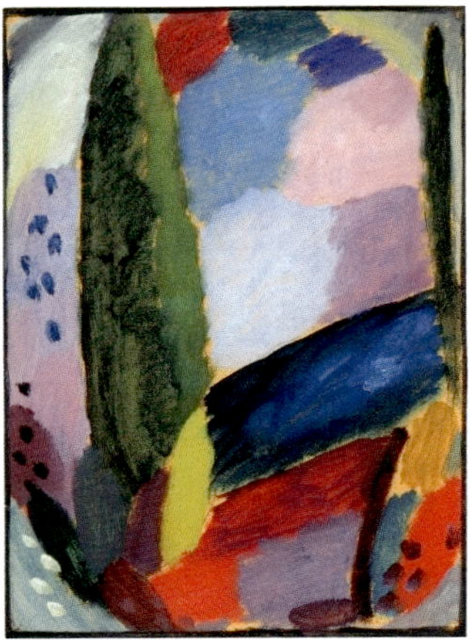

In 1914 Jawlensky, as a Russian living in Germany, was forced to leave the country. Together with his family he had to leave Munich within forty-eight hours. He went into exile in Switzerland. At first he settled at St. Prex on Lake Geneva, and later in Zurich, before moving to Ascona on Lake Maggiore, where he lived

ALEXEJ VON JAWLENSKY 1864–1941

Variation – Summer Night, c. 1918
Oil on linen-finish paper laid down on cardboard, 37.5 × 28 cm
CR Jawlensky 1023

Variation – Winter, c. 1918
Oil on linen-finish paper laid down on cardboard, 36.5 × 28.5 cm
CR Jawlensky 1016

Variation – Red Path with Black Gate, 1915
Oil on linen-finish paper laid down on cardboard, 37.5 × 26 cm
CR Jawlensky 673

from 1918 to 1921. "My soul had changed because of much suffering, and this forced me to seek other forms and colours ..." He could not simply continue with his series of "Heads". In close relation to his biography, he created over the next seven years nearly 400 *Variations on a Landscape Theme*. The motif which Jawlensky varied like a composer was based on his new immediate environment: it is the view from his window in St. Prex of a narrow path with tree and garden gate, as seen in the *Red Path with Black Gate* of 1915. Jawlensky internalised this image to such an extent that he no longer needed the actual view; he could rather give shape to his subject in a new and free way, again and again. In doing so, he always maintained the same dimensions of the small panels. Starting with an impression of nature, his pictures became more and more abstract and he finally reached the stage of compositions of pure form and colour only remotely suggestive of the original starting point. The constitutive trait of many of these variations is the slim silhouette of a cypress rising on the left-hand edge of the image.

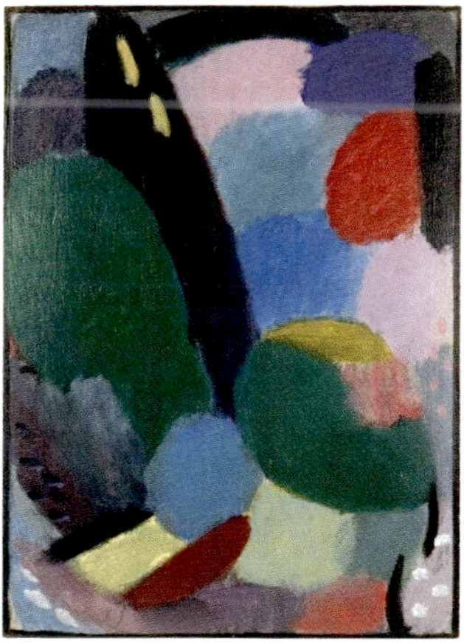

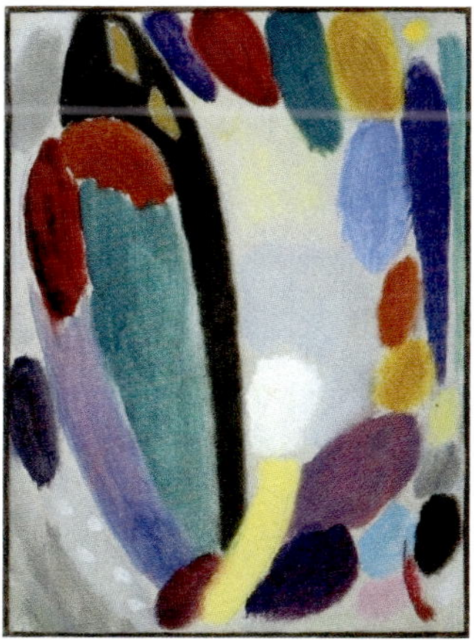

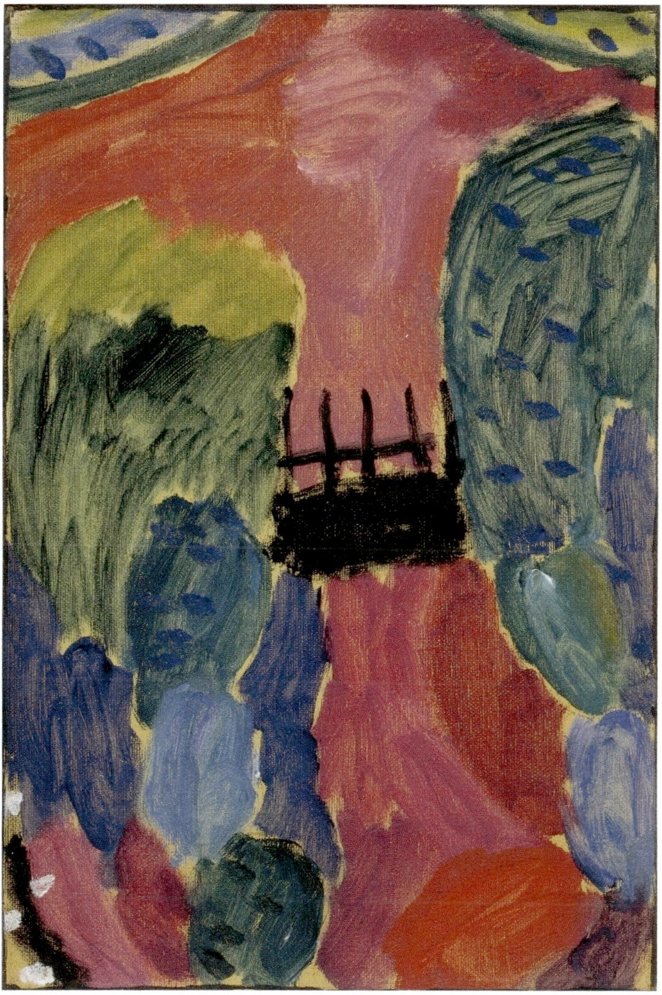

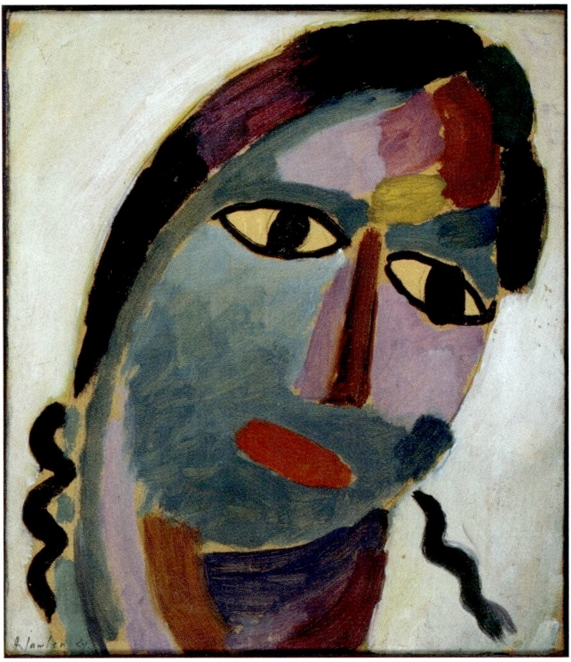

ALEXEJ VON JAWLENSKY 1864–1941

Mystical Head:
Red Mouth –
Green Face, 1917

Oil on cardboard, 41 × 36.5 cm
CR Jawlensky 882

Saviour's Face, c. 1921

Oil on cardboard, 33.6 × 26 cm
CR Jawlensky 1137

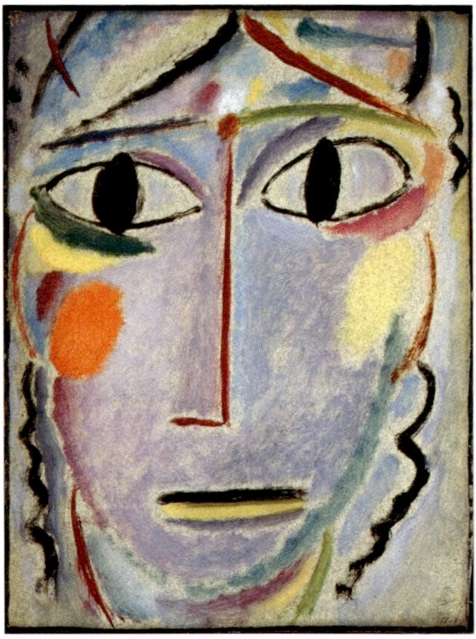

With his exile to Switzerland and the beginning of his work on the "Variations", the theme of the human face receded for a time in Jawlensky's work, but it never entirely disappeared. In 1916 Jawlensky met the young painter Emmy Scheyer (known as Galka), whose appearance inspired him to create a number of portraits. However, it was not until his move to Wiesbaden in 1921 after he and Marianne von Werefkin had separated that Jawlensky produced variations on the theme of Galka and the further reduction of the human head in the form of a new series. From 1922 he painted the so-called "Constructive Heads", beginning with the faces of saints and the Saviour from the early 1920s. His starting point, as with the "Variations", was the model of nature, in this case the figure of Galka with her narrow, inclined head, curved nose and locks of hair. Jawlensky increasingly gave abstract form to these characteristics, finally reaching the stylisation of a curved vertical line for the nose and horizontal and diagonal lines for the mouth and eyes. The constituent elements of the series are placed in a well-thought-out arrangement of lines and surfaces between the edges of the cardboard that border the composition. These themes preoccupied him up to 1933.

Dreamy Shining (Saviour's Face), 1921

Oil on cardboard, 36.6 × 26.5 cm
CR Jawlensky 1140

Abstract Head (Revelation), 1927

Oil on cardboard, 42 × 33 cm
CR Jawlensky 1274

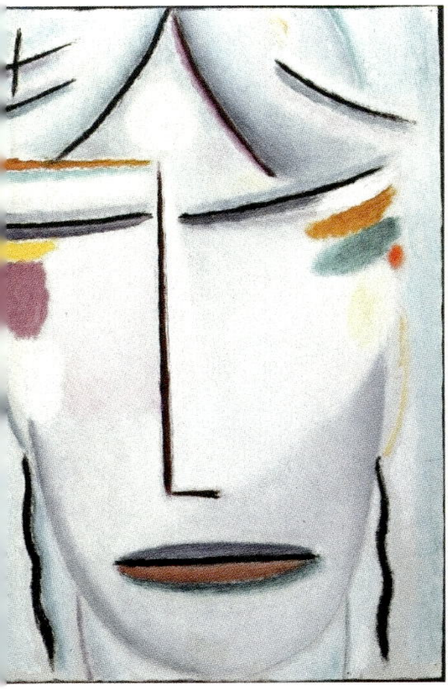

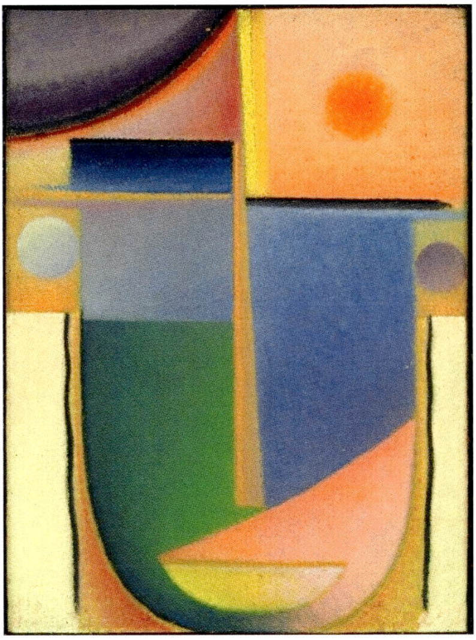

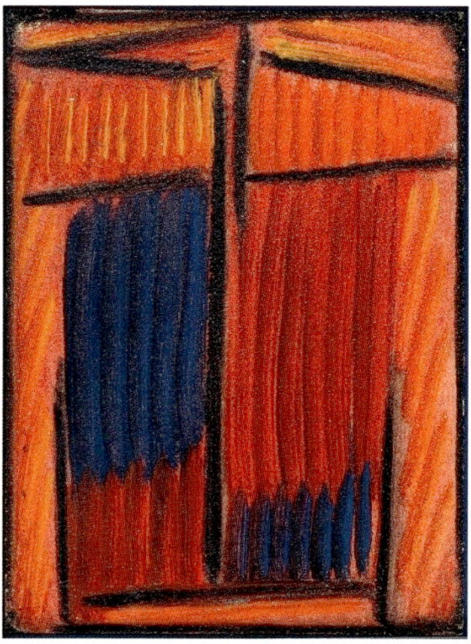

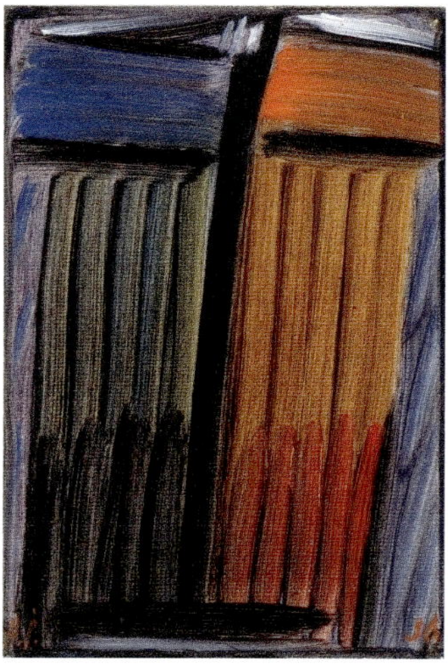

ALEXEJ VON JAWLENSKY 1864–1941

Meditation – Harmony in Red and Blue, 1936

Oil on cardboard, 17 × 12.5 cm
CR Jawlensky 1785

Meditation – Slavic Song, 1936

Oil on linen-finish paper laid down on cardboard, 17.7 × 12.7 cm
CR Jawlensky 2061

In 1929 Jawlensky was diagnosed with arthritis deformans. This meant severe pain for the artist in the years that followed, as well as a progressive stiffening of the joints. Like one "possessed", as he wrote in a letter, he worked until 1937/38, when it became physically no longer possible for him to do so. This last phase of Jawlensky's creative activity were dominated by a further series, the most extensive one of all: the "Meditations" – mostly postcard-size works on paper, which he fastened side by side next to each other on the easel. Later the sheets were mostly mounted on card or cardboard. In some four years of work on the "Meditations" he created more than 1,000 variations on this theme. Stylistically, this third series in the artist's oeuvre is a further development of the "Constructive Heads". In it, he further reduces the form he adopted up to 1933 so that a cross determines the structure of the painting's surface, stylising the eyes, nose and mouth elements. In between, with clearly visible brushstrokes, Jawlensky employs the whole upper part of the body to apply delicate layers of paint, creating areas of colour which

Large Meditation – Yellow Blue Red, 1936

Oil on linen-finish paper laid down on cardboard, 25.1 × 17.8 cm
CR Jawlensky 1850

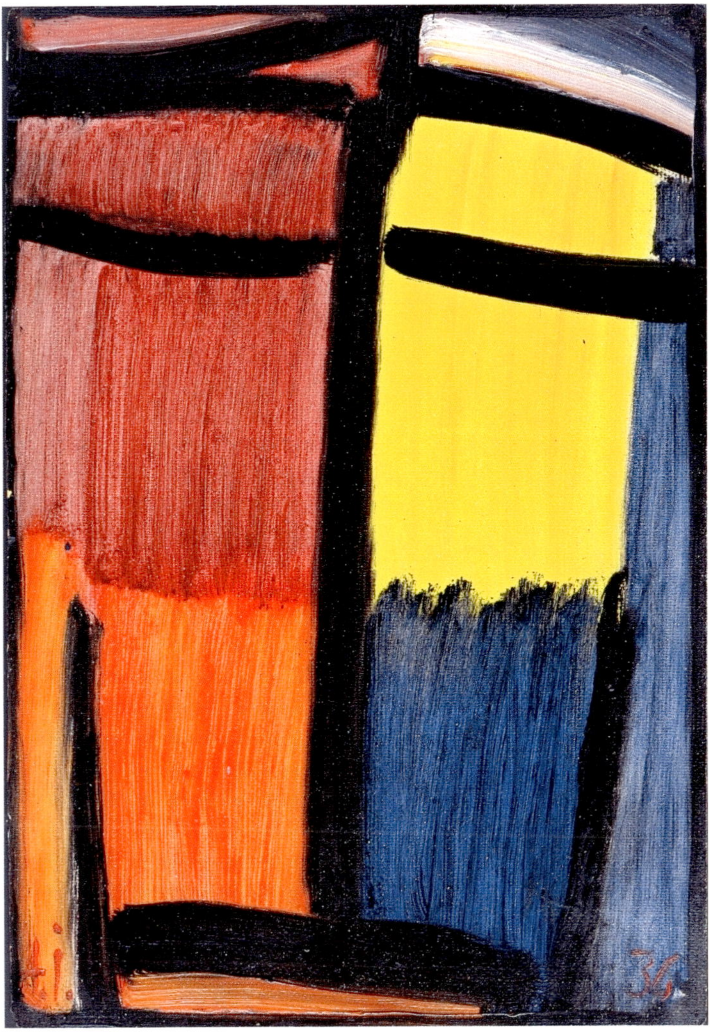

express different basic moods. This remains the most radical form of abstraction for the painter; Jawlensky deliberately never took the final step towards freeing himself from the representational. In the centre of his creativity stands the expression of what is hidden deep within, which for him is constantly linked with the starting point of his work, the human figure.

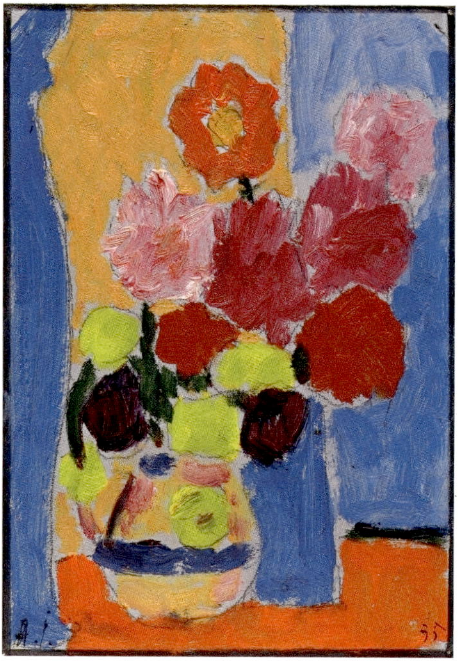

ALEXEJ VON JAWLENSKY 1864–1941

Still Life (Small Flowers), 1935

Oil on linen-finish paper laid down on cardboard, 18.8 × 13.5 cm
CR Jawlensky 1741

Like all the Expressionist artists, Alexej von Jawlensky was affected by the National Socialists' reactionary doctrines concerning art. As early as 1933, he was totally prohibited from exhibiting his work. His paintings were denounced at the "Degenerate Art" exhibition in 1937 in Munich and removed from German museums. In addition the artist, living in Wiesbaden, was burdened by the progressive arthritic condition which increasingly hindered his painting. Nevertheless, during this time he began work on the "Meditations", his most spiritual series. But, after a long hiatus, he also began to create still lifes again, using flower arrangements as the motif for a number of paintings. The juxtaposition of these two still lifes of 1935 and 1937 makes it clear how important it was to Jawlensky to free himself in this area too from the model of nature, and to transform what he saw into a synthesis of form, line and colour. The *Large Still Life* is an example of his typical glazing technique during his last years. It is one of the artist's last works before the stiffening of his joints from 1938 made it impossible to continue working.

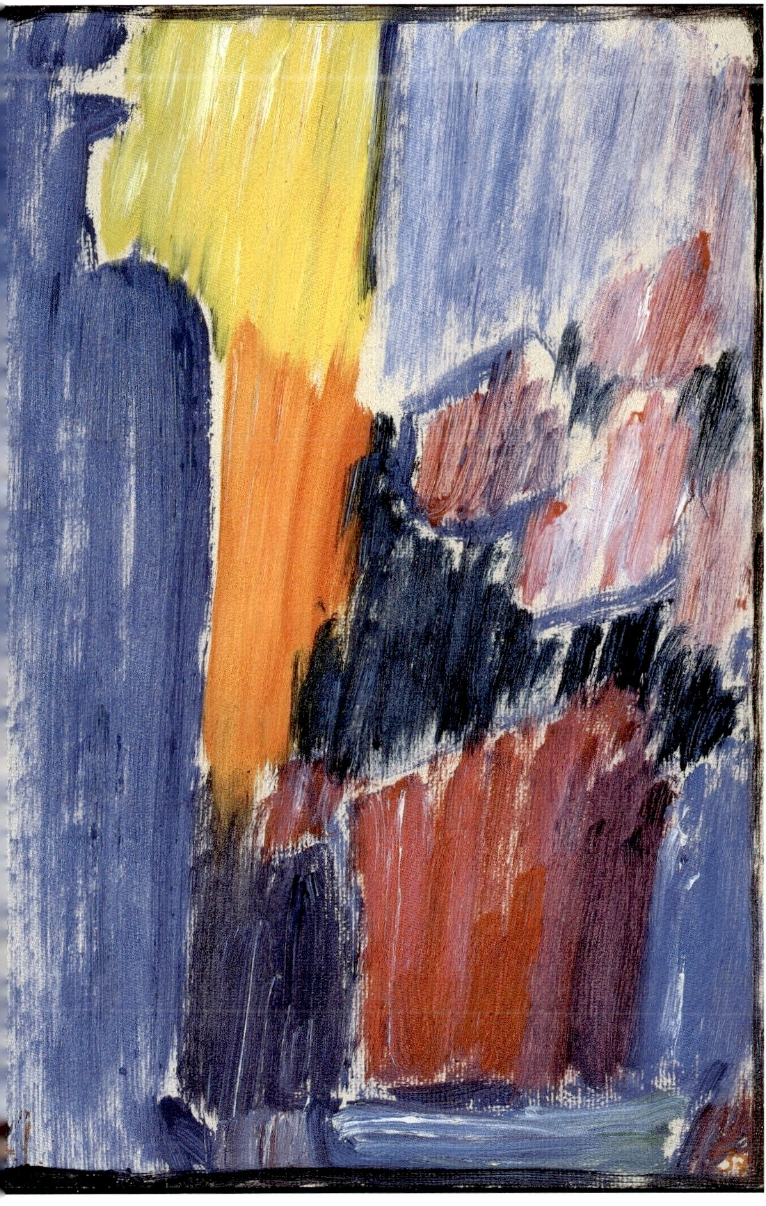

Large Still Life
(Sunny Window), 1937

Oil on cardboard, 24.7 × 17.3 cm
CR Jawlensky 2136

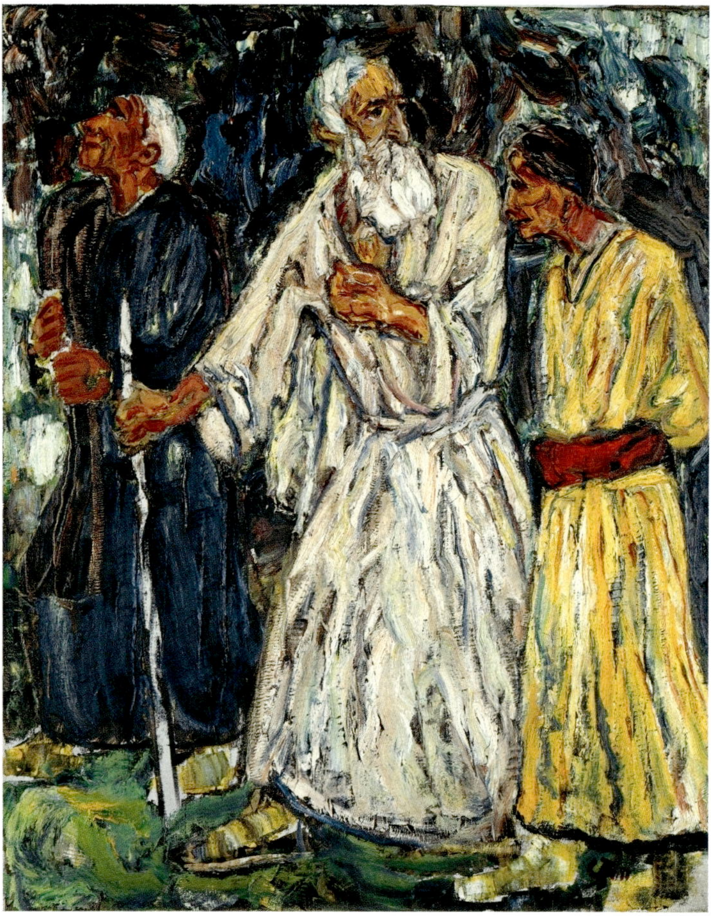

Three Wanderers (The Blind Tobias), 1911

Oil on canvas, 98 × 80 cm
CR Köcke 495

The painting of Christian Rohlfs developed initially at the Weimarer Kunstschule (Weimar Academy of Art), where he progressed from academic realism through open-air painting to a free Impressionist way of expressing himself. A contemporary of Cézanne, Van Gogh and Gauguin, in the early twentieth century he assimilated the influences of the French avant-garde, and developed in his sixties his own contribution to the new art of the Expressionists. In the years that followed, his artistic work manifests a disparate form that hovers between almost lyrical abstraction and Expressionist figure painting. An example of the latter genre is the *Three Wanderers* from the artist's time in Munich. The scene, also known as *The Blind Tobias*, shows three men striding forwards, the middle one being the blind father of the boy in the yellow garment, who is going on his Biblical journey together with the unrecognised archangel Raphael, in the background in a blue garment. The painting's composition is well thought out, based on the diagonals of the image, and skilfully restricts figures and space through carefully matched colours. In terms of painting technique, it demonstrates Rohlfs' characteristic scraping technique.

This landscape from Rohlfs' time in Polling, Bavaria, represents the painter's decorative, lyrical development before the First World War. Landscape was a lifelong preoccupation of the artist. In his early work he usually focuses on a detail, without great extension into depth of space. This characteristic posed compositional problems for the artist in the face of the monumental Alpine landscape. His letters attest to his difficulties in composition without foregrounds supplied by the landscape. Rohlfs resolved his creative dilemma by

Mountains (Bavaria), 1911
Oil on canvas, 50.5 × 65 cm

CHRISTIAN ROHLFS 1849–1938

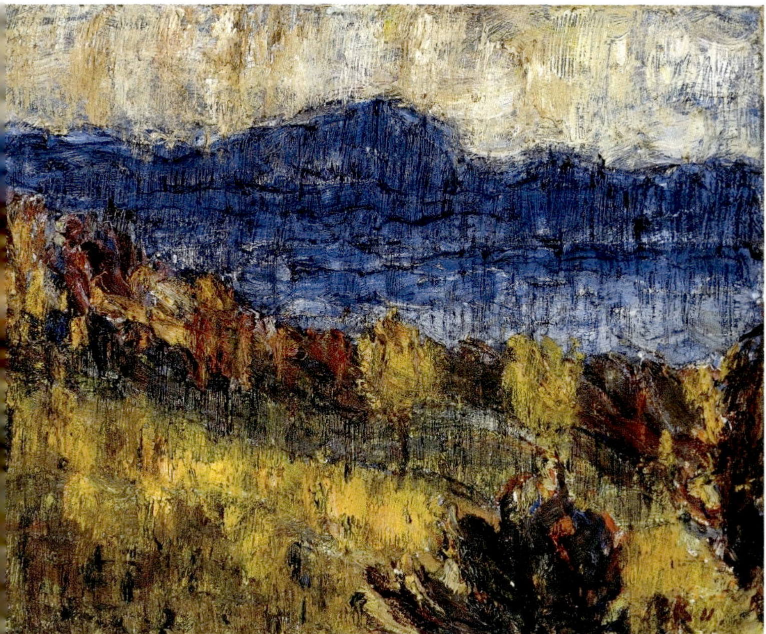

creating unusually free, almost abstract images, to an extreme extent removed from the model of nature. Only close examination of the *Mountains* of 1911 reveals an autumnal foreground with a row of trees ascending diagonally to the left, behind which rise the range of dark-blue mountains. Lacking depth, the composition has the effect of an abstract zonal layering of colours, whose structure only gradually becomes apparent to the viewer.

CHRISTIAN ROHLFS 1849–1938

In 1901, Rohlfs moved from his Thuringian home of many years to Hagen in Westphalia at the invitation of the collector Karl Ernst Osthaus. In addition to his patron's collection of contemporary art, he discovered the city of Soest as a source of many future subjects. In 1905/06 he spent the summer months there and recorded his impressions in his sketchbook. This important fund of pictorial motifs resulted in the following years in paintings that depict individual districts of the town and its famous church towers.

In this way in 1913 he created this picture of the *Steeple of St Paul's*, which he had already painted in 1906 from a similar perspective. While at that time he still cultivated a style of painting based on Van Gogh – colour-intensive, Impressionist, nervously iridescent – this painting produced seven years later clearly shows changes in Rohlfs' artistic perception. On his return from Bavaria he sought to reorient himself and overpainted some works he had completed before 1910. They included this painting, which he reconstructed in tempera in 1913. Individual colour surfaces structure the horizontally

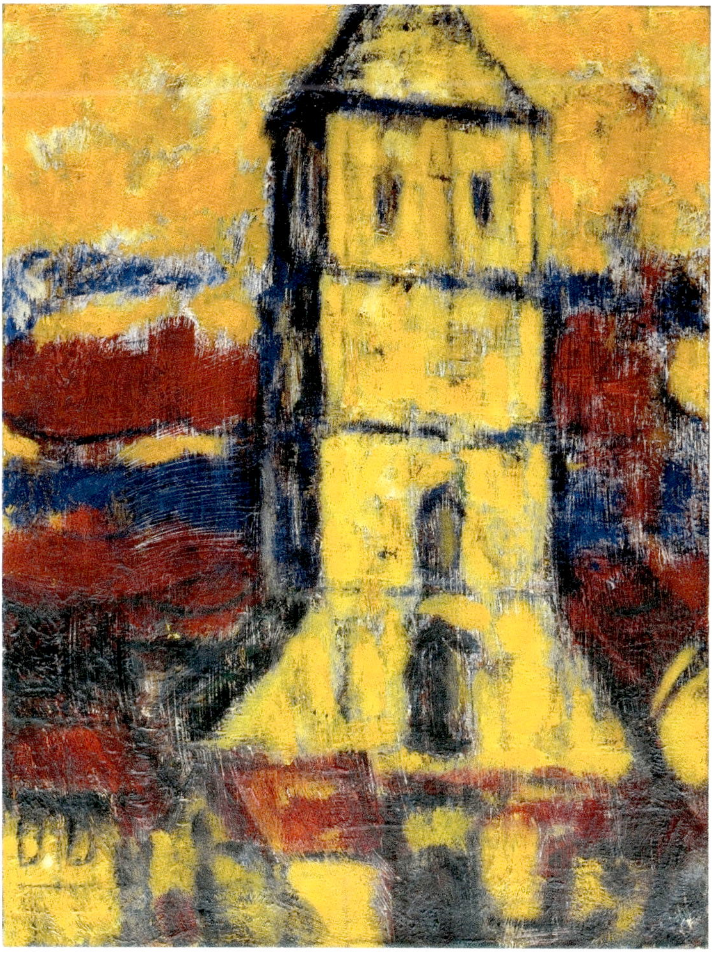

layered painting and lead from the earth-bound lower level, dominated by dark red, along the steeple, upwards into the lighter, yellow-toned areas above the roofs of the houses. Thus the composition gains an inner tension from the blend of weight and lightness of the two basic colours.

Steeple of St Paul's in Soest, 1913

Tempera on canvas, 78 × 60 cm
CR Köcke 535

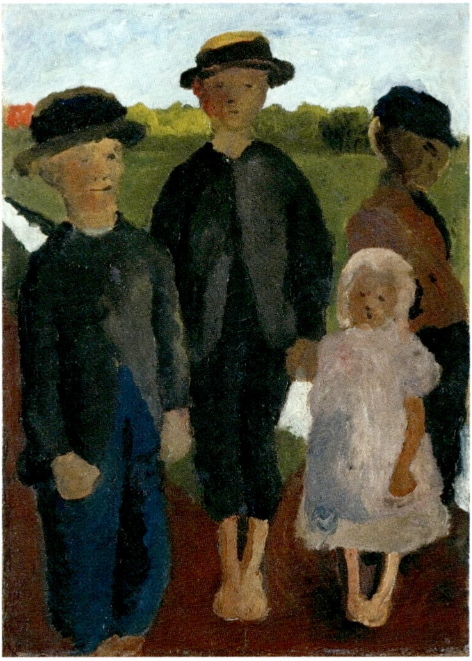

PAULA MODERSOHN-BECKER 1876–1907

Four Children in a Landscape with a Moorland Canal, c. 1900

Oil on cloth-lined board on wood, 55.8 × 41 cm
CR Busch/Werner 69

Paula Modersohn-Becker lived her short life to the full before her premature death at the age of 31. She was active as a painter for a good decade of that period, and her works made a significant contribution to the development of Expressionism in Germany. Her main themes were always people and nature, but it was the child that interested her most of all. Depictions of peasant children are found from 1898 onwards, the year in which she settled in the little artists' colony of Worpswede in the Teufelsmoor (Devil's Moor) near Bremen. Born in Dresden, in 1901 she married the painter Otto Modersohn. She gave birth to a longed-for child in 1907 by but died from postnatal complications.

Major changes in her artistic oeuvre took place from 1900, when she stayed in Paris for the first time. Freeing herself from the traditional role of the woman, in the years that followed she developed an increasingly self-determined life as an artist and often stayed in France for many months, far from her family. Here she became familiar with the most recent developments of the avant-garde and above all became an enthusiast for the art of Cézanne and Gauguin. Everything she saw had such an effect on her that around 1904 she began to simplify her painting with regard to form and colour.

These two depictions of children in Worpswede from the time of her first stay in Paris show them framed by the typical landscape of the Teufelsmoor, with its broad meadows traversed by drainage canals. Modersohn-Becker's strong interest in a clearly structured composition is evident. As with most of her works, in these early depictions a quiet melancholy of her own already pervades the scene. The artist succeeds here in empathising deeply with the tender souls of the young children and giving form to what she feels.

Girl Leaning on Birch-Tree Trunk in a Landscape, c. 1902

Oil on cardboard on canvas, 72 × 49 cm
CR Busch/Werner 294

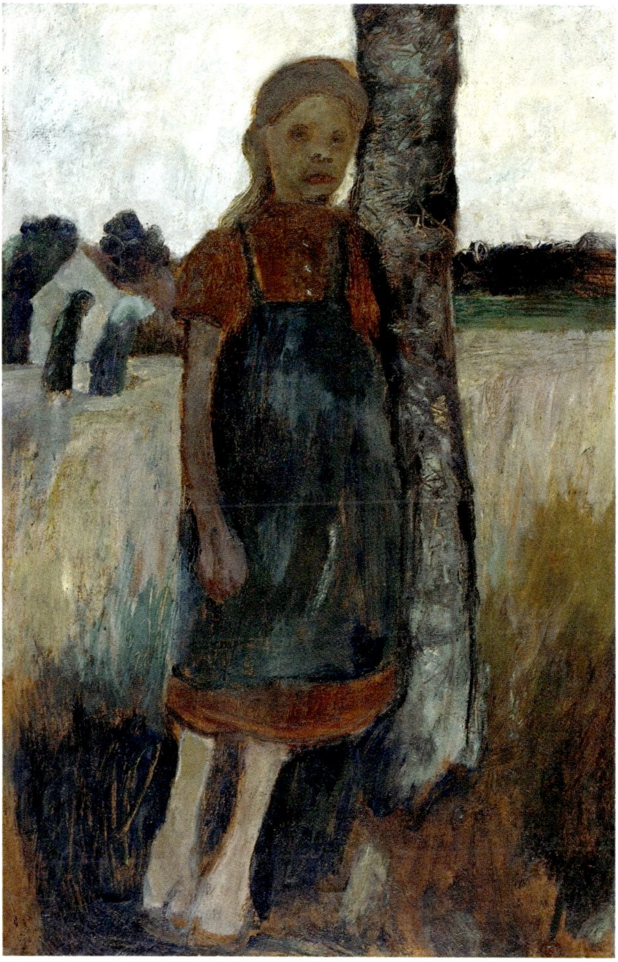

Helmut Kolle, like Rohlfs, Beckmann and Paula Modersohn-Becker, is among the Expressionist artists who belong to no group. In addition he is hardly known to the public at large today. In his short life, which included a creative period of only one decade, he developed his own characteristic style, which adopts and makes use of Expressionist and Cubist influences. As a painter, in his early works Kolle used the pseudonym Helmut vom Hügel. *The Sailor's Farewell* dates from his period of lyrical-poetic Expressionism in the early 1920s. The sailor is seen in a rocky landscape, gazing longingly, lost in thought, at the roses in his right hand. This image, whose basic mood is expressed in dark, muted colours, draws its emotional effect from the glowing red of the shirt and the mediating yellow of the collar against the brown rock of the background as well as from the harmonious placement of the figure of the sailor within the square picture frame.

The Sailor's Farewell
(American Sailor), 1923

Oil on canvas, 82 × 82 cm
CR Chabert 24

HELMUT KOLLE 1899–1931

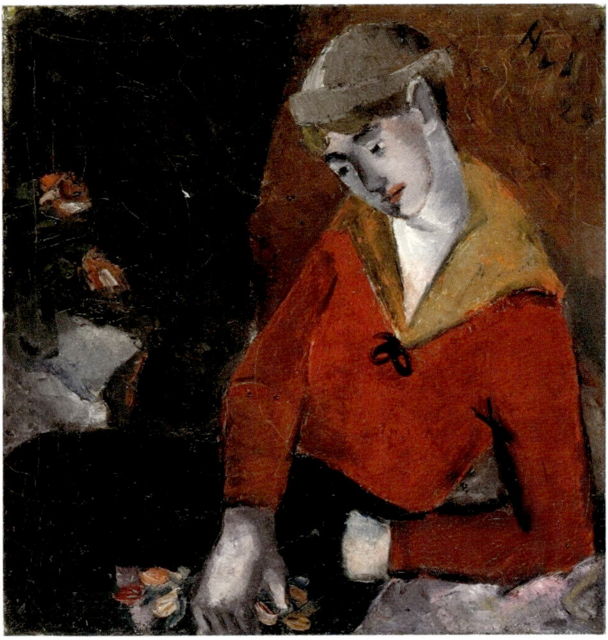

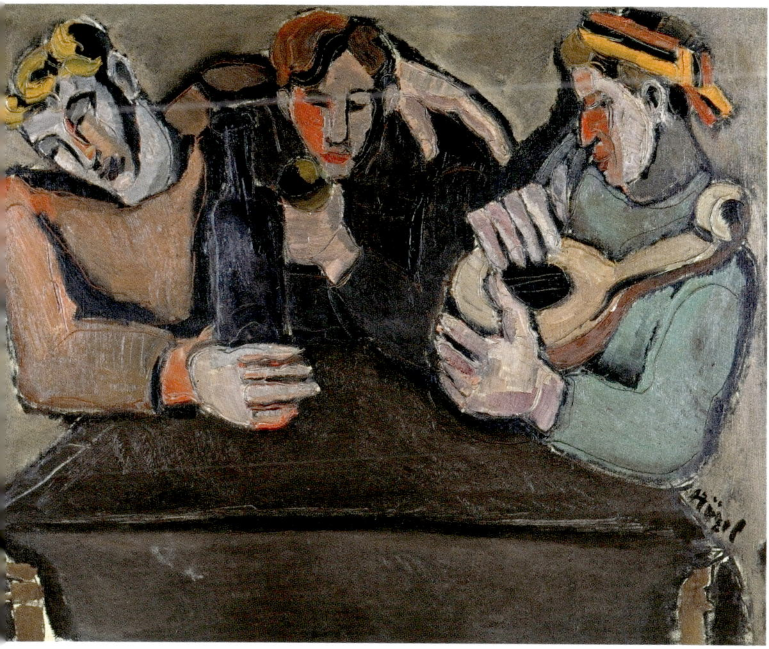

In his monograph on Kolle of 1935, Wilhelm Uhde describes *The Three Drinkers* as a "composition of monumental effect". This large-format work, with its perspective that draws the viewer into the depth of the space, possesses great suggestive power and concentrates the attention on the central figure of the three. This group of figures is skilfully restricted by its spatial arrangement and by the deployment of colour, accentuating the central figure, which stands out from the group and which radiates a mixture of despair and resignation.

In 1924 Kolle and Uhde moved to Paris. There the young painter received recognition, exhibited successfully and gained contact with the contemporary art of France, which subsequently left clear traces in his artistic works.

The Three Drinkers,
c. 1925/26

Oil on canvas, 114 × 146 cm
CR Chabert 110

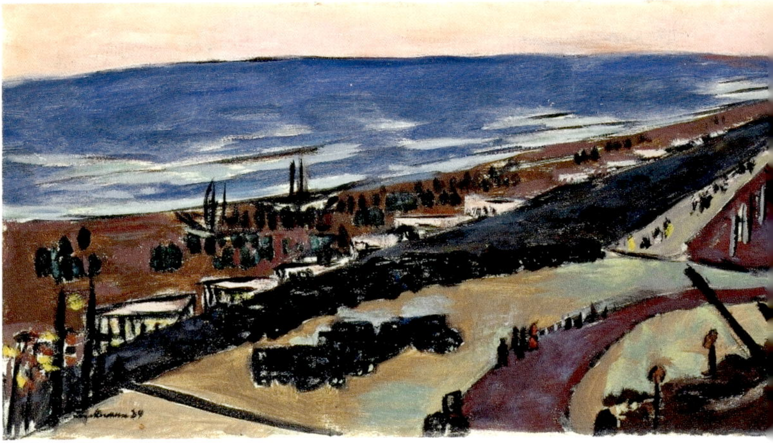

View of Zandvoort in the Evening, 1934

Oil on canvas, 40.5 × 100.5 cm
CR Göpel 399

During the years before the outbreak of World War II Max Beckmann often travelled with his wife; he stayed with friends, including a visit to Gstadt on Lake Chiemsee with Lilly von Schnitzler, who supported the painter by purchases of his works, and from 1934 several times to Zandvoort in the Netherlands, where the collector and art patron Eduard Freiherr von der Heydt owned a house in the dunes. While the early landscapes of Beckmann came into being directly from nature, from the 1920s he also worked from postcards and private holiday photographs. Such an origin can be assumed for the *View of Zandvoort in the Evening*, which shows the extended promenade of the Dutch seaside resort.
From 1932 the attacks of the National Socialists on Max Beckmann increased noticeably. After their seizure of power he was dismissed from his teaching post at the Städelschule (Städel School) in Frankfurt; his paintings were removed from public collections and condemned in 1937 at the "Degenerate Art" exhibition.

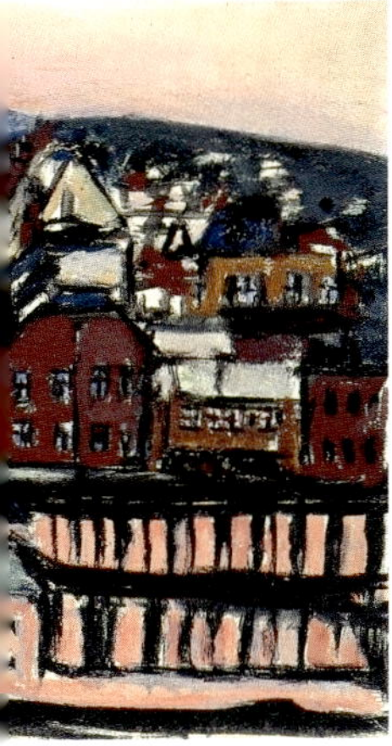

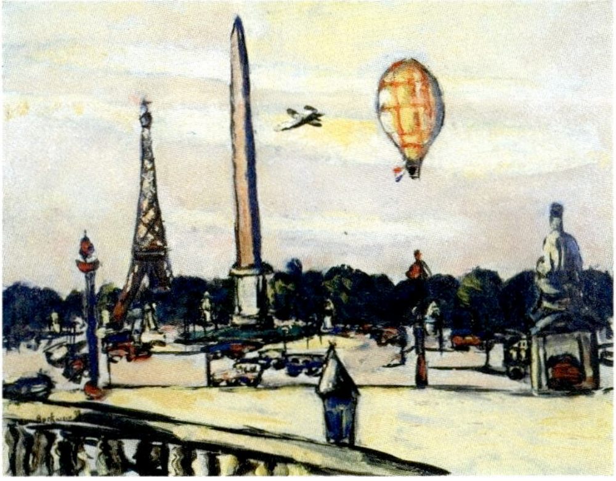

MAX BECKMANN 1884–1950

In July 1937, one day after Adolf Hitler's speech on the opening of the "Degenerate Art" exhibition, Beckmann left Germany with his wife to go into exile in Amsterdam. Since his youth the painter had visited Paris several times. From the Netherlands he rented a small flat in October 1938, near the Bois de Boulogne, where he lived and worked until the summer of 1939. During these months he created various Paris cityscapes, among them two paintings showing the Place de la Concorde by day and night. The day version is a view of the famous Paris square determined by the horizontals and verticals of the picture. The peace and quiet of the observer standing in the distance is abruptly disturbed by the martially towering objects – the obelisk, the Eiffel Tower, and the sculptures and street lamps. Created shortly before the outbreak of war, this depiction has the effect of a suggestion of things to come in the "nightmarish world" (Max Beckmann).

Place de la Concorde by Day, 1939

Oil on canvas, 47 × 61 cm
CR Göpel 524

Three-dimensional sculpture occupies no more than a marginal place in the work of Max Beckmann. Only in the 1930s and 1950s did he produce a small number of cast bronzes whose subjects blend harmoniously into the figurative universe of his oeuvre as a whole. Nevertheless, a number of his paintings contain two-dimensional representations of sculptures.

Sculptural forms have always been associated with the divine or Promethean act of creation. The interpretation of this subject in Max Beckmann's work – like that of the relationship between man and woman – undergoes a number of changes over the years. In his late works it takes on a comparatively violent form: the human body appears deformed and often adopts unnatural positions.

For Beckmann, the theme of the mythical act of creation is closely bound up with the relationship between the sexes. The parallels become abundantly clear in *The Sculptor's Dream*. The picture was created on a rejected piece of old canvas between July 1946 and January 1947 in the artist's studio in Amsterdam. It was a time when Beckmann experienced great mental anguish in the face of the uncertainties of the immediate post-war period. Reminiscent of Pygmalion, the creator/artist/man, who remains invisible, attempts to take violent possession of the helpless woman, who has no will of her own – perhaps a metaphor for life itself – and to 'grasp' her, or it, for himself. It is the attempt to gain security and therefore power (over oneself) by looking to the future when surrounded by uncertainty and danger on all sides.

MAX BECKMANN 1884–1950

The Sculptor's Dream, 1947
Oil on canvas, 135 × 70 cm
CR Göpel 737

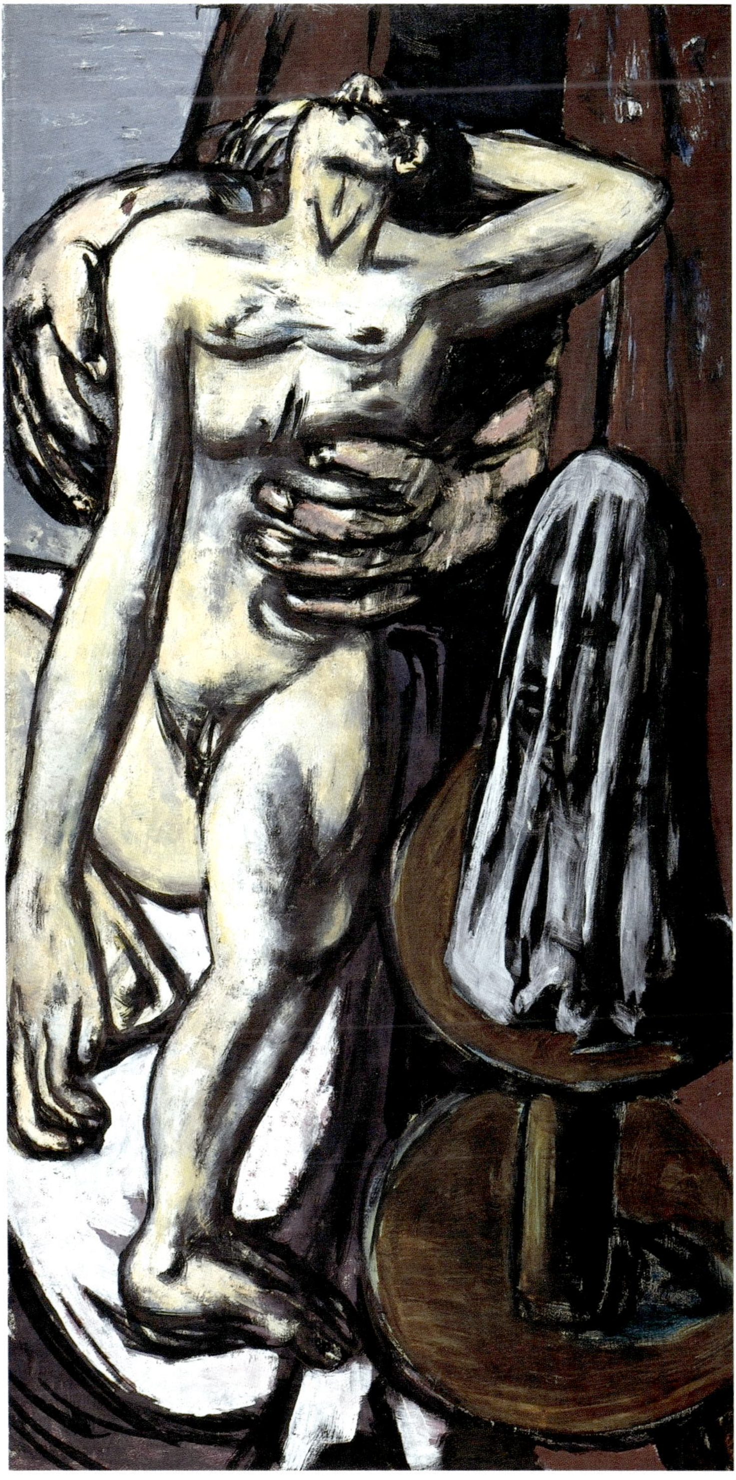

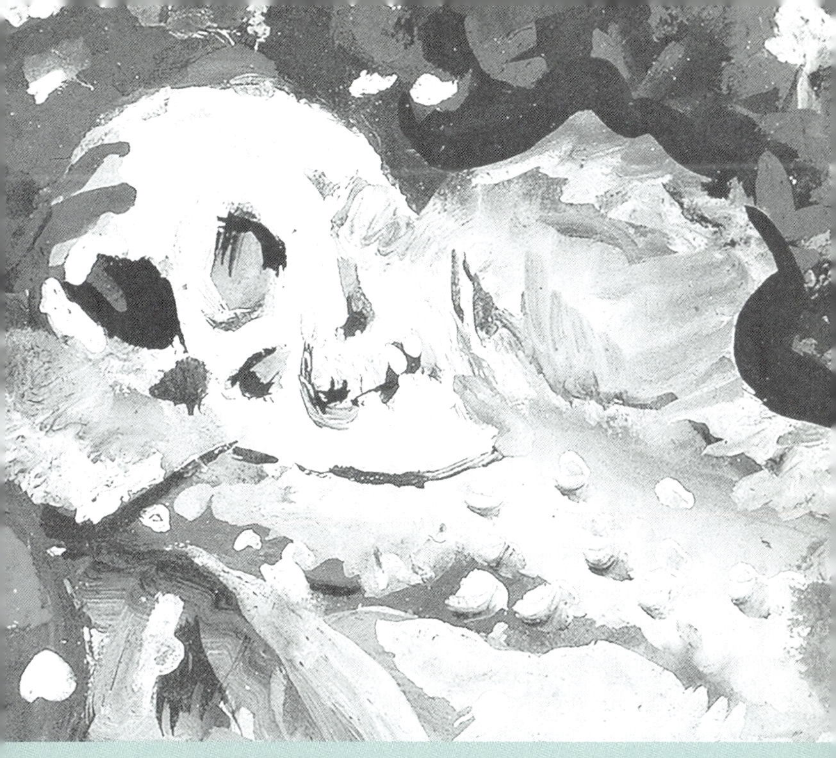

OTTO DIX

CONRAD FELIXMÜLLER

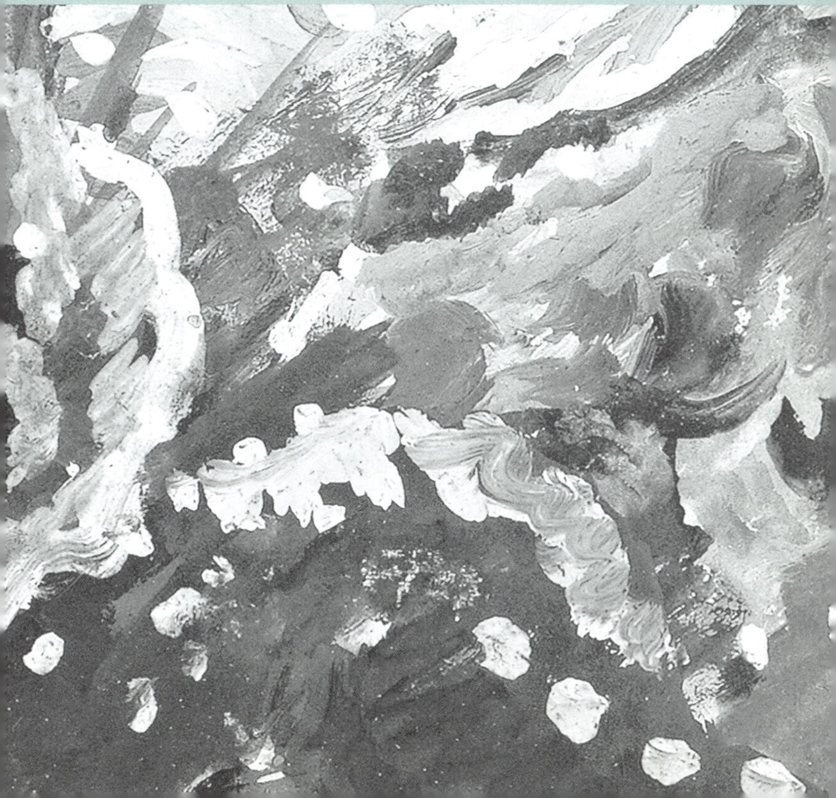

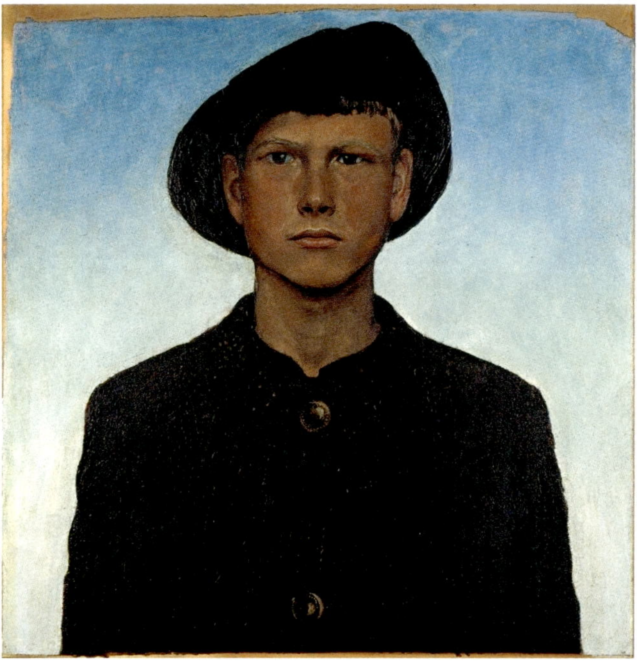

OTTO DIX 1891–1969

Self-Portrait with Walker's Hat, 1912

Oil on paper mounted on cardboard, 51 × 49 cm
CR Löffler 1912/2

Otto Dix's confrontation with his own personality in his work began in 1911/12. Up to the outbreak of the First World War he created a bare dozen self-portraits in oil, of which this work at Chemnitz is the very first. A contemporary photograph of Otto Baumgärtel, his closest friend at the time, shows the twenty-one-year-old painter, who had been studying at the Königliche Kunstgewerbeschule (College of Applied Arts) in Dresden since the autumn of 1910, in a similar pose. Dix portrays himself as a "Wandervogel", that is, a member of the youth movement of around 1900 that sought to distance itself explicitly from its parents' generation and undergo a conscious self-education in a community of others of the same age. As an expression of his sense of belonging to this group he has chosen its typical clothing, consisting of a light coat and walker's hat. While Dix, in his work from 1913 onwards, primarily worked from Expressionist models, this work represents a first attempt at the Old Master-like manner he perfected after 1920. In seven preparatory sketches he searched for the right format.

Between his schooldays in Gera and his years at the Königliche Kunstgewerbeschule in Dresden from 1910 to 1914, the artist repeatedly took his native landscape as his theme in drawings and paintings, creating streets, house-fronts and landscapes in a free Impressionist manner.

In February 1912, Dix very probably visited the Van Gogh exhibition at the Arnold Gallery in Dresden; its influence is evident in the Expressionist development in his art from this time. The *Snow-Covered Wood* is the first landscape he painted in this new style. The unusual perspective shows the vineyard in the Untermhaus district of Gera, near his parental home. Like a wall of tree-crowns, the wood rises up with its snow-covered fir-tree tops, above which birds circle against a wintry grey sky.

Snow-Covered Wood (Vineyard), 1912

Oil on paper mounted on cardboard, 53.5 × 59.5 cm
CR Löffler 1912/4

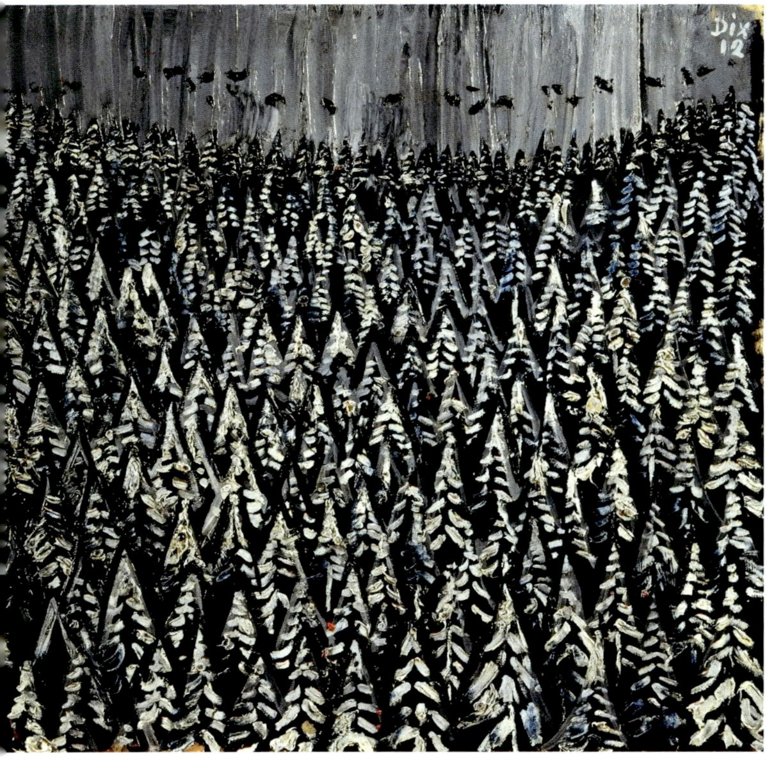

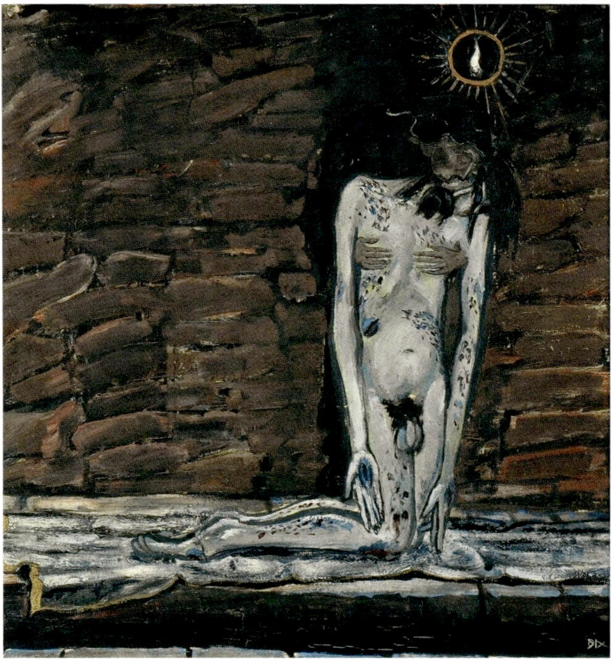

OTTO DIX 1891–1969

Pietà, 1912

Oil on paper mounted on Novopan, 50.5 × 49.5 cm
CR Löffler 1912/1

Religious themes are found in Otto Dix's early work as in the years of the Inner Emigration and in the late work starting in 1945. The *Pietà* is the only painting with a Biblical motif that he created before the First World War, and it occupies a key position within this group of works. While the artist's allegorical confrontation with his personal experience and his recent past is in the foreground of his late work, his early works are characterised by an experimental, open approach. Dix, as a young man, empathises with the primeval themes of humanity: suffering, pain and death, represented by the Passion of Christ. The scene is placed on an open road in front of a brick wall in tones of blood-red and brown. As though under the impact of overpowering grief and love, Mary holds the wounded body of her son over the shroud, kissing it in her anguish. When questioned towards the end of his life about parallels with Gustav Klimt's painting *The Kiss* (1907/08), which could be seen in the Great Art Exhibition in Dresden in the summer of 1912, Dix identified his *Pietà* as "a little in the *Art Nouveau* manner".

This depiction of the Dresden prison is also one of the young student's first paintings. The work is one of the group of pre-war paintings and was presumably created before Dix was called up at the end of August 1914. It shows the Mathildenstrasse prison in the Pirnaische Vorstadt district near the Elbe, not far from the historic centre of the city. Up to 1907 this striking building on Holbeinplatz was the main prison for the district court; after that it functioned as a branch of the prison on Münchner Platz. Dix's 'portrait' of the notorious establishment largely coincides with reality, but dramatises the motif by viewing it from below with exaggerated perspective and simplification of forms in the depiction of the prison block. In this way he stages the building in an unusual manner, making it appear massive and impregnable, but also menacing, like the bow of a great ship.

Prison in Dresden, 1914
Oil on cardboard, 68 × 82 cm
CR Löffler 1914/19

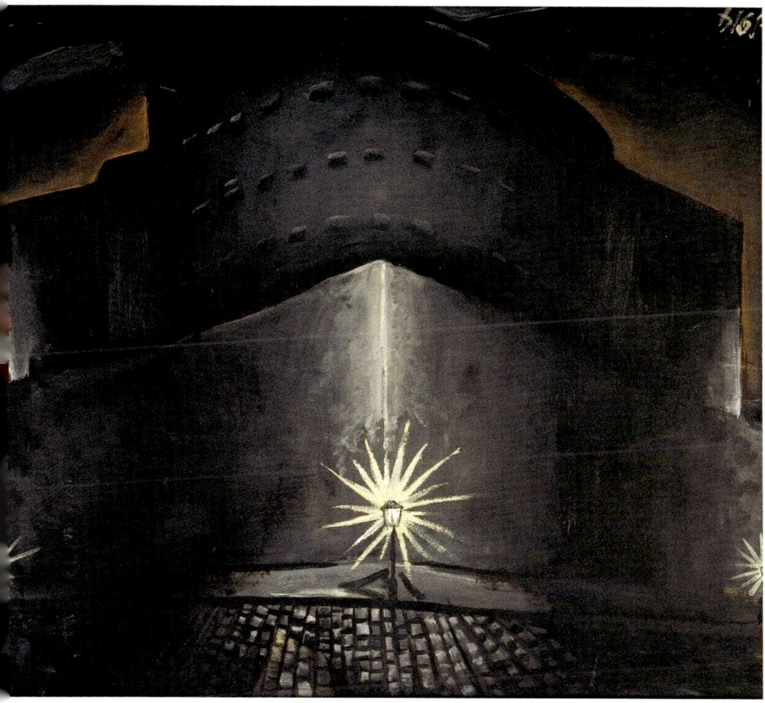

While in the early landscapes up to 1912 it is the open-air play of light in the forests and meadows of the Elbe that the young painter sought to capture, from 1913 it is the motif of the city – and specifically the city by night with its lights – that is featured in the work of Otto Dix. The experiences of the trail-blazing exhibitions of international contemporary art in Dresden of 1912/13 opened up to him a new approach to colour and motif. Up to the outbreak of war, he created twelve paintings in the Expressionist *alla prima* method which have the city or interior spaces by night as their subject. In his two variations on the motif of gas street lamps,

House by Night II, 1914
Oil on paper, 66 × 55 cm
CR Löffler 1914/18

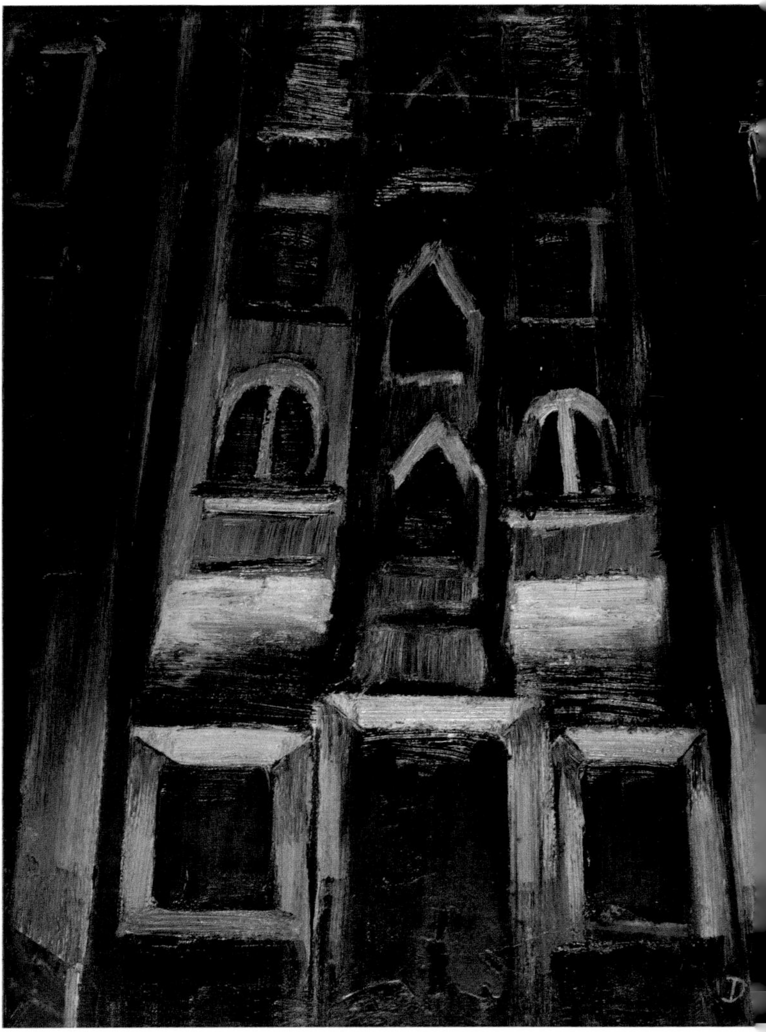

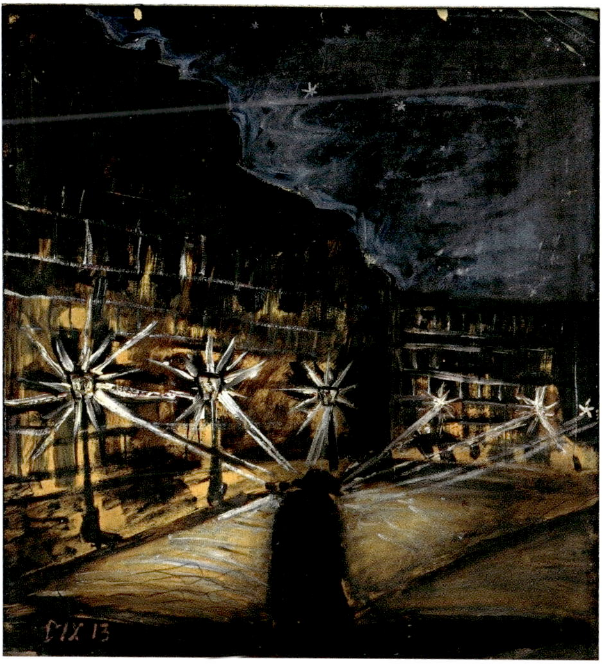

OTTO DIX 1891–1969

Dix is chiefly concerned about the atmospheric rays of light in the dark. Actual observation of these phenomena in the foggy haze of the city by night may have been the source of this theme, while the figure seen from behind in the centre of the composition can be interpreted in the Romantic tradition as a symbol of the isolation of the individual in the modern city. Compared with this, in *House by Night II* the young painter is primarily interested in the sculptural play of light on the richly structured house façades.

Street with Gas Lamps, 1913

Oil on paper mounted on cardboard, 40 × 40 cm
CR Löffler 1913/17

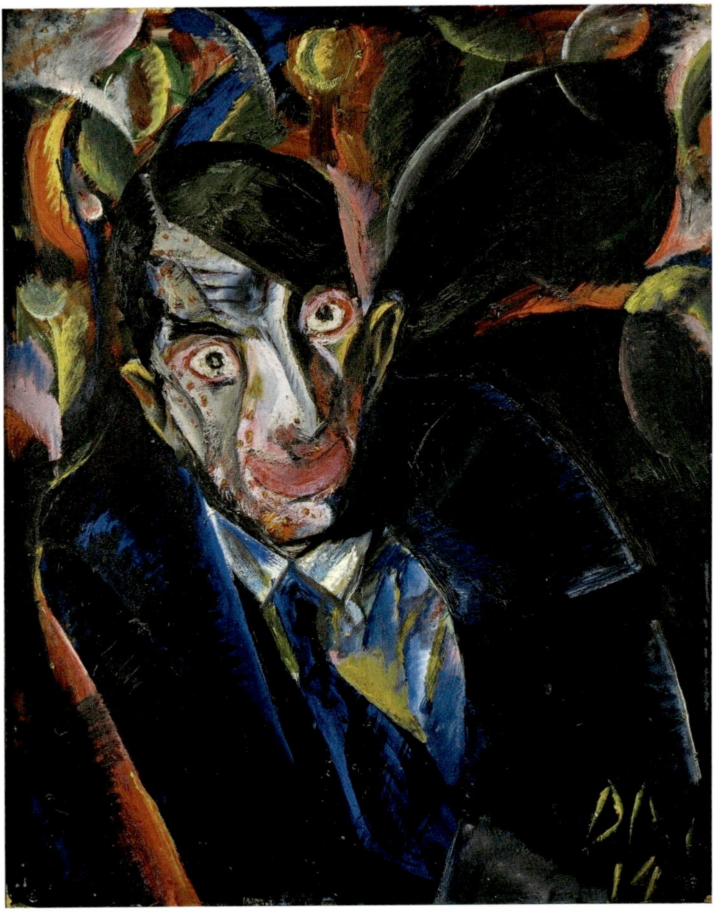

Portrait of the Painter Zienert, 1914

Oil on canvas, 64 × 52 cm
CR Löffler 1914/10

This portrait is of the painter Walter Gustav Zienert. The artist, born in Annaberg in the Erzgebirge (Ore Mountains), also studied from 1914 to 1915 at the Kunstgewerbeschule (Academy of Applied Art) in Dresden. This work is one of a series of portraits of artists in Dix's circle of friends, executed before the outbreak of war. It shows Zienert hovering, blurred, against a background landscape in largely abstract, Expressionist style, using the opportunities provided by contemporary modern composition. In the year when this painting was created, the Arnold Gallery in Dresden held the Expressionist Exhibition, which had an inspiring and encouraging effect on Dix and his fellow-students. During that year he predominantly characterised his friends by means of experimentation with various artistic media.

Like many of his generation, Otto Dix at first positively welcomed the outbreak of the First World War. True to his motto – "I am such a realist that I have to see everything with my own eyes in order to confirm that it is so" – as early as the August of the year of his call-up he joined the 48th field artillery regiment in Dresden as a reservist. In May 1915 he had himself transferred to the machine-gun company XII at Bautzen, before reporting voluntarily in the autumn to go to the front. From September 1915 Dix was sent to the western front in the Champagne district and spent the majority of his army service up to 1918 in France and Flanders.

During this time, between battles he created more than 400 drawings, gouaches and field postcards. It was particularly in the gouaches that he dealt with the appalling experiences of action at the front: "Barbed wire, fleas, grenades, bombs, holes, corpses, blood, schnapps, mice, cats, gas, cannons, dirt, bullets, mortars, fire, steel, that's war!"

Soldier's Head, 1917
Gouache, 32 × 23.5 cm
CR Pfäffle G 10erJ/3

OTTO DIX 1891–1969

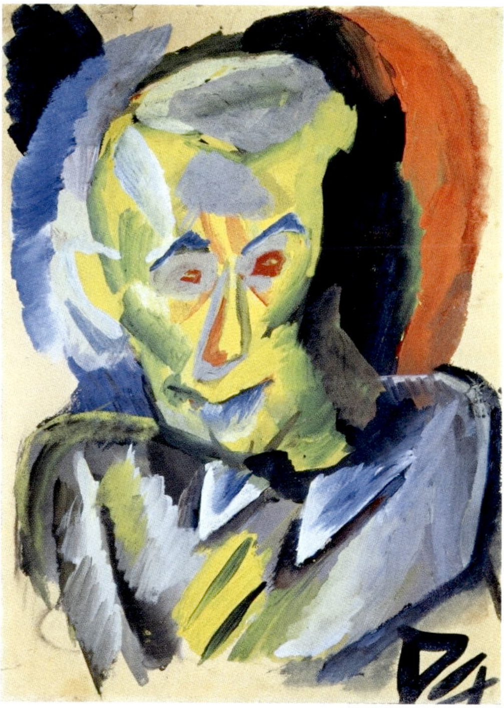

While recording his experiences in documentary form in his drawing, Dix tried in his gouaches to express the horrors of war in artistic terms with thickly applied paint. The *Soldier's Head* is one such work, couched in the Expressionist language of forms and colours. While the *Trench* suggests death and destruction by means of its choice of colours, in its pendant, *Concrete Trench with Flowers* Dix takes as his theme the absurd in human behaviour, contrasting the trench with the eternally recurrent cycle of blossoming nature.

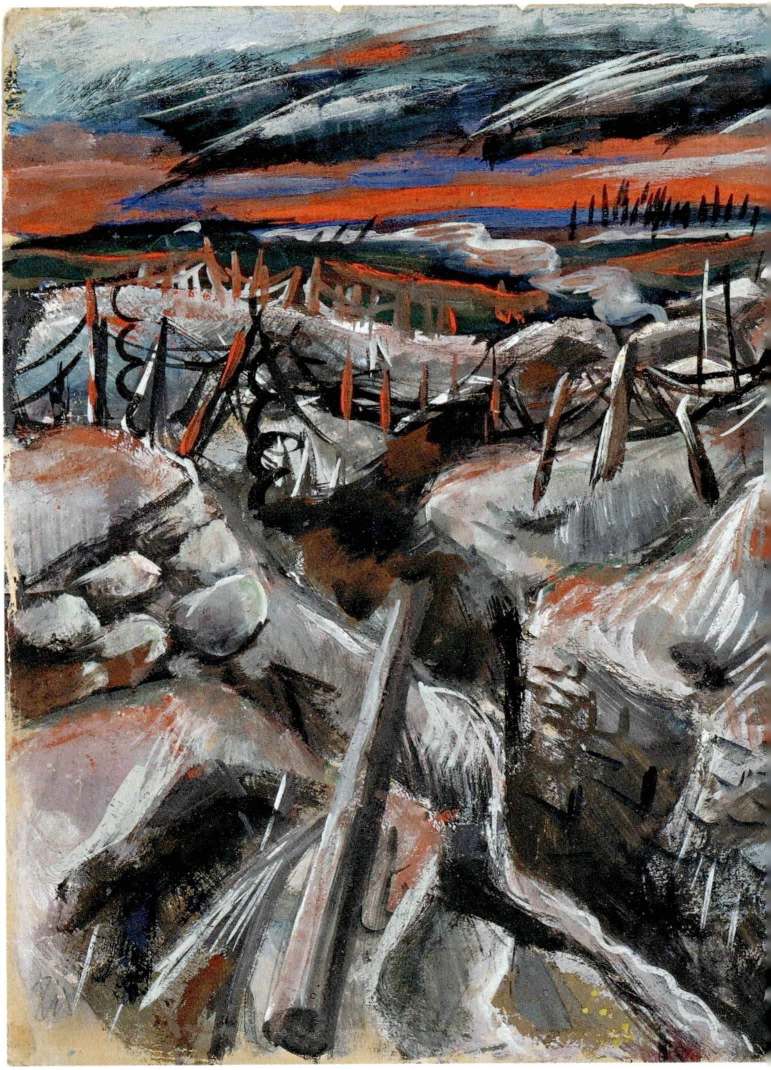

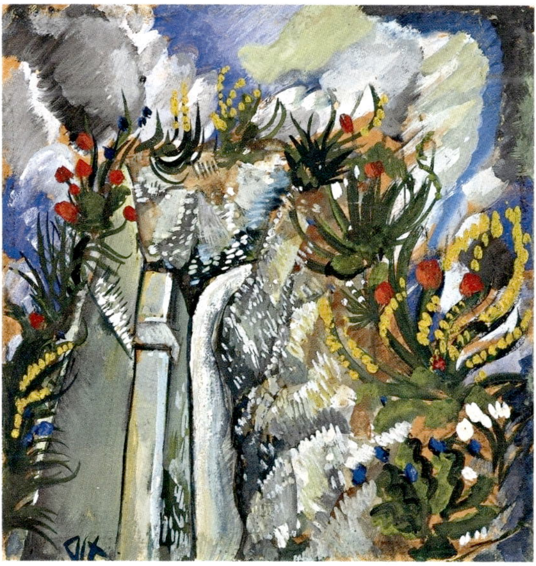

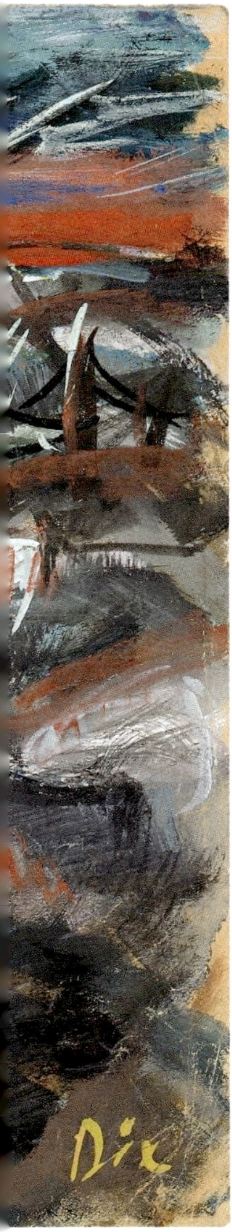

OTTO DIX 1891–1969

Trench, c. 1916

Gouache and opaque white, 29 × 29 cm
CR Pfäffle G 1917/25

Concrete Trench with Flowers, 1916

Gouache, 28.8 × 28.6 cm
CR Pfäffle G 1916/18

Grave of a Frenchman (Champagne), 1915

Gouache over pencil,
29.9 × 28.5 cm
CR Pfäffle G 1915/8

Night Scene, 1918

Gouache, 39 × 40 cm
CR Pfäffle G 10erJ/1

OTTO DIX 1891–1969

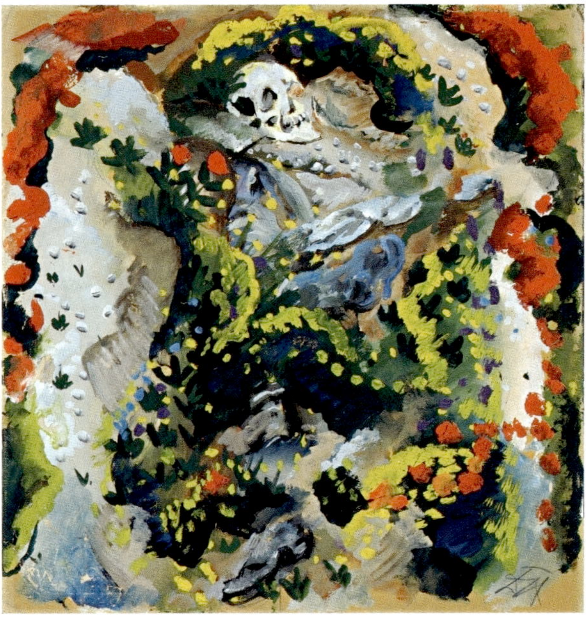

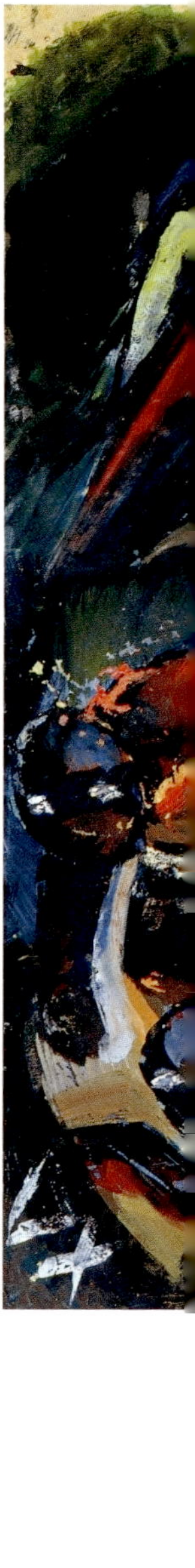

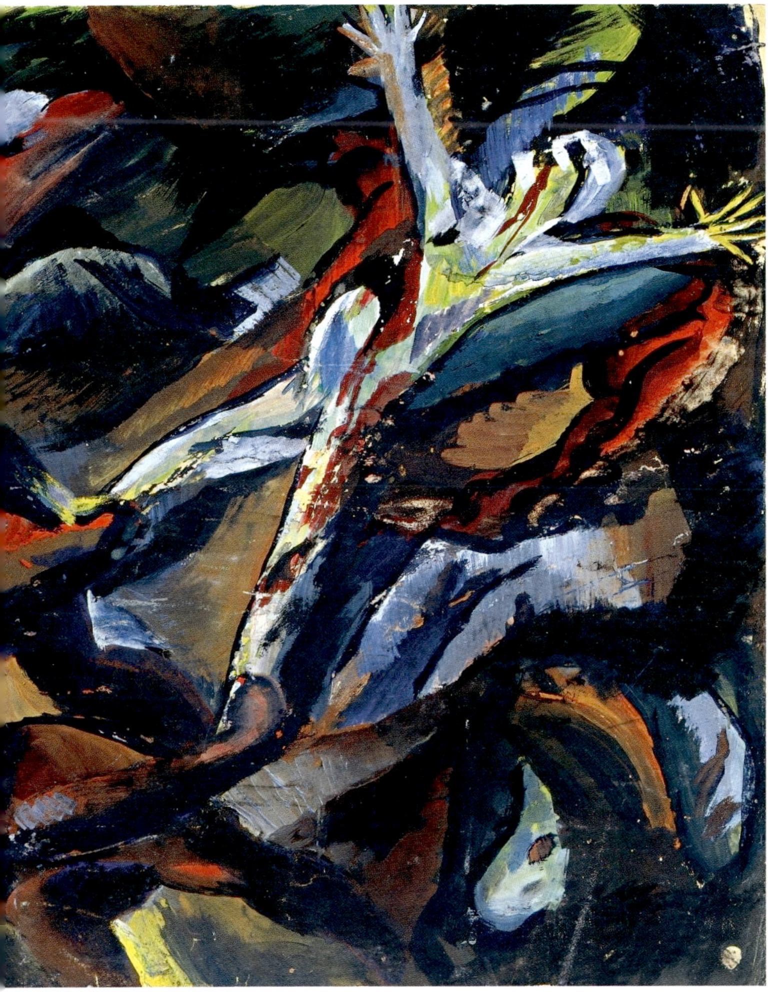

The dying soldier in *Night Scene*, luridly illuminated by grenade fire and flares, illustrates the countless losses of the trench warfare on the western front.
On the sheet *Grave of a Frenchman* Dix wrote in a letter of 17 January 1916: "It was here, on this spot, that he fell. He was laid in the large 21 grenade crater and covered with plenty of earth. His helmet on top!"

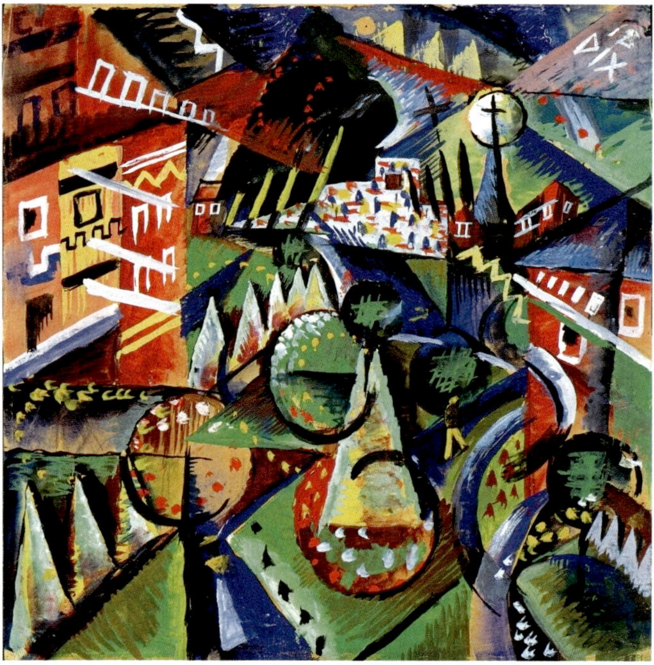

OTTO DIX 1891–1969

Going for a Walk in a Small French Town, 1918

Watercolour and gouache over pencil, 39.2 × 39 cm
CR Pfäffle A/G 1918/2

Before the war Dix had already encountered Futuristic painting through an exhibition at the Richter Art Gallery in Dresden. He created gouaches in that style particularly towards the end of the war, when he broke up his *Going for a Walk in a Small French Town* into pointed forms in the Cubist manner. The observer is confronted with loneliness and a world turned upside down.

In 1919 Dix returned from the war to Dresden to find himself in the middle of the revolutionary activities in the city. Disappointed with the results, he radicalised his artistic methods and made his way towards a drastic formulation of taboo topics. At this time he broke away entirely from the bourgeois system of values. Around 1920 'Dada-Dix' was active within the Dresden Dadaist group and executed provocative collages, drawings, paintings and graphics.

It was in this context that the painting *Red Head* was created in 1919. A reddish-purple head, surrounded by eleven yellow stars, rises in front of a silhouetted city by night. In the interior of the skull, instead of the brain, are images of thoughts on themes such as love and sexuality. In the same year Dix varied this motif in his first portfolio of prints called *Werden* (Becoming) in the woodcut *I Dix am the A and the O.*

Red Head, 1919

Oil on cardboard, 72 × 66 cm
CR Löffler 1919/8

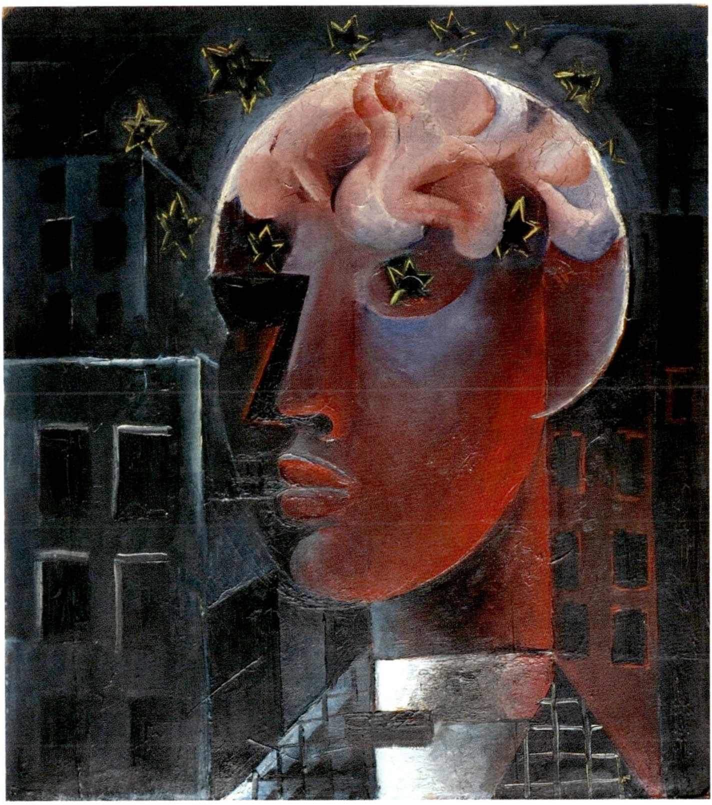

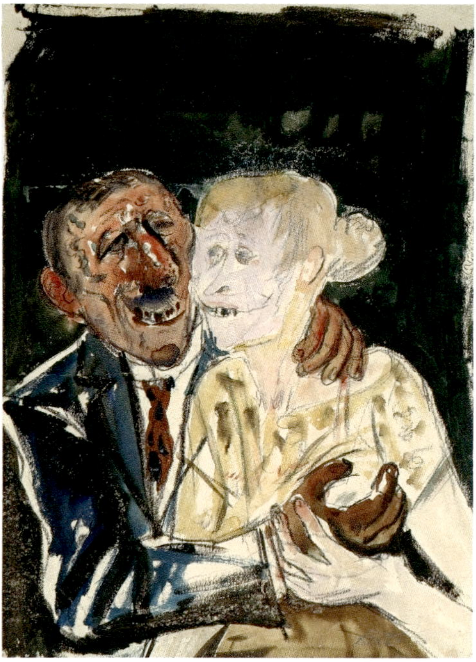

OTTO DIX 1891–1969

Study for
'Lovers in the Bar', 1921

Watercolour and opaque white over pencil, 55.1 × 41 cm
CR Pfäffle A 1921/8

The new decade saw basic changes in Otto Dix's work. His painting style developed from an Expressionist *alla prima* painting method to a glazing technique based on the practice of the Old Masters. Along with this went a change in Dix's world view: instead of his youthful intoxication with the richness of life, Dix from now on contemplated every form of human togetherness with great sobriety and objectivity. His *Lovers in the Bar* is one of these somewhat unflattering depictions of interpersonal feelings. Dix used drawings and watercolour studies to prepare for this painting, executed with the use of paint layering. The painting itself unfortunately became a casualty of war. Only a drawing and this watercolour are preserved, with its free-form composition, in which Dix bluntly portrays the coarse eroticism in suburban bars.

Between 1919 and 1923, Dix created various formulations of the theme of 'sailor and girl', which included three oil paintings. *Farewell to Hamburg* stands at the point of transition between Dix's Expressionist and Dadaist experiments and his New Objectivity painting. This composition is indebted to the collage principle of Dadaism: seashore, jetty and lighthouse, and departing ship symbolise the sailor's farewell to the harbour city of Hamburg. The sailor himself is seen in head-and-shoulders portrayal, floating in the centre of the composition, with a shirt-button in the form of a globe surrounded by flags. What he was doing during his shore leave is related by a photograph-like image inserted at the front, in the lower left corner, which gives an insight into the well-known Dix interior, in which prostitution and rape are played out. In the manner of a "veristic Surrealism" (Fritz Löffler) the seashells on the shore indicate the sexual connotations of the composition.

Farewell to Hamburg, 1921

Oil on canvas, 84 × 59 cm
CR Löffler 1921/1

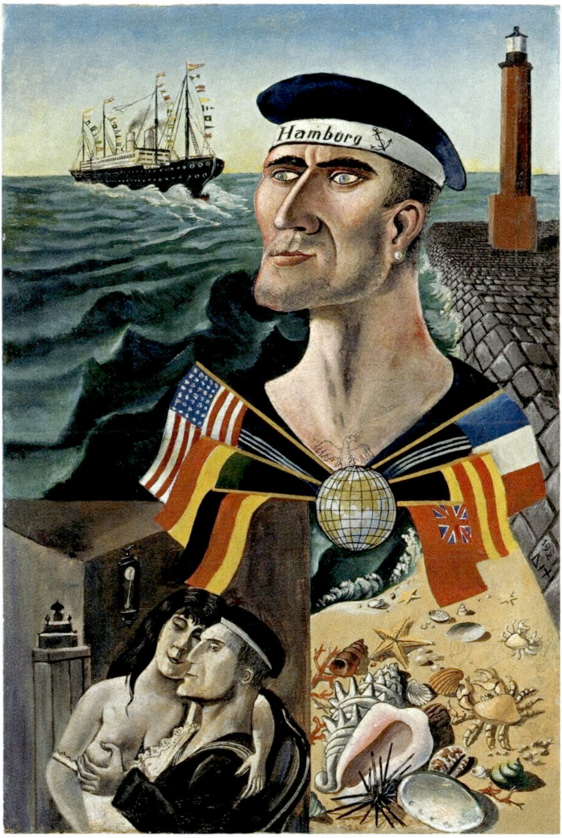

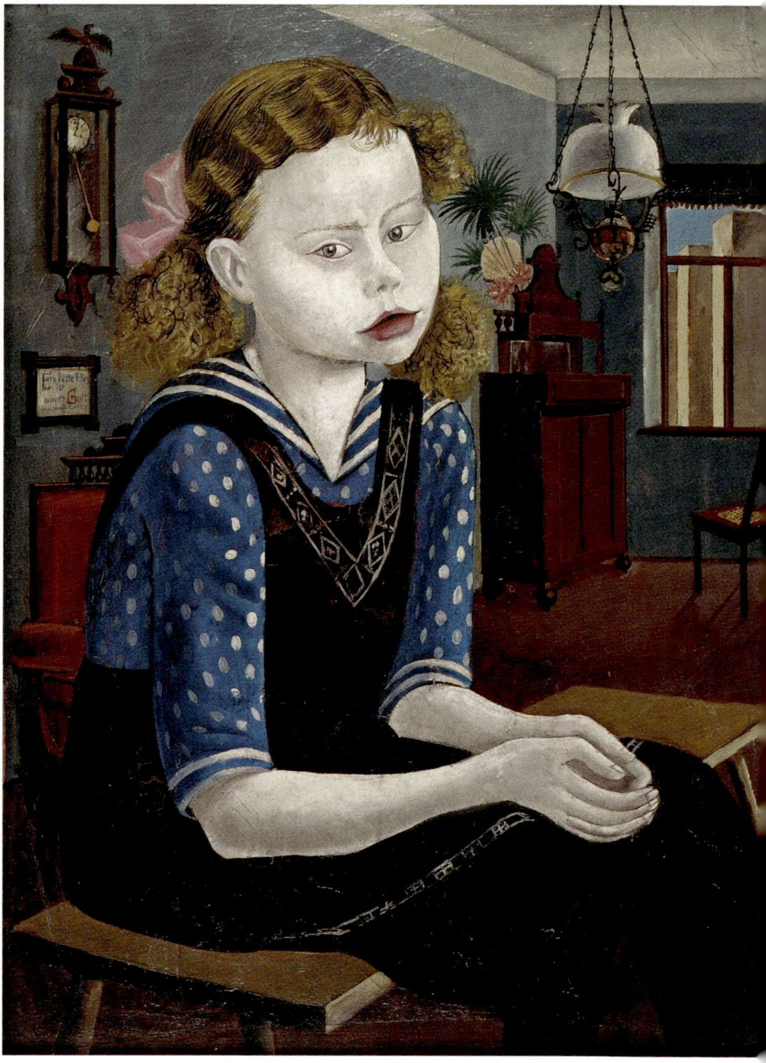

Girl on Sunday, 1921

Oil on canvas mounted on cloth lined board and hardboard, 83 × 66.5 cm

CR Löffler 1920/1

This *Girl on Sunday* stands at the beginning of the New Objectivity paintings of Dix's oeuvre of the 1920s. Its carefully thought-out composition is evident above all in the details of the spatial structure, as well as the application of paint, modelled on Cranach and Dürer. The greater part of the picture is occupied by the figure of a girl wearing her Sunday best, sitting on a rough wooden bench, surrounded by a typically bourgeois living space in the style which Dix repeatedly contrived between 1920 and 1922 with the help of characteristic set-pieces, such as the decorated cabinet, pendulum clock, chair and lamp as well as the potted palm and window with view. In this dreary petty-bourgeois world the girl is growing up without a perspective, but this is also where Dix's scenarios such as rape and prostitution are played out.

Watercolour painting occupies a central role in Dix's oeuvre of the 1920s. In 1922 alone, he created no fewer than 219 watercolours, and in 1924 another 153. It was at this time that Dix was living in Düsseldorf and working with the *Junges Rheinland* (Young Rhineland) group and the gallery owner Johanna Ey. The high point in the artist's official recognition was formed by the large exhibition in the Kronprinzenpalais in Berlin in November 1924. Ludwig Justi, the director of the

Maud, 1922
Watercolour over pencil,
49.6 × 37.6 cm
CR Pfäffle A 1922/151

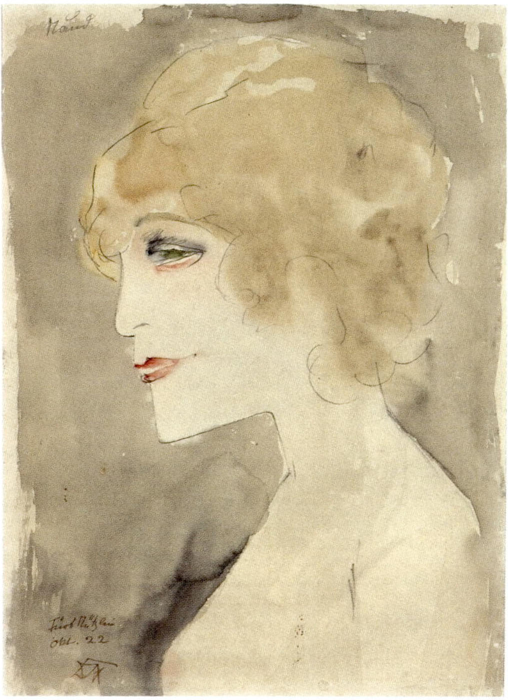

Nationalgalerie, presented Otto Dix as a contemporary artist with a selection of 100 watercolours.
Using delicate colour schemes Dix depicted a number of subjects which were controversial at the time as well as portraying prominent persons and anonymous models including *Maud*. Dix's contemporaries clearly appreciated works of this kind, since Justi asked Dix's art dealer Karl Nierendorf whether the artist would be prepared to donate the work to the museum. The fact that it had a particular value for the Dix family is shown by the dedication to his wife, using her pet name: 'Fürs Mützlein'.

OTTO DIX 1891–1969

In 1922 Dix moved to Düsseldorf. In the environment of 'Mutter Ey's' art gallery and the *Junges Rheinland* (Young Rhineland) group he quickly established himself and became a respected portraitist. Through the collector Hans Koch he also became acquainted with art dealers such as Alfred Flechtheim and Karl Nierendorf, whose portraits he later painted. This was the origin of the 1923 portrait *Nierendix*, as Nierendorf was called in Berlin because of his passionate championing of Otto Dix. In the same year he put the artist under contract and supported him as a patron up to the time of his move to New York in 1936. Dix frequently made drawings of his art dealer, as well as painting him in oils and watercolour. Two of these watercolours record the view of the Severin bridge, as seen from the first-floor window of Nierendorf's Cologne gallery at 16, Gürzenichstrasse. This sheet, which was shown in the watercolour exhibition of 1924 and which was much prized by Dix, was already at that time one of his most expensive works, at a sale price of 120 gold marks.

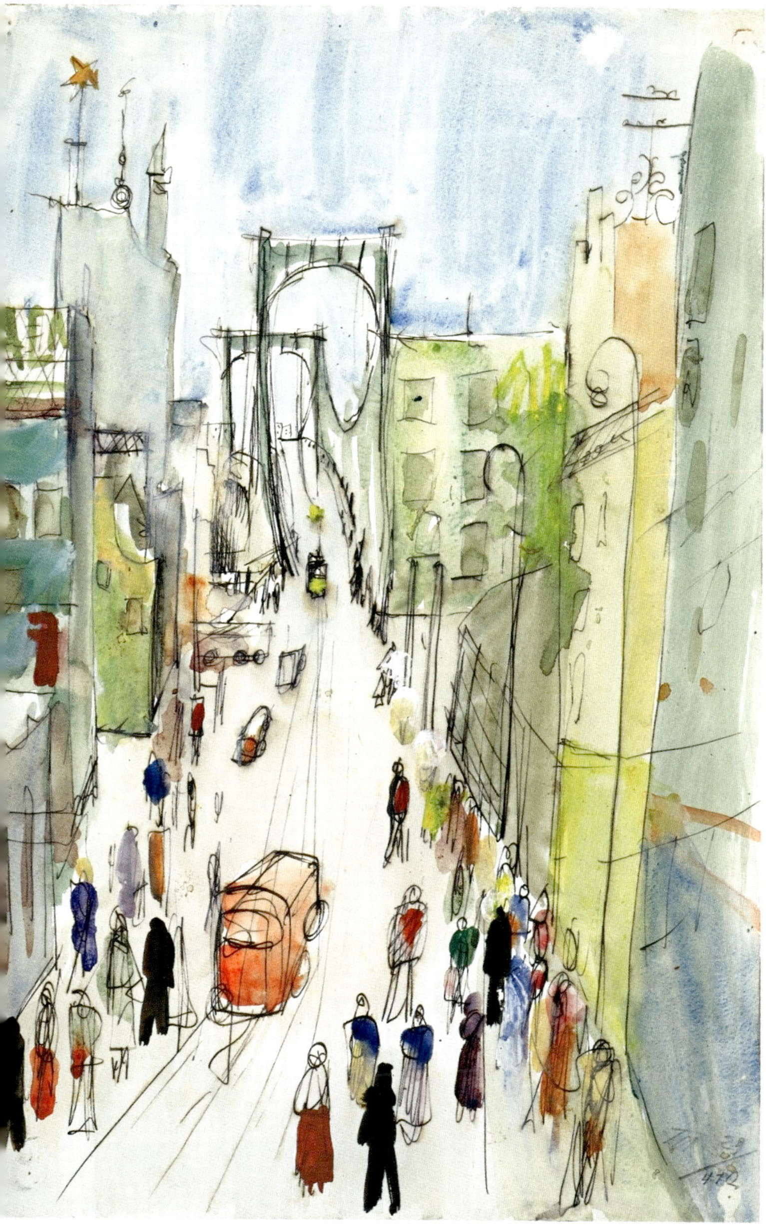

Gürzenichstrasse
Cologne, 1923

Watercolour, Indian ink, opaque white, 49.4 × 33.7 cm
CR Pfäffle A 1923/104

Apart from the large portrait paintings, which were mostly created to commission, in the 1920s Dix produced numerous anonymous watercolour portraits. While his paintings bring out the characteristics of his subjects by exaggerated sharpening and distortion of their outstanding features, in the lightness of the watercolours it is the atmospherically emotional that dominates their appearance. By means of conscious exaggeration of facial peculiarities and the play of iridescent paint surfaces, Dix is able to create expressive portraits of models unknown to us today.

Meta is one of the most impressive sheets in this context. In 1923 Dix twice portrayed this model in watercolour, dedicating one sheet to the writer Alfred Wedekind. What fascinates Dix about Meta is her remarkable facial structure with her protruding chin, thick lips and pointed nose. Dix always sees the inner person mirrored in the outward appearance. For this reason the colouring, especially in the watercolours, always plays a part in laying open the psyche of the

Head II, c. 1923
Watercolour and silver bronze, 49.9 × 33.3 cm
CR Pfäffle A 1923/143

OTTO DIX 1891–1969

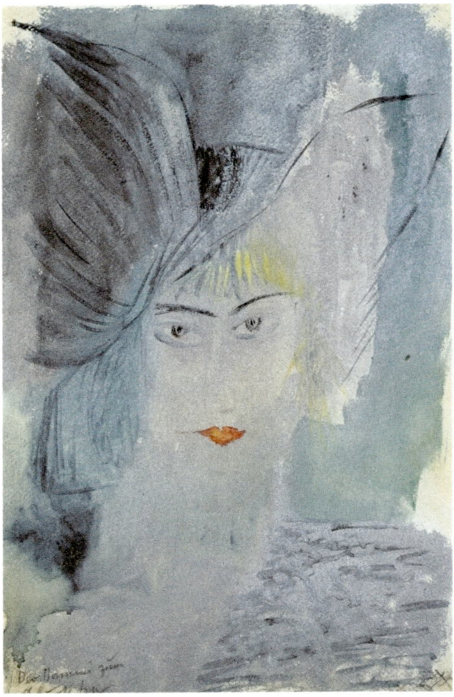

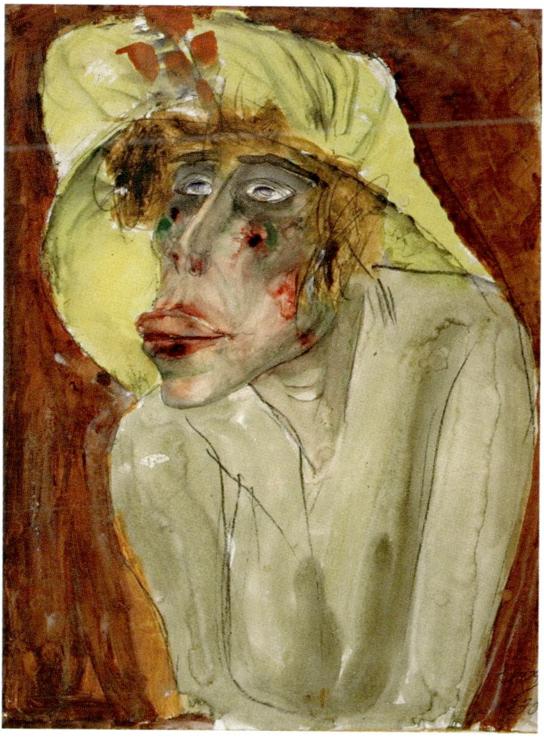

subject. In *Meta* the almost colourless body of the woman retreats behind the head in the centre of the picture, which is additionally accentuated by the yellow hat of the title: clothing, make-up and composition thus underline the oddity of the subject's appearance.
In contrast to this is the *Head II*. Similar in theme, this too features a woman with a hat, but this time she is a society lady wearing costly headgear with heron feathers. While in *Meta* it is the beauty of ugliness that Dix has elaborated, in this sheet he succeeds in heightening the elegance of the woman through delicate colouring and the use of silver bronze. Dix exhibited both works at the watercolour exhibition in Berlin in 1924, placing *Meta* at the highest level of prices for his watercolours at 150 gold marks, while *Head II* was in addition dedicated to his mother on her birthday.

Meta (Woman with Yellow Hat), 1923

Watercolour over pencil, 48.1 × 37.9 cm
CR Pfäffle A 1923/98

The intimate character of the small-format watercolours enables Dix to portray themes he cannot handle with the same degree of clarity in his large oil paintings. What seems today – eighty years later – only too well-known from films and television gave the most violent offence to the bourgeois system of values and moral understanding in the 1920s. Paintings such as *Girl at the Mirror* and *The Salon II* (both 1921) led to court action, in which Dix was accused of obscenity and the distribution of indecent representations. What had already been perceived as objectionable in the paintings was handled in a decidedly more explicit and risqué manner in the watercolours. Here he breaks taboos and openly depicts prostitution in all its variations.

In many portraits of prostitutes he dedicates himself to the figures on the margins of society, even though the prostitution trade flourished in the supposedly Golden Twenties and was used by the losers as well as those who profited from the war. As if on a stage or in a gallery window, the viewer is confronted with a *Parade* of

The Parade, 1923

Watercolour over pen
with Indian ink, 33.8 × 25 cm
CR Pfäffle A 1923/99

OTTO DIX 1891–1969

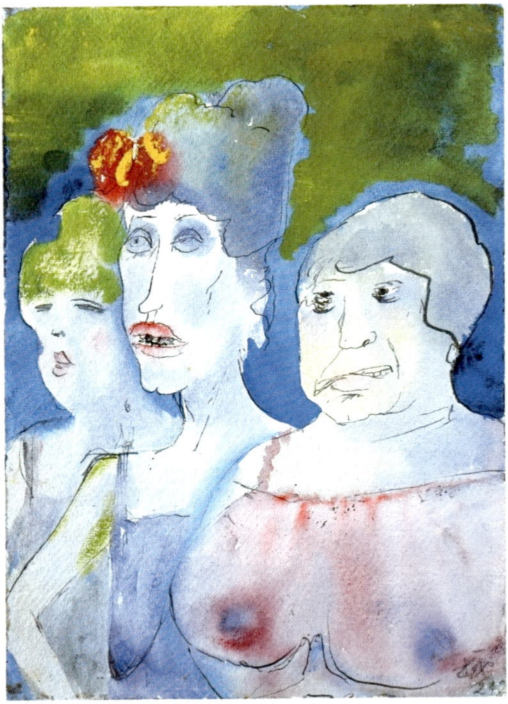

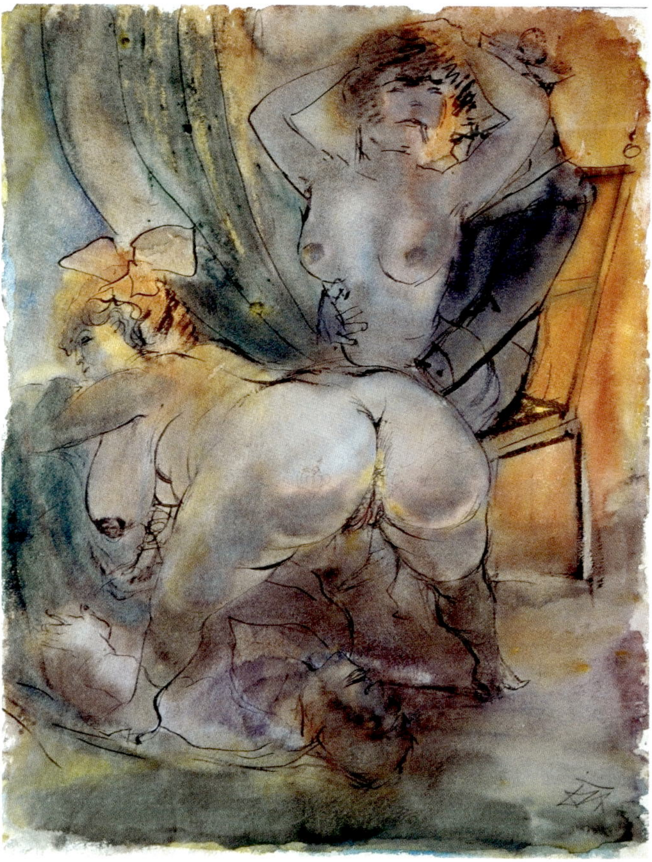

three prostitutes, who look as if they are posing in front of him like goods offered for sale. It is not a question of beauty; these are women offering bodies worn out by their profession and heightened by make-up. The coldness of their work is echoed by the cool colouring of the watercolour.

In some of these sheets Dix portrays aspects of sexuality that were entirely new in the art of the time: sexual extremes such as fetishism, sadism, masochism and rape. Not infrequently, these scenes take place in brothels or in the milieu of the port. The happenings in the *Brothel at the Port* show variants of sexual satisfaction in which Dix often emphasises the full breasts and naked buttocks of the prostitutes by means of special lighting values.

Brothel at the Port, c. 1926

Watercolour over pen with Indian ink, 61.1 × 48.6 cm
CR Pfäffle A 1926/3

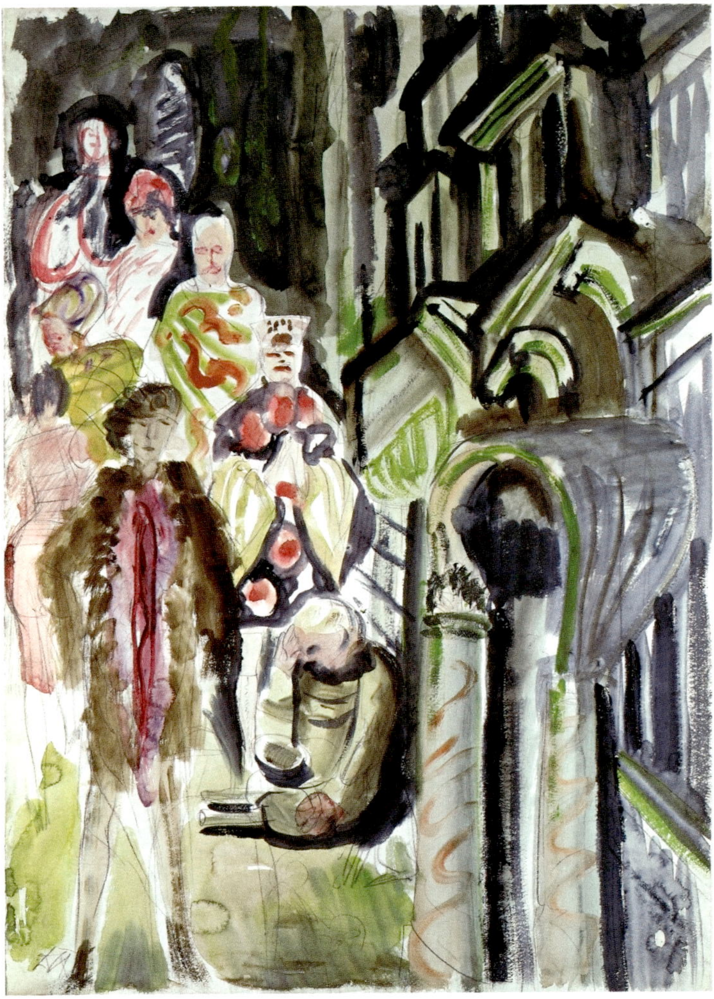

Metropolis
(Study for the Right Wing of the Triptych 'Metropolis'), 1927

Watercolour and pencil,
78 × 56.5 cm
CR Pfäffle A 1927/17

The *Metropolis* triptych (1927/28), today in the Stuttgart Museum of Art, is one of the major works in Dix's oeuvre of the 1920s. In its outer design it takes up the form of winged church altars, thus creating an ironic interpretation of its own time, the so-called Golden Twenties. Dix had been working out the theme in various sketches and watercolours since 1925/26. In the central panel the smart set, with their jazz and Charleston, try to forget the everyday reality depicted in the side panels: the power of money in the form of prostitution and the results of war in the form of crippling injuries.

From the immediate time of creation of the executed work, apart from detailed studies there is evidence of various sketches for the individual panels. A pencil sketch for the left-hand panel has been preserved, which already contains the essentials of the executed composition. Dix produced a watercolour study for the right-hand panel which is the only preserved colour study for the triptych. Here too – both works are the last stages immediately before the draft cartoons – the composition very largely coincides with the painting. As a whole, however, the dominating principle of composition of these sheets is a pronounced accentuation of the diagonals, which Dix abandoned in the execution of the painting.

Metropolis (Sketch for the Left Wing of the Triptych 'Metropolis'), 1928

Charcoal, heightened with white, and pencil, 64.2 × 47 cm
CR Lorenz NSk. 7.2.16

OTTO DIX 1891–1969

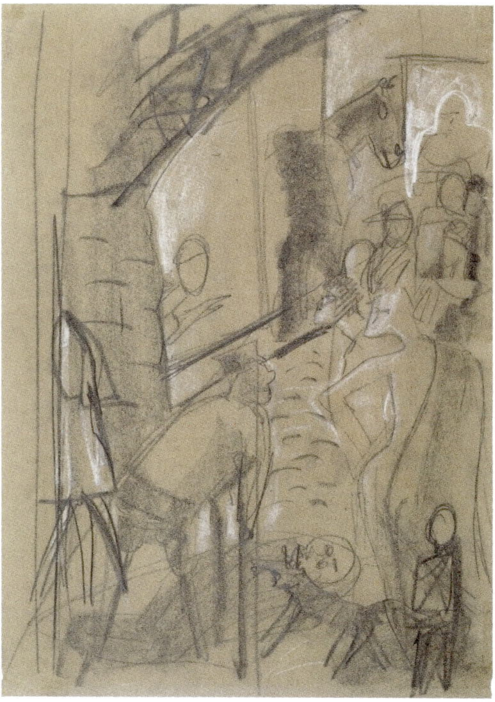

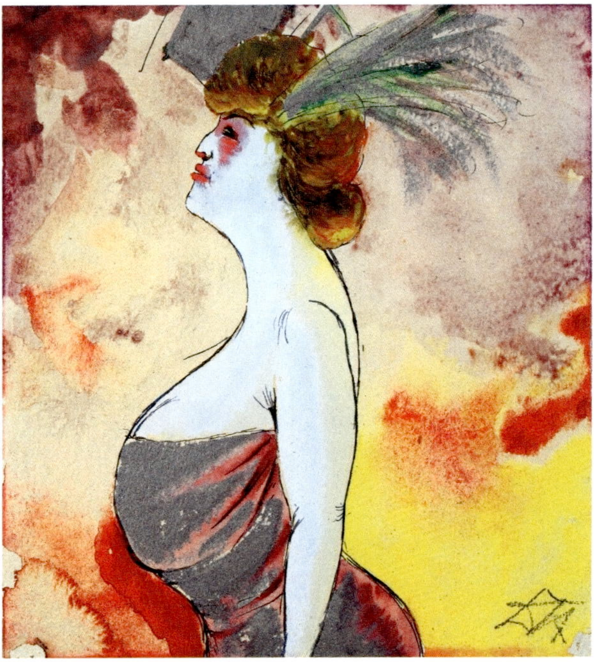

OTTO DIX 1891–1969

Woman Artiste (Artiste in Silver Dress), c. 1923

Watercolour and silver bronze over pen with Indian ink, 21.5 × 19.8 cm
CR Pfäffle A 1923/147

During 1922/23, Dix was preoccupied, in twenty-six watercolours alone, with the theme of the circus, to which he also dedicated the fourth part of his etching oeuvre. The sheet called *Woman Artiste* is among the qualitatively most valuable in this group. In front of a marbled abstract background, which is reminiscent of the blurring of the coloured lights in the circus ring, the clearly contoured profile figure of the artiste stands out. In the manner peculiar to him, Dix stresses by conscious exaggeration the unique and special in the woman's appearance.

One recognises quite clearly in this sheet the varying use of media in Dix's watercolours: first he borders the figure in a clear outline drawing with pen and Indian ink, after which, using the wet-in-wet technique, he creates the background and adds small areas for the face, dress and flesh-colour. Using a covering technique he then adds the hair, before giving the sheet its particular charm by using silver bronze in the area of the head decoration and the artiste's dress.

In the autumn of 1926 Dix was appointed professor at the Academy of Art in Dresden. In 1927 he returned to the place where he had spent his student years, and taught there up to 1933, when the National Socialists seized power. This period produced the major works of his creative career, the triptychs *Metropolis* and *War*. In parallel to these, the violent verism of his work abated, and the craft of the Old Masters increasingly

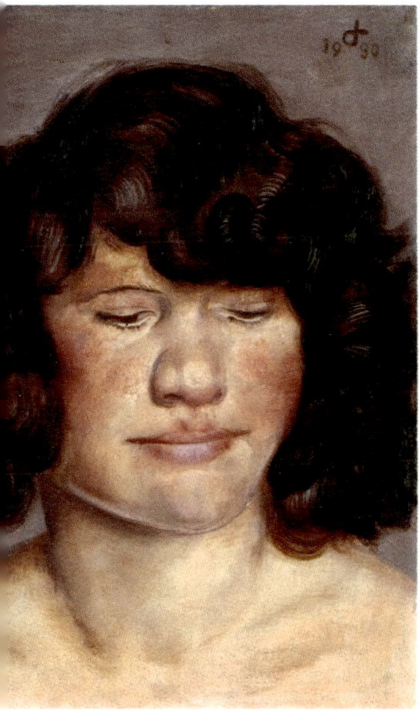

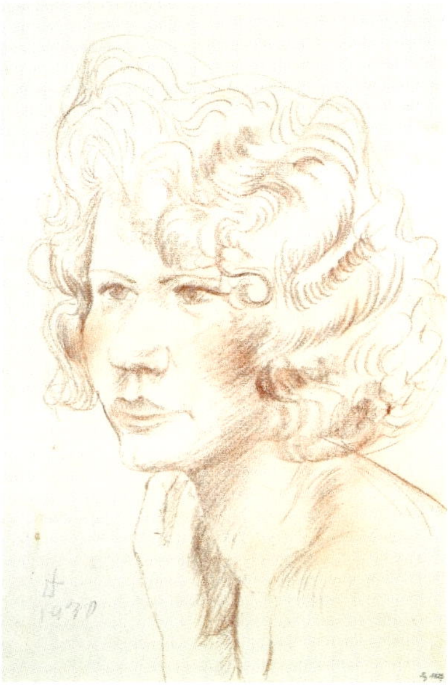

influenced him, particularly in his drawings. Red and white chalk and silver pencil are the new materials he worked with; the portrait drawing of the model Erna II very clearly shows this new method. His new tendency towards the style of the Old Masters can however also be observed in the oil painting of this time. The painting *Girl's Head with Curly Hair* shows one of Otto Dix's favourite models of the early 1930s. Erna I and Erna II sat for him as life models, both when he was teaching students at the academy and for his own private work. In his total oeuvre, this little portrait stands as a turning-point to his new style. The execution is reminiscent of the small-format portraits by Dürer and Cranach, with whose works in the Dresden collections Dix had been intensively engaged since his youth.

Girl's Head with Curly Hair, 1930

Mixed technique on wood, 35.5 × 24.1 cm
CR Löffler 1929/7

Girl's Head Erna II, 1930

Red chalk, 44.5 × 30 cm
CR Lorenz NSk. 11.5.6

The portrait of a red-haired woman against a blue background, like the *Girl's Head with Curly Hair*, stands at the turning point of Dix's change to the style of the Old Masters. The calmer approach to composition of those years is also found in the portraits, in which Dix increasingly renounces the eloquent embedding of the subject in expressive pictorial contexts in favour of a neutral background, from which the psychologically perceived appearance of the subject stands out. In parallel, he developed his stonemason-like monogram which marks the works of the Inner Emigration.

The high point of this phase of his work is the portrait of the actor Heinrich George, completed in 1932. Also in the same group is this impressive portrait of a red-haired woman, consisting almost without exception of the three primary colours. In front of an intense, brilliant blue background, the slight figure of the woman stands out, with her softly shimmering yellowish silk dress. Dix directs all his attention at the head, with its red hair, and the face with its reddened eyes. The

OTTO DIX 1891–1969

woman's gaze is directed at the viewer, who cannot avoid it and who is spellbound by its profound air of melancholy.

Immediately after the National Socialist seizure of power in 1933, Otto Dix was dismissed from his teaching post at the Dresden Academy. He left the city and moved with his family to Schloss Randegg near Singen, which belonged to his brother-in-law Hans Koch. The loss of his teaching post and his departure from Dresden to the peaceful Hegau landscape robbed Dix of one of his most important sources of inspiration: the metropolis. The years of Inner Emigration that followed are thus marked by landscape painting. Dix created 700 drawings alone. With his sketchbook, he wandered through forests and mountains and recorded the many subjects he encountered. In the old-masterly drawing style that he had already developed in Dresden, from 1934 he developed his large landscapes, which he often prepared in detailed drawings.

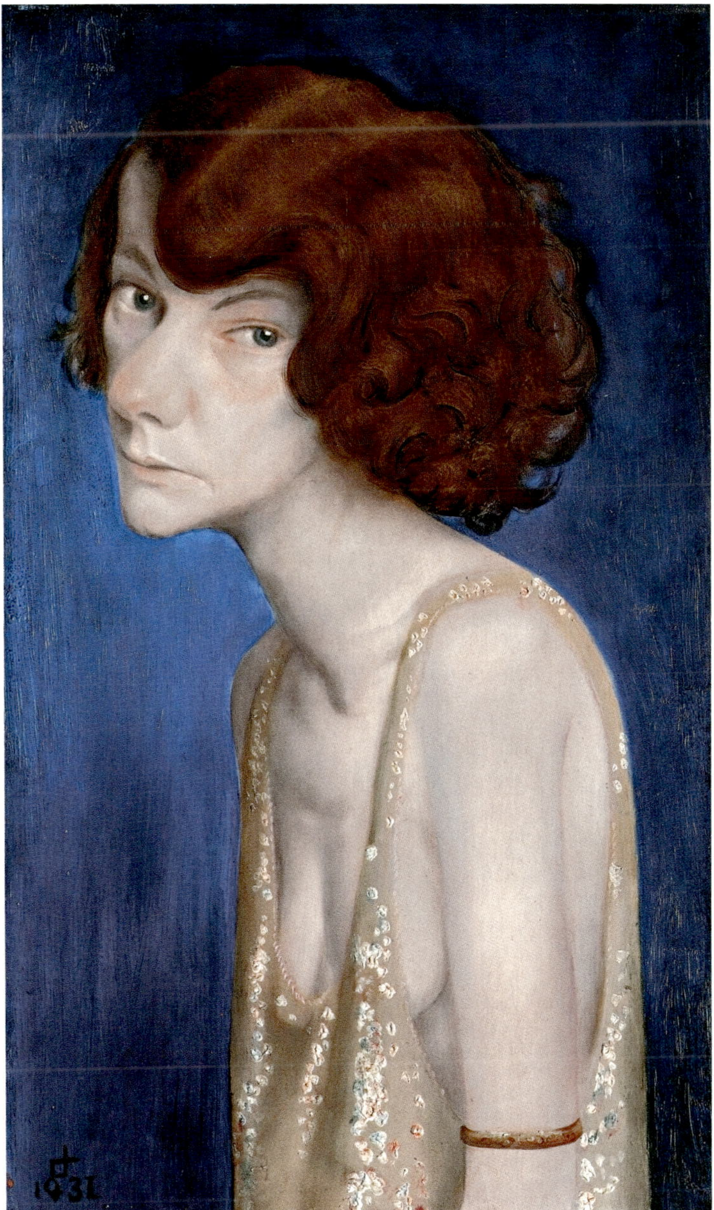

Red-Haired Woman
(Portrait of a Lady), 1931

Mixed technique on canvas
on wood, 60.5 × 36.5 cm
CR Löffler 1929/4

The connection between these works is impressively demonstrated by the painting *Randegg – Evening Mood* of 1934 and the watercolour and pen drawing of 1936. In each case the village is seen from the same point of view. The painting was one of the first to be completed by Dix after his move from Dresden. In light, delicate colours it shows his new home in spring. Two years later Dix left Randegg but preserved the memory in this remarkable pen drawing. It is reminiscent of the Innsbruck drawings by Albrecht Dürer in its rich detail and in the quality of its execution.

Randegg – Evening Mood (Spring Evening), 1934

Mixed technique on plywood, 60 × 80.1 cm
CR Löffler 1934/3

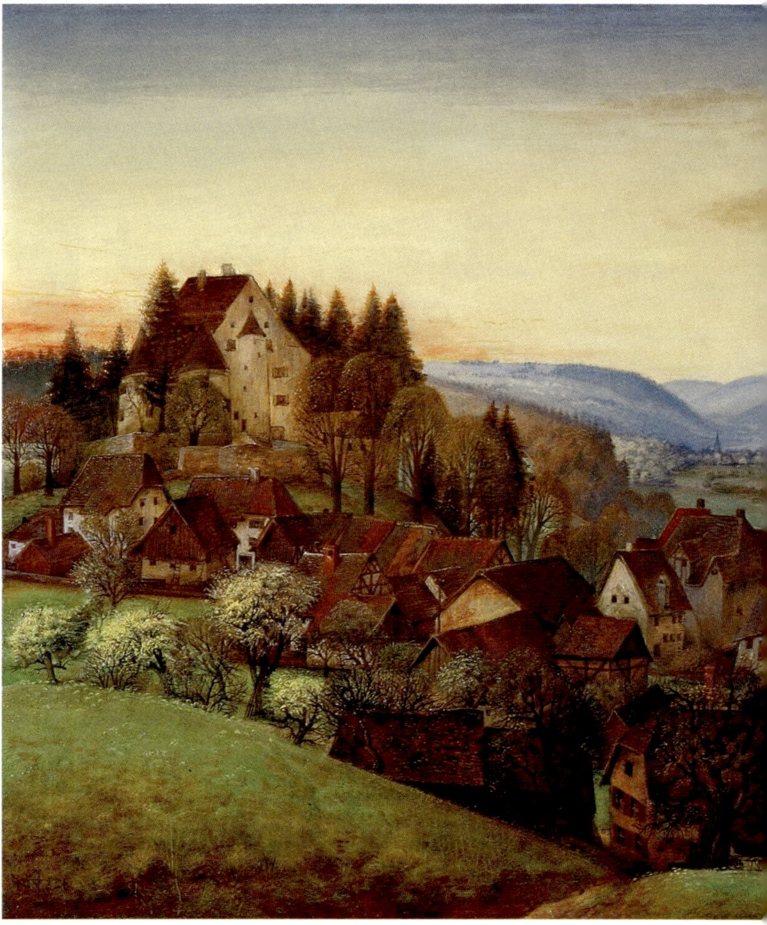

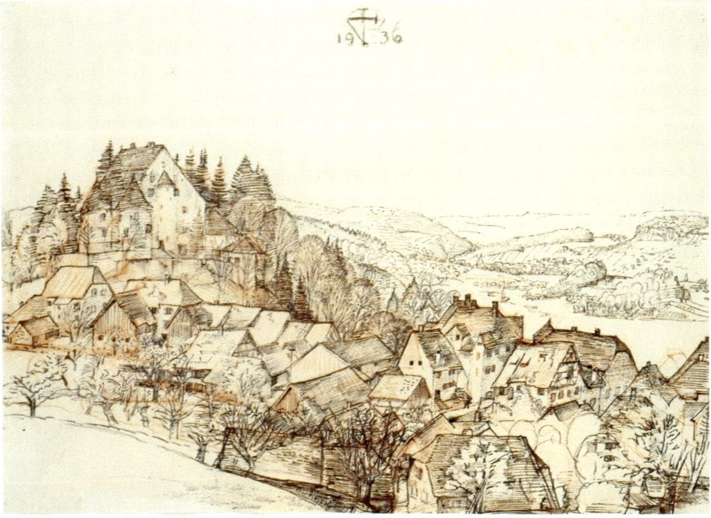

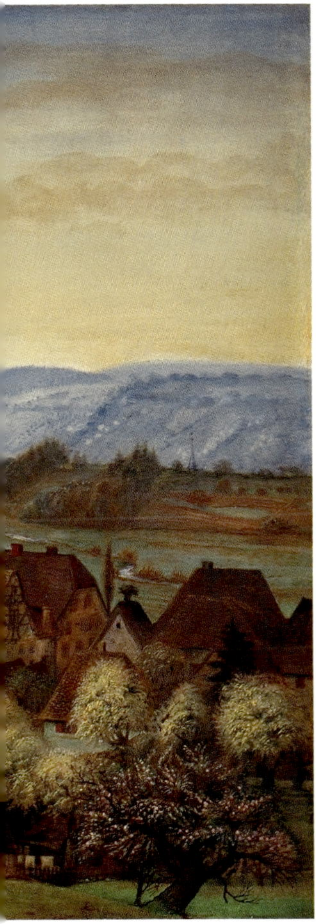

OTTO DIX 1891–1969

Randegg Castle, 1936

Watercolour over Indian ink,
50.4 × 72 cm
CR Pfäffle A 1936/1,
CR Lorenz IE 7.3.14

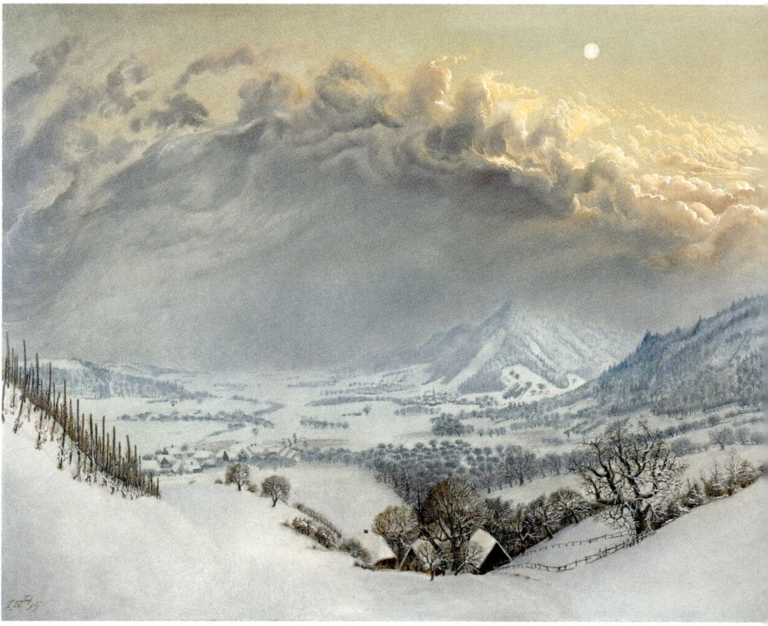

OTTO DIX 1891–1969

Winter Landscape with Moon (Winter Evening in the Hegau), 1935

Mixed technique on wood,
60 × 80 cm
CR Löffler 1935/5

The dominance of landscape in the work of Dix in the years of the Inner Emigration was not only a chance for him to continue after the loss of Dresden; it also gave him the opportunity to reflect his own times.

The landscapes of 1934 to 1944 do not portray his homelands with pure naturalism; but are rather detailed studies precisely composed by Dix, to which he sometimes lends the moods corresponding to the political events of the day. Often the point of view within the picture occupies a raised position, from which one can observe the expanse of the landscape, which from this perspective has a more monumental and awe-inspiring effect.

This is the case with the paintings shown here: *Winter Landscape with Moon* was created in early 1935 and exhibited in the same year in New York. In the preceding year, Dix was banned from exhibiting in Germany, which robbed him of all public presence. An atmosphere of menacing insecurity hangs over the snow-covered plain with the mighty cloud formations looming over it. Questionable, too, is the promise radiating from the yellow light. Like the emotionally charged landscapes of the Dresden Romantics, especially Caspar David Friedrich, depictions such as that of the *Gloomy Landscape* indicate more profound levels of meaning beyond themselves.

The great complex of landscapes in the work of Otto Dix can be categorised according to the various places where he lived or stayed. Apart from the Hegau and the landscape of Lake Constance, where Dix lived from 1936 in his house in Hemmenhofen, it was mountain ranges in the Alps and the Riesengebirge or Giant Mountains (Krkonose Mountains) that stimulated him to create large-format paintings. In 1938 he spent several weeks in the Engadine in Switzerland. Seven paintings resulted from his experience of the High Alps. In the *Valley at Pontresina with Bernina Group,* Dix portrays the Central Alps of Switzerland: dead trees in the foreground, and in the background above blue valleys the Bernina massif covered with snow and ice. It is the bleak world in which Friedrich Nietzsche spent his

Gloomy Landscape (Upper Rhine in the Evening), 1940

Mixed technique on wood, 65 × 85 cm
CR Löffler 1940/18

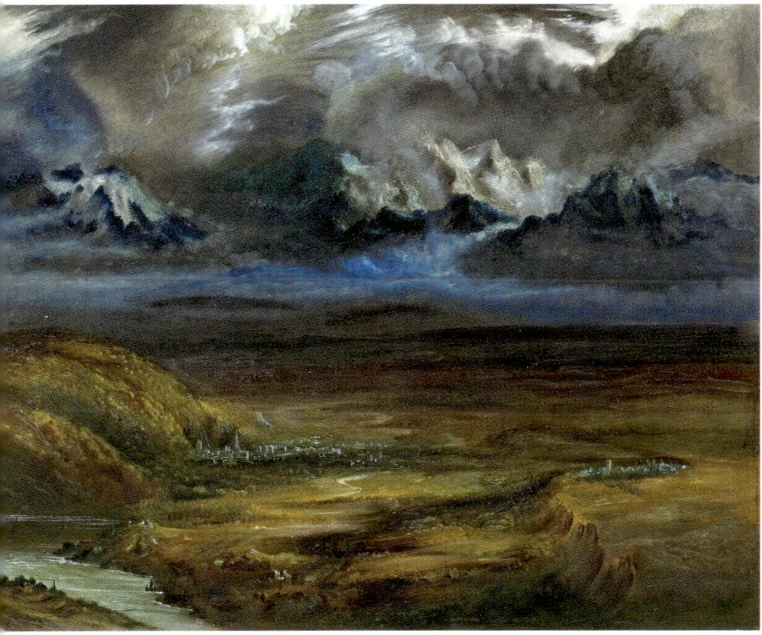

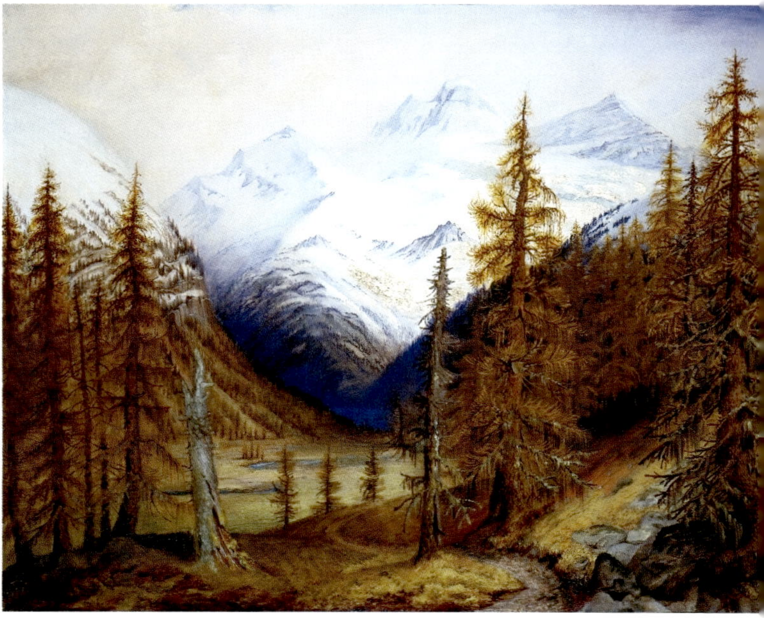

OTTO DIX 1891–1969

Valley at Pontresina with Bernina Group, 1938

Mixed technique on wood,
70 × 80 cm
CR Löffler 1938/13

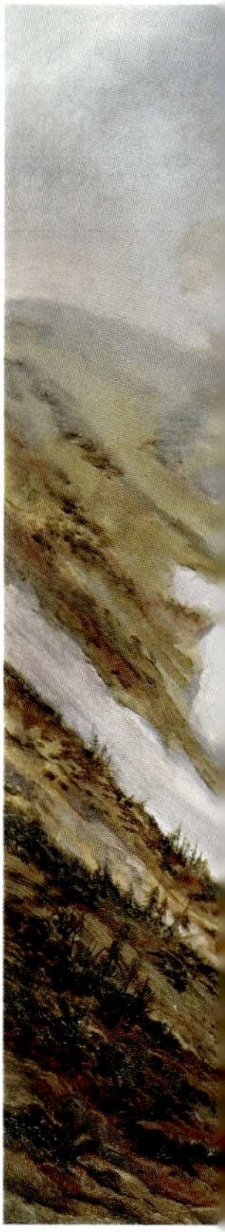

summer months in the 1880s, the philosopher whose writings inspired the young painter in the early years of the century.

In 1941/42 Dix made several trips to the low-mountain region of Bohemia and the Krknoše Mountains. Again he recorded his experiences in more than a dozen paintings. There are two versions of the *Little Pond in the Riesengebirge*. While the smaller one shows the basin of the valley approximately at the level of the lake, the larger, Chemnitz version shows the familiar, high-lying viewpoint of the observer, and guides the gaze both downwards into the valley with the lake and also high above the mountain ridge into the dim and misty expanse of the mountains.

Little Pond in the Riesengebirge II (The Little Valley), 1942

Mixed technique on wood, 75 × 100 cm
CR Löffler 1942/23

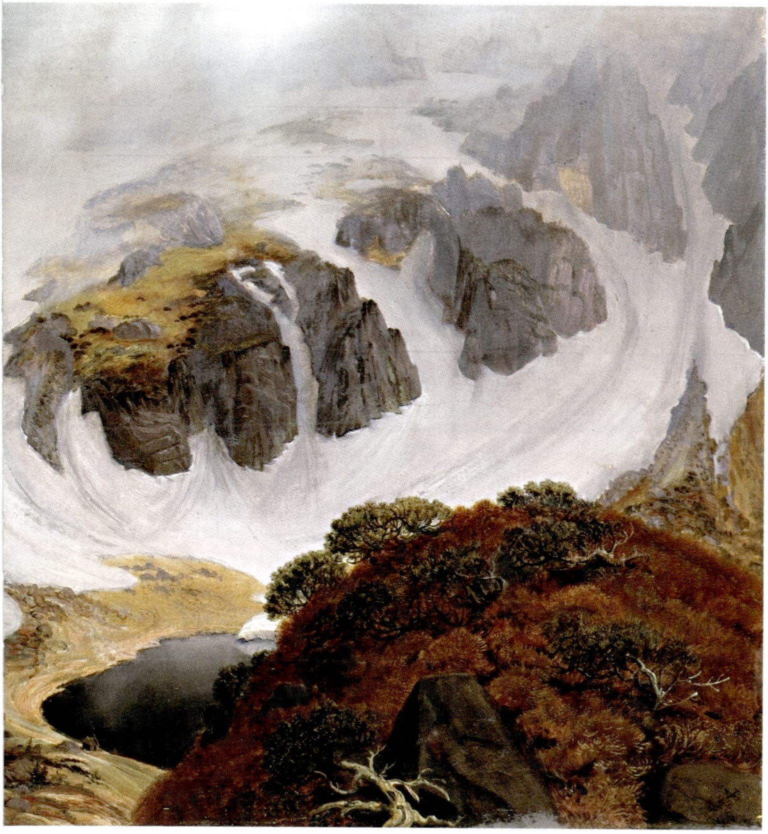

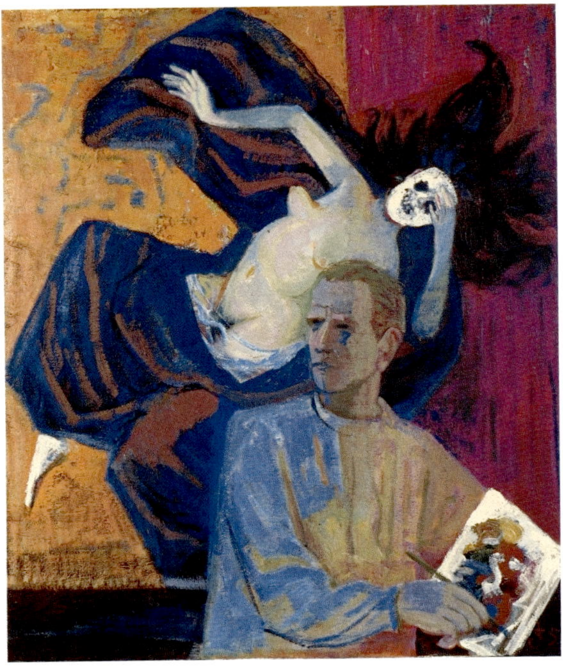

OTTO DIX 1891–1969

Self-Portrait with Masked Woman Dancer, 1945

Oil on wood, 118 × 105 cm
CR Löffler 1945/3

During the period of Inner Emigration Dix's attention was concentrated primarily on the landscape, and he also tested the Christian myths for their usability for his own work. Only in the 1940s did he turn his attention again to his own person. Between 1942 and 1945 he produced three similarly designed self-portraits. They all have in common Dix's portrayal of himself in his white painter's smock with brush and palette in hand, with drapery and a female figure in the background. The artist himself in each case turns his back on the subject and looks out of the picture. In all three works the painter's eyes lie in deep shadow in the dark sockets of his ageing face. In the Chemnitz self-portrait, painted shortly before his call-up to the Volkssturm militia in February 1945, Dix develops the recumbent female nude of the version of the previous year into a dancer with a death mask held in front of her face. If the figure of 1944 can still be interpreted as the Muse protecting the artist absorbed in his work, in 1945 she is transformed into a Whore of Babylon, hovering menacingly above him and promising death.

In the spring of 1945, Otto Dix was to experience for the second time in his life the horrors of war that he had hitherto described so impressively in his work. Towards the end of the war he found himself imprisoned in France until 1946. Returning to Hemmenhofen a year later he created two self-portraits, of which one shows the painter as a prisoner in Colmar, in Alsace. In the second, Dix portrays himself in a wintry, bare, snow-covered landscape in a sheepskin coat and fur cap. Again the artist's eyes lie darkly in his face, which is overshadowed by his cap, as he looks out of the picture, sullenly questioning what the future holds in store. From 1942 a last change of style appeared in Dix's work: he turned his back on the glazing technique he had perfected since the 1920s and developed an *alla prima* style of painting which was to characterise his late artistic work from 1945.

Self-Portrait with Fur Hat in Front of a Winter Landscape, 1947

Oil on wood, 81 × 60 cm
CR Löffler 1947/3

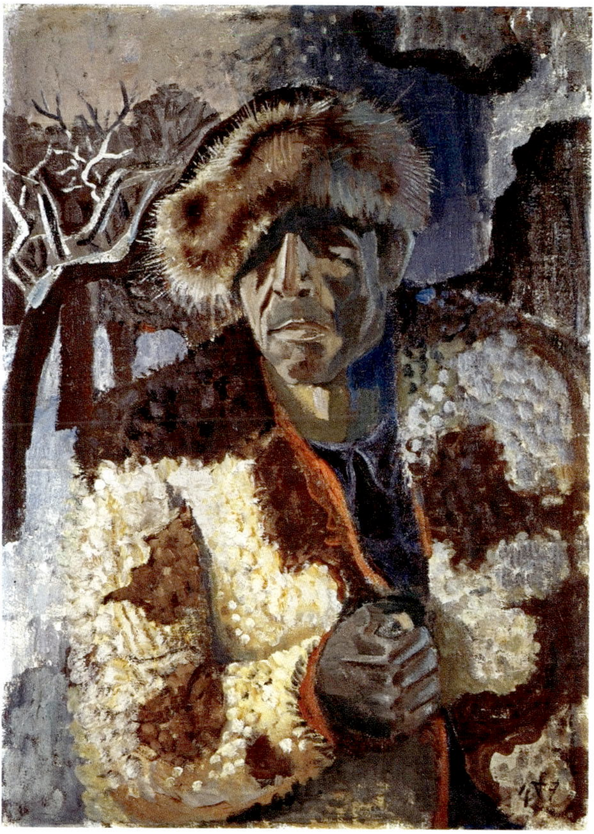

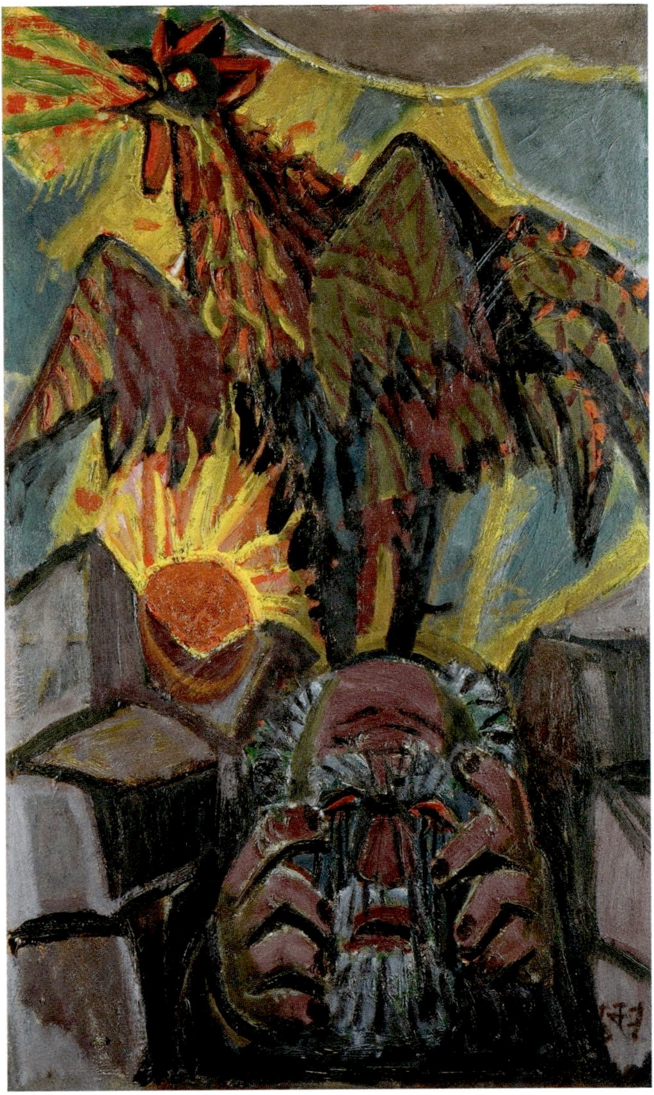

St Peter and the Cock II, 1957
Oil on wood, 92 × 64 cm
CR Löffler 1957/3

Dix's late work is marked by three cycles of motifs: his native landscape, the portrait and Christian themes. These had already preoccupied him at the time of his Inner Emigration. After 1945 they offered him the chance to reflect in artistic terms on his wartime experiences and the question of German guilt. From 1946 he created more than four dozen paintings on the Passion of Christ and on scenes from the Old and New Testament. The intensity of this confrontation becomes clear when one notes that Dix often used one and the same theme in all the techniques available to him.

In this way, the theme of the apostle Peter's denial of Christ resulted in two works in oil, as well as drawings, pastels, lithographs and glass windows for the church at Kattenhorn on Lake Constance. His first version of *Peter and the Cock* was created in 1950. In front of a brick wall, truncated by the lower edge of the picture, Peter's head is visible with his hands held in front of his weeping eyes; above him, sitting on his shoulder, is the cock crowing his betrayal to the world. In the great Chemnitz version of 1957, Dix has dramatised the composition with Peter and the cock now arranged one above the other, slightly moved away from the centre of the picture. The wall has given way to a formation of broken stones, behind which shine the menacing rays of the blood-red rising sun. In the version of 1958 as pastel and lithograph, Dix again picks up the painting of 1950 with slight variations.

St Peter and the Cock, 1958

Pastel, 57 × 44 cm
CR Lorenz SW 3.10.8

OTTO DIX 1891–1969

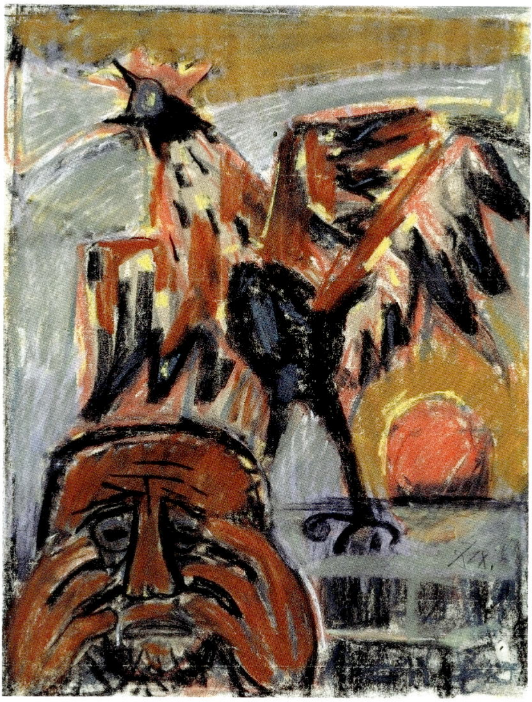

The substantial graphic work of Otto Dix, represented in this collection by important works and complete portfolios, falls into two parts according to biographical criteria – before and after its enforced interruption by the Third Reich. After his return from wartime imprisonment, an enormously productive period, particularly with regard to lithographic work, set in and lasted from 1947 until his death in 1969. Apart from themes used by Dix for oils, pastels and lithographs, including the *Contessa* of 1962, he repeatedly completed highly expressive self-portraits up to the final year of his life.

After the war, Dix resumed his regular trips to Dresden. There, using the Erhardt printing press at the Academy on the Brühl Terrace, he created his expressive, painterly

Contessa, 1962

Colour lithograph on six stones, 62.5 × 40.5 / 75 × 50.5 cm
CR Karsch 291

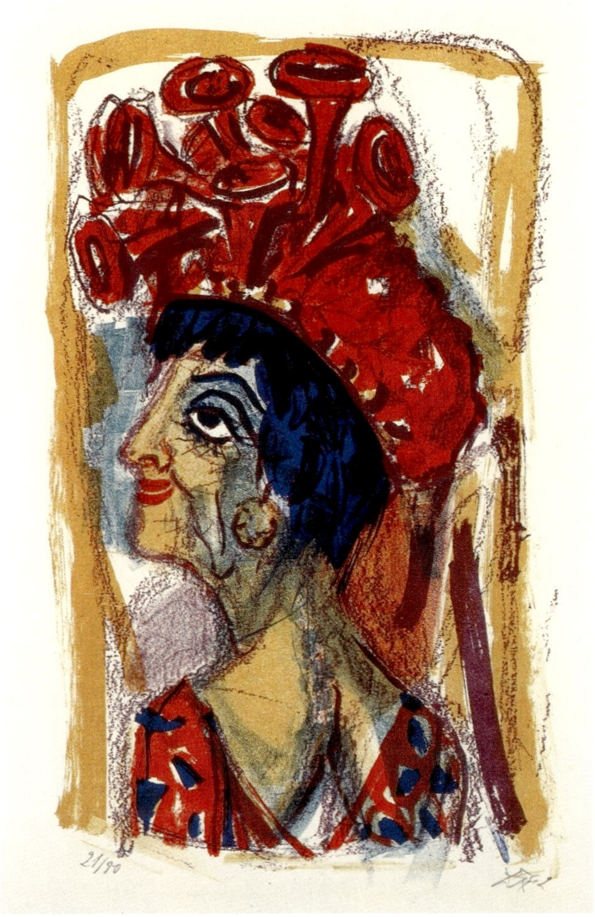

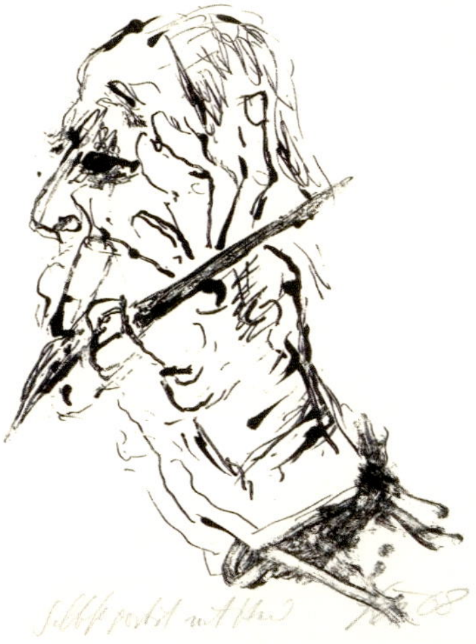

OTTO DIX 1891–1969

black and white chalk and colour lithographs. It is in the coloured sheets, often printed using up to six stones, that the artistic expressivity of his late work is evident, as it developed in his oil paintings from 1942. In a parallel development, one can observe especially in the annually created self-portraits a gradual move away from form, approaching a freedom almost reminiscent of Art Informel in the last sheets before his death.

Self-Portrait with Hand, 1968

Lithograph, 32 × 24.5 / 52 × 37.5 cm
CR Karsch 320

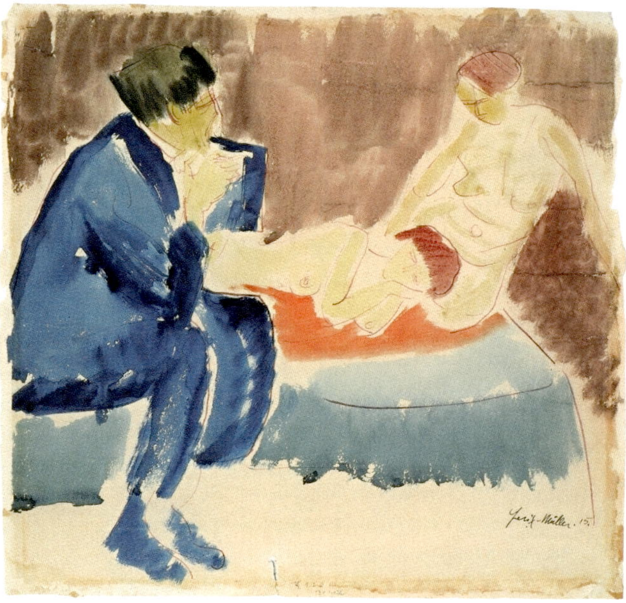

CONRAD FELIXMÜLLER 1897–1977

Studio Scene, 1915

Watercolour, 36.5 × 39.9 cm

This little watercolour study is one of Felixmüller's earliest works. In 1912 the Dresden painter Ferdinand Dorsch had noticed the young artist, and enabled him to be accepted by the Königliche Kunstakademie (Royal Academy of Art). Within a short time Conrad Felix Müller freed himself from the style of his teacher and achieved an Expressionist form language. At seventeen years of age he left the Academy and from then on was active as a freelance artist under the name Felixmüller. From this period comes the *Studio Scene*, which shows his friend the painter Paul Kother with two female models. In 1915 Felixmüller portrayed his friend several times; they both visited Kirchner at his Berlin studio, and in the following year they exhibited with Lyonel Feininger at Herwarth Walden's Sturm Gallery. This watercolour shows how much Felixmüller was beginning to free himself from the rigid composition and painting style of his teacher at the beginning of the First World War. With a few sparse strokes of the pencil he sketches the scene and builds it up with just a few colours.

As a freelance painter and in close exchanges with his friends, Felixmüller found his way during the war years of 1915 to 1918 to an expression of "absolute form", as he himself defined it. The artist's first success was when using the Cubist mode, specifically in the medium of graphic prints. In numerous woodcuts, etchings and lithographs he expressed what moved his mind. Throughout his life, this remained the human figure – either alone or embedded in its environment. In this early Expressionist phase it is above all the human in its relationship with nature that Felixmüller explores in many of his graphic works. Broken up into several horizontal layers, the *Couple in a Hilly Landscape* appear closely entwined while seated in the landscape, only to melt into it, in form as well as colour. Ecstatic Expressionist experience of nature and forward-pressing, avant-garde striving after form find an adequate, personal shape in these early lithographs.

Couple in a Hilly Landscape, 1916

Colour lithograph, 65 × 55 cm / 70 × 55.5 cm
CR Söhn 89

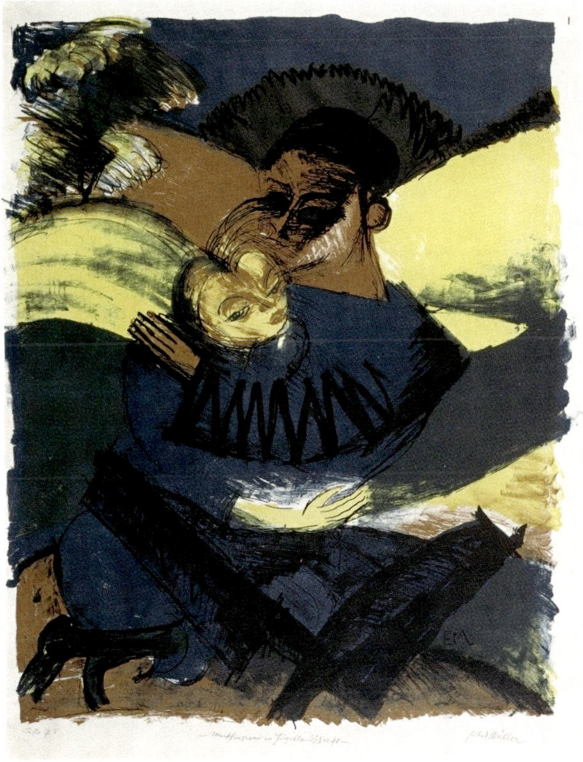

The artist achieved his greatest success in the year in which he created his *Self-Portrait with Sports Cap*. For his painting *Pregnant Woman in Autumn* (destroyed during World War II) he received the prize of the state of Saxony which traditionally enables the winner to spend two years in Italy. Since the war years Felixmüller had been not only an artist, but also an active participant in revolutionary activities. He decisively supported the workers' cause, for example by means of agitative prints for Franz Pfemfert's periodical *Die Aktion*. Thus in 1920 Felixmüller went not to Rome, but to his brother's house in the Ruhr district, where he studied the living and working conditions of the working population. This energetic and decisive frame of mind is unmistakably conveyed by the painter in his self-portrait. Determined and strong-willed, he clenches his hands into fists, standing in the bare space, as though just about to undertake some activity. Stylistically this work marks the beginning of the turning point towards an objective confrontation with reality.

CONRAD FELIXMÜLLER 1897–1977

The *Coal Miner* is Felixmüller's central work, reflecting his experiences in the Ruhr district in 1920. In a letter to the collector Heinrich Kirchhoff he writes: "How the first sight of a mine in the middle of the town affected me – I cannot describe in a few words. My heart and mind practically stood still…" In many graphic works Felixmüller makes use of his impressions of the world below ground and the miners. This sheet, with the half-length portrait of the gaunt old collier, is built entirely on the intense contrast of red, blue and black. In front of the red brick of the colliery and the steel blue of the conveyor and the factory courtyard, the worker's silhouette stands out impressively, blackened

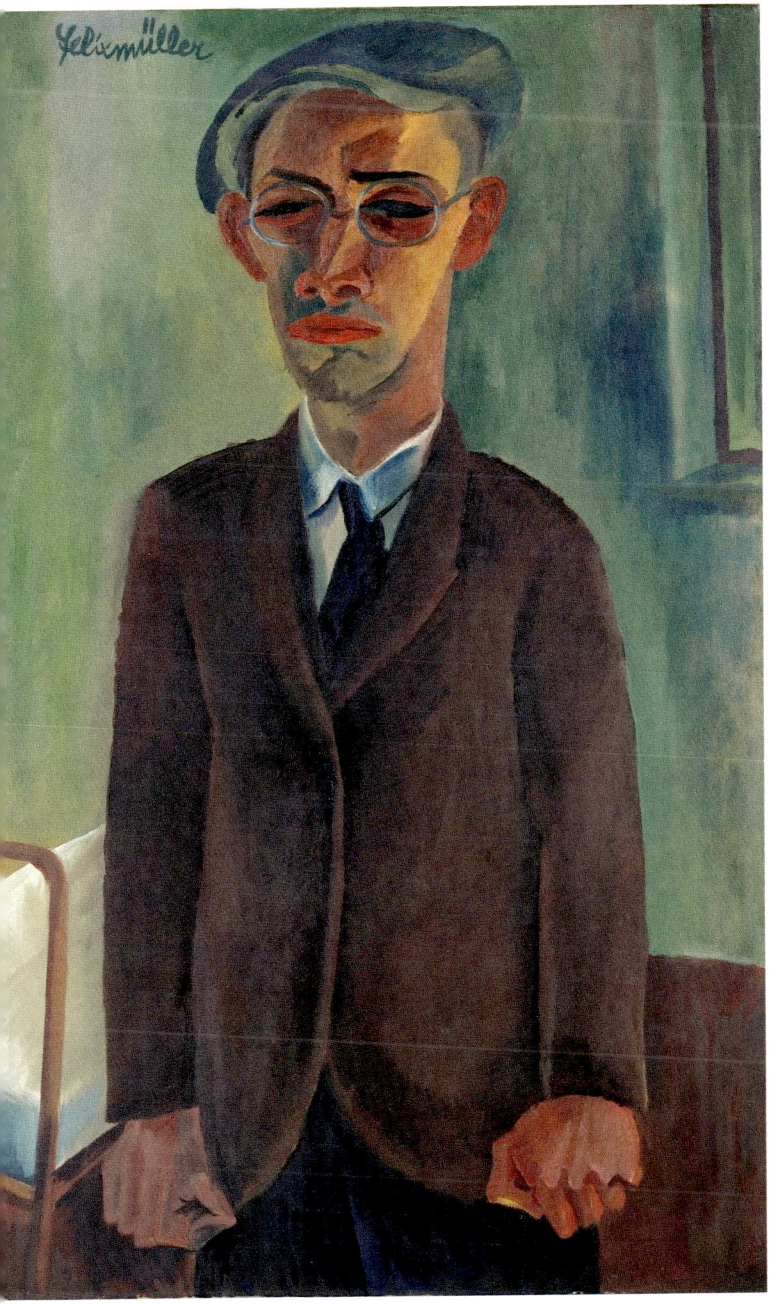

Self-Portrait with
Sports Cap, 1920

Oil on canvas, 115 × 75 cm
CR Felixmüller 199

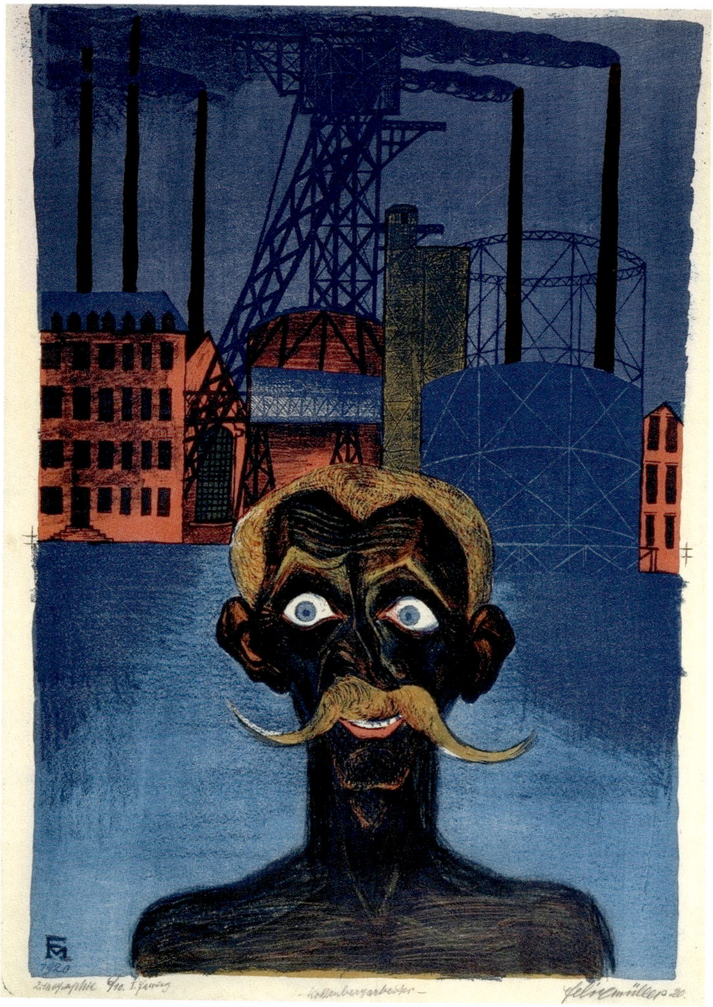

Coal Miner, 1920

Colour lithograph, 57.2 × 39 / 58.5 × 43 cm
CR Söhn 211

by coal dust. From his soot-blackened face the whites of his eyes shine out in ghostly fashion. "I saw men who aroused my greatest admiration, because after long years of work below ground, grown old and bowed, they shuffled across the colliery yard ..." Around 1920 with his portraits of working-class people Felixmüller succeeded in moving to a realistically descriptive art, free from all Expressionist exaggeration.

Felixmüller began his studies of the working environment in the mining districts of Saxony. After his return from his first trip to the Ruhr district, he wrote at the end of 1920 that he was "stuffed as full as a sandbag" with impressions. In the years that followed he found in the working man, in particular the industrial factory workers, *his* theme, to which he repeatedly gave shape using all the techniques at his disposal. Unlike his painter friend Dix, he was interested not in the strata of the prostitutes and the losers of the First World War, but rather in the portrayal of the working-class environment. While he followed his agitative goals with his work for Pfemfert's *Aktion*, his depictions of the industrial workers and miners of the 1920s were determined by a factual, objective view of their milieu. The watercolour, *Unemployed Man*, for example, shows the hopelessness of the worker in front of a deserted factory. It makes a statement rather than a direct accusation.

Unemployed Man, 1921

Watercolour and opaque colours, 57 × 44 cm

CONRAD FELIXMÜLLER 1897–1977

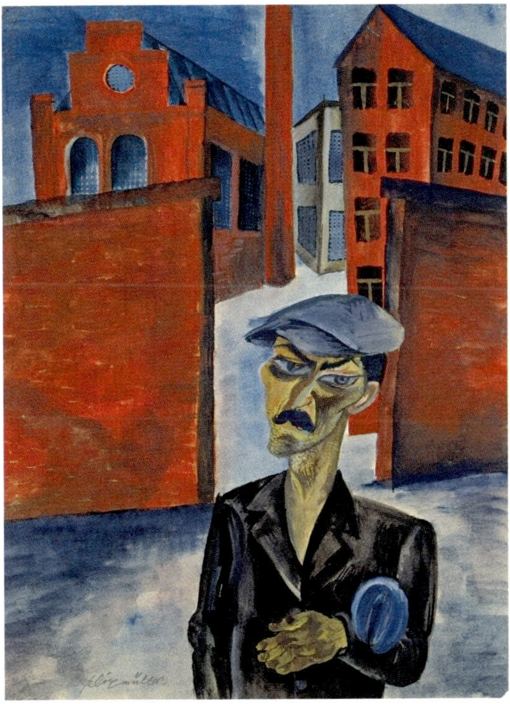

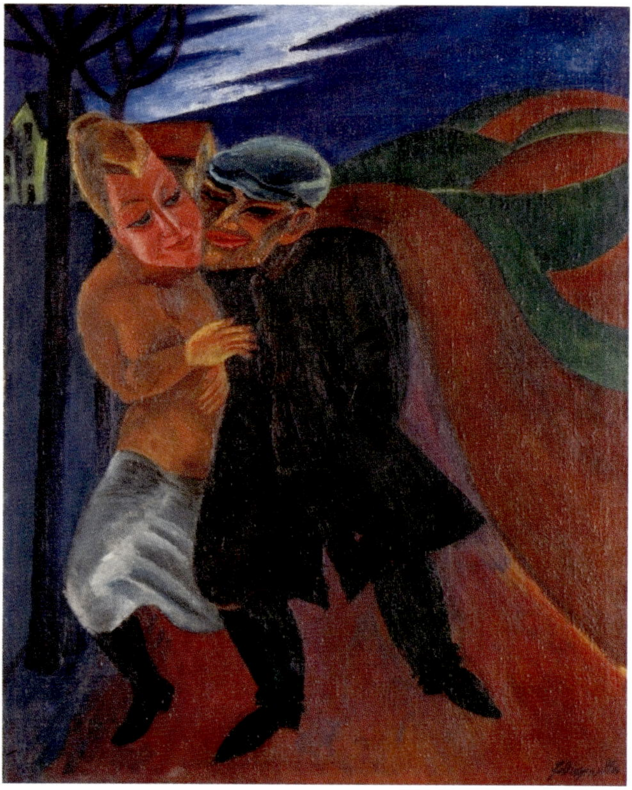

In the Spring Wind, 1920

Oil on canvas, 95 × 78 cm
CR Felixmüller 205

Conrad Felixmüller and Londa Freiin von Berg were married in June 1918. Before the couple moved into their apartment in the Klotzsche suburb of Dresden, they spent the summer with the Wiesbaden collector Heinrich Kirchhoff. Over the next three years Kirchhoff secured the material existence of the young couple by entering into a contract with the painter, which granted him a general right of first refusal and guaranteed the artist a monthly income. In this way, *In the Spring Wind* came into Kirchhoff's possession. The painting shows the couple on a stormy spring walk. Together they brace themselves against the wind that rushes towards them in the open hilly landscape. The painter's sports cap, which he also wears in his self-portrait of the same time, is clearly recognisable.

A comparison of the painting with the watercolour *Lovers in the Rain* reveals Felixmüller's special painterly qualities. The treatment of colour in some of his oil paintings during these years recalls the intense brilliance of the hues in his watercolours. Moreover, the comparison of these two works shows the recovery of form, from the early 1920s, in the artist's work after its Cubist disintegration since 1916.

Like Otto Dix, Felixmüller repeatedly explored individual motifs using various techniques, with drawings and watercolours serving as compositional studies for larger paintings. This is the case with the *Blue Circus Rider.* While Dix in 1922 devoted a whole portfolio of prints to the theme of the circus among others, the subject of the travelling show people plays no such prominent role in the work of Felixmüller.
The occasions for such depictions were his own experiences together with his family. Thus, in 1921, he and his son Titus visited the Leyseck circus in Dresden. The visit

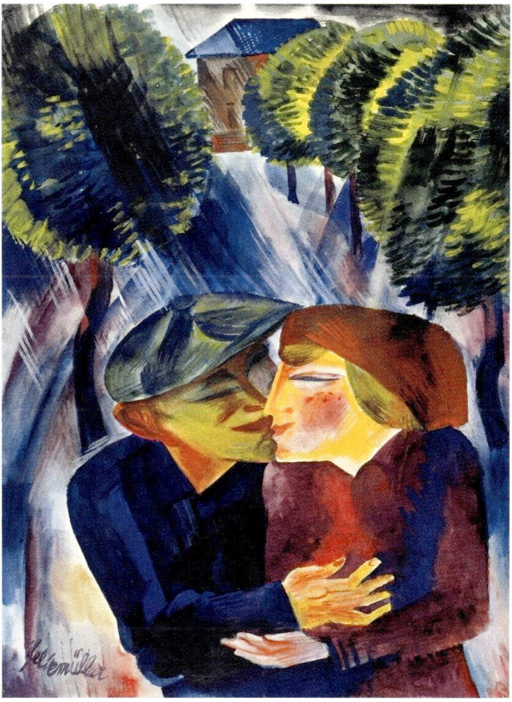

Lovers in the Rain, 1922
Watercolour, 64 × 48 cm

resulted in various drawings, watercolours, etchings and paintings. The motif of the circus rider seems to have particularly fascinated the artist. He dedicated works in all techniques to this subject, including two paintings. The Chemnitz watercolour is a study for the painting *The Circus Rider*, which today belongs to a private collection. The two works correspond with regard to the composition of the group of figures, although this is more closely knit here than in the almost square painting.

Blue Circus Rider (Study for the Painting 'Woman Circus Rider'), 1921

Watercolour, 56.5 × 43 cm

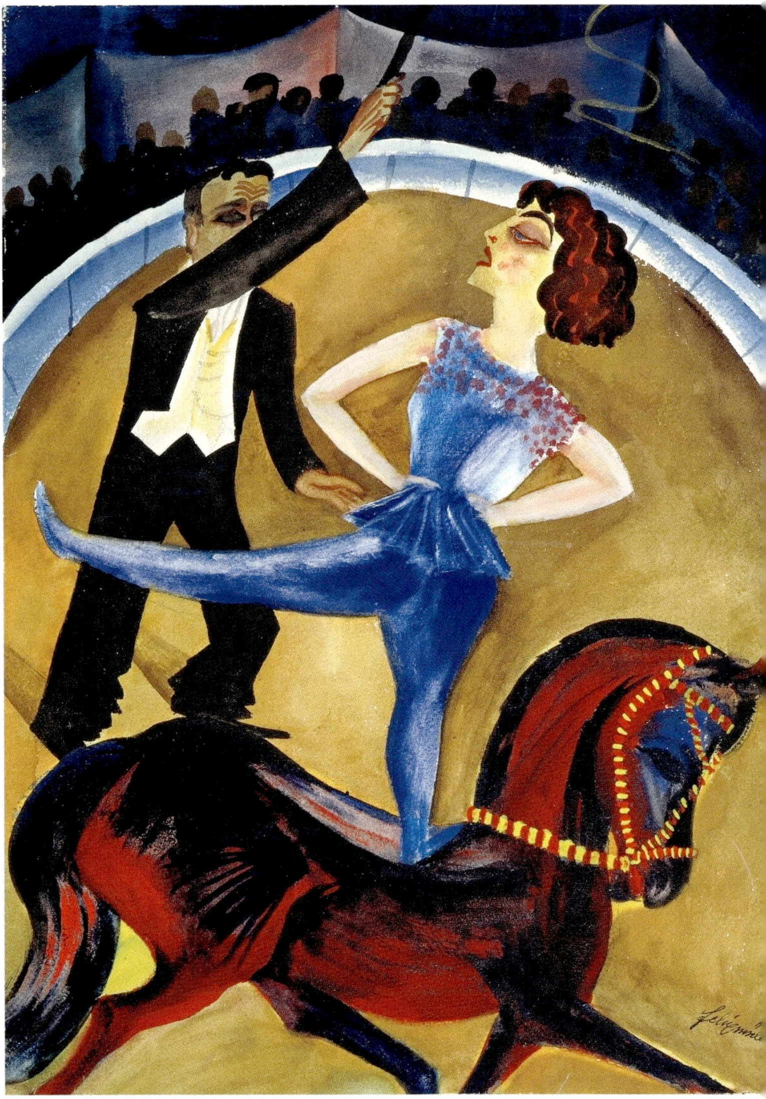

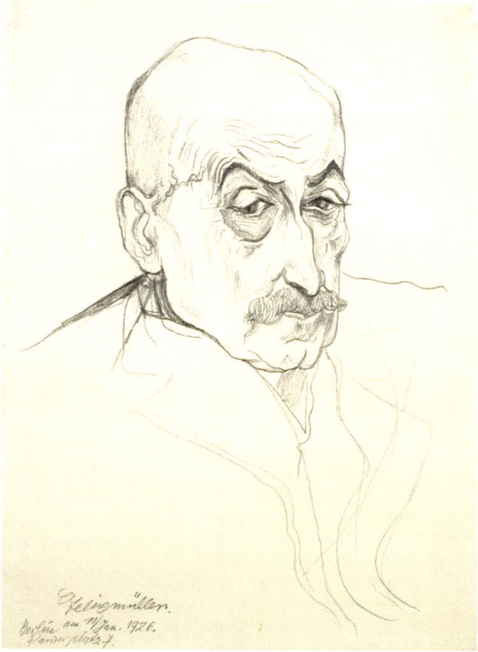

CONRAD FELIXMÜLLER 1897–1977

This portrait study is impressive evidence of Conrad Felixmüller's skill as a draughtsman. His pronounced talent for drawing was discovered and encouraged at an early stage. The artist himself frequently commented in the course of his life on the extent to which the command of drawing formed part of his concept of the artist's profession. Drawings such as this portrait of Max Liebermann show the mastery with which Felixmüller's hand guides the pencil, and without major corrections captures the characteristic features of the subject's appearance, "how incredibly finely his [Liebermann's] head is formed, covered with a thin smooth skin, and rhythmically enlivened by veins and folds" (Conrad Felixmüller). The drawing is a study for the portrait of the painter that was executed as a woodcut. Like the portraits of Lovis Corinth (1925) as well as Christian Rohlfs (1927), Felixmüller created this work "as a memorial of my respect and gratitude".

Portrait of Max Liebermann, 1926

Pencil on thin cardboard, 42.1 × 32.5 cm

This watercolour from the early 1930s shows the garden at Felixmüller's house in the Klotzsche suburb of Dresden, where the painter lived with his family from his marriage in 1918 up to 1931. The immediate living environment is a repeated theme in the artist's work, in the context of his many portrayals of himself and his family. The motif of the garden is also frequently found in his views from windows or direct depictions of landscape. Using the special potential of the watercolour technique, Felixmüller succeeds in this sheet in conveying the atmosphere of the wintry snow-covered garden. In finely nuanced tones of blue, white and purple he renders the snow and the sky above the house, giving an impression of cold weather. Since the late 1920s Felixmüller had already left Expressionism behind, in order to turn with renewed strength to a realistic rendition of what he saw, felt and experienced.

Klotzsche –
Garden in Winter, 1931

Watercolour, 53 × 43 cm

CONRAD FELIXMÜLLER 1897–1977

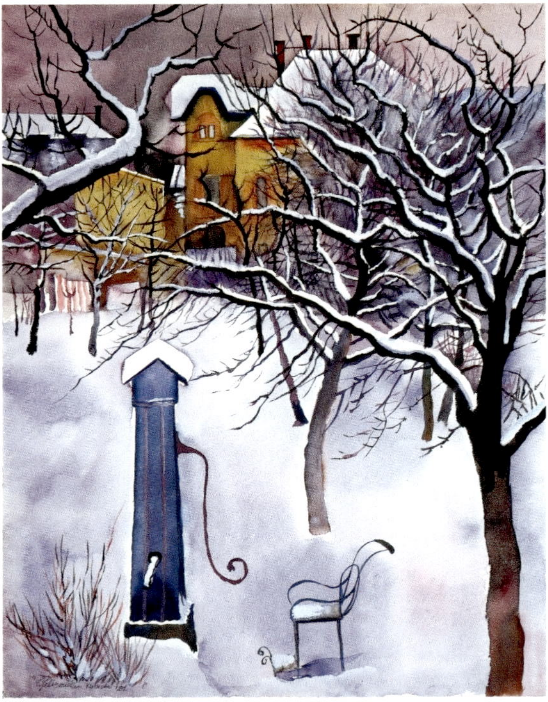

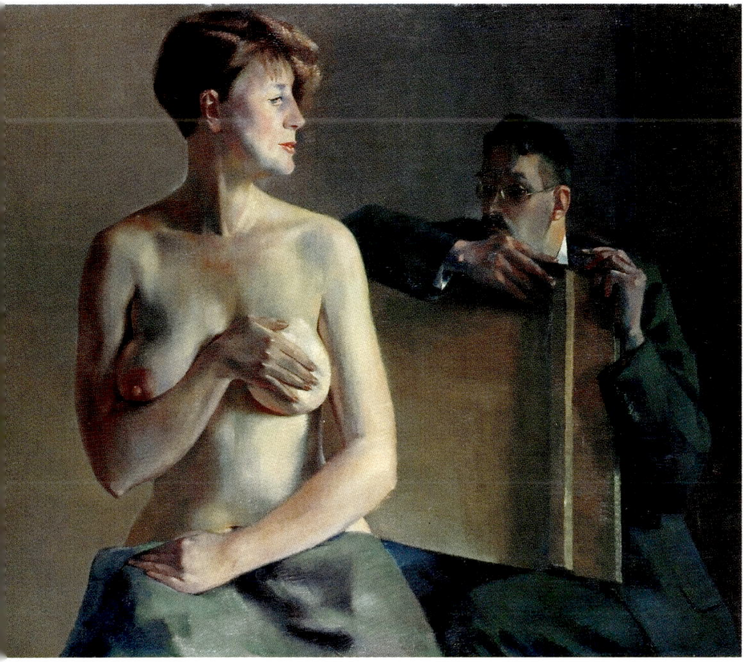

This painting, a self-portrait of the painter drawing his wife in the nude, marks a turning-point in the artist's life. Stylistically it is characteristic of the new realism which Felixmüller developed from the 1930s onward. Far from his earlier Expressionist exaggeration of form and colour, Felixmüller here attempts to render reality with as objective a description as possible. Compositionally fitted into a clearly structured framework, the painting shows the seated frontal nude figure of Londa and the reflective painter during a break from his drawing.

The artist's pause for thought and the woman's gaze sliding off into the distance suggest the time of the work's creation and the family's uncertain future. As early as 1933 the defamation of Felixmüller by the National Socialists began in the exhibition "Spiegelbilder des Verfalls der Kunst" (Reflections of the Decline of Art) in Dresden, in which forty of his works were shown. The family then left Dresden and moved to Berlin, where they lived until the loss of their apartment and studio in April 1941.

Londa, Seen from the Ai – Semi-Nude, 1933

Oil on canvas, 110.5 × 90.5 cm
CR Felixmüller 562

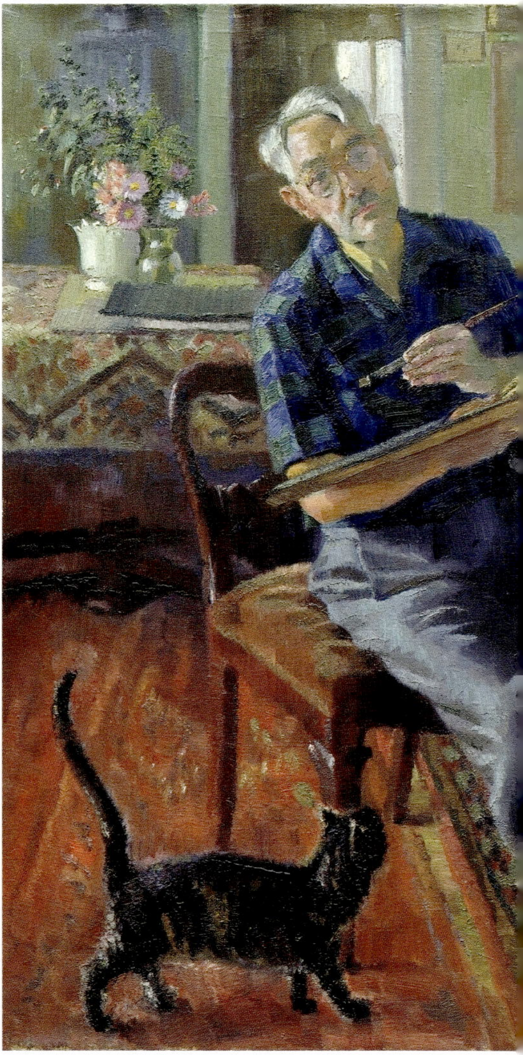

Throughout his creative career, Felixmüller was preoccupied with his own personality. As with Otto Dix, his confrontation with himself can be followed in the collection from the early beginnings (1916) up to a few years before his death (1972) by means of drawings, watercolours, prints and paintings. One of his late works is the self-portrait in oil, which he created in 1959 at Tautenhain, south of Leipzig, where the painter lived with his family from 1944 to 1961. After the war he was appointed to a professorship in painting and drawing in the faculty of education of the University of Halle an der

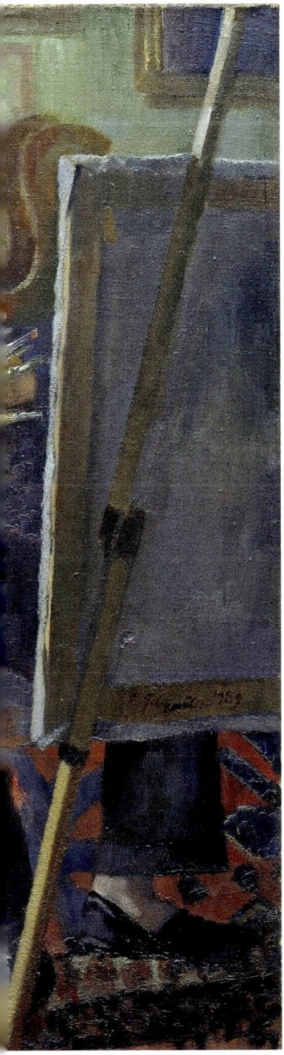

Self-Portrait in Blue-Green Shirt, with Bussy, 1959

Oil on canvas, 67.5 × 58.5 cm
CR Felixmüller 1424

CONRAD FELIXMÜLLER 1897–1977

Saale, which he occupied until his retirement in 1962. More and more dissatisfied with political developments in East Germany, however, he gradually retreated into his private life. This painting shows the 62-year-old in his domestic environment with the cat Bussy at the moment when he glances in the mirror to check his appearance. At the same time it exemplifies the homogeneity and consistency of the style he found around 1930 and which marks his mature and late work of the 1930s to 1970s. Felixmüller records the world immediately around him with sharp observation and a fine glazing technique of painting.

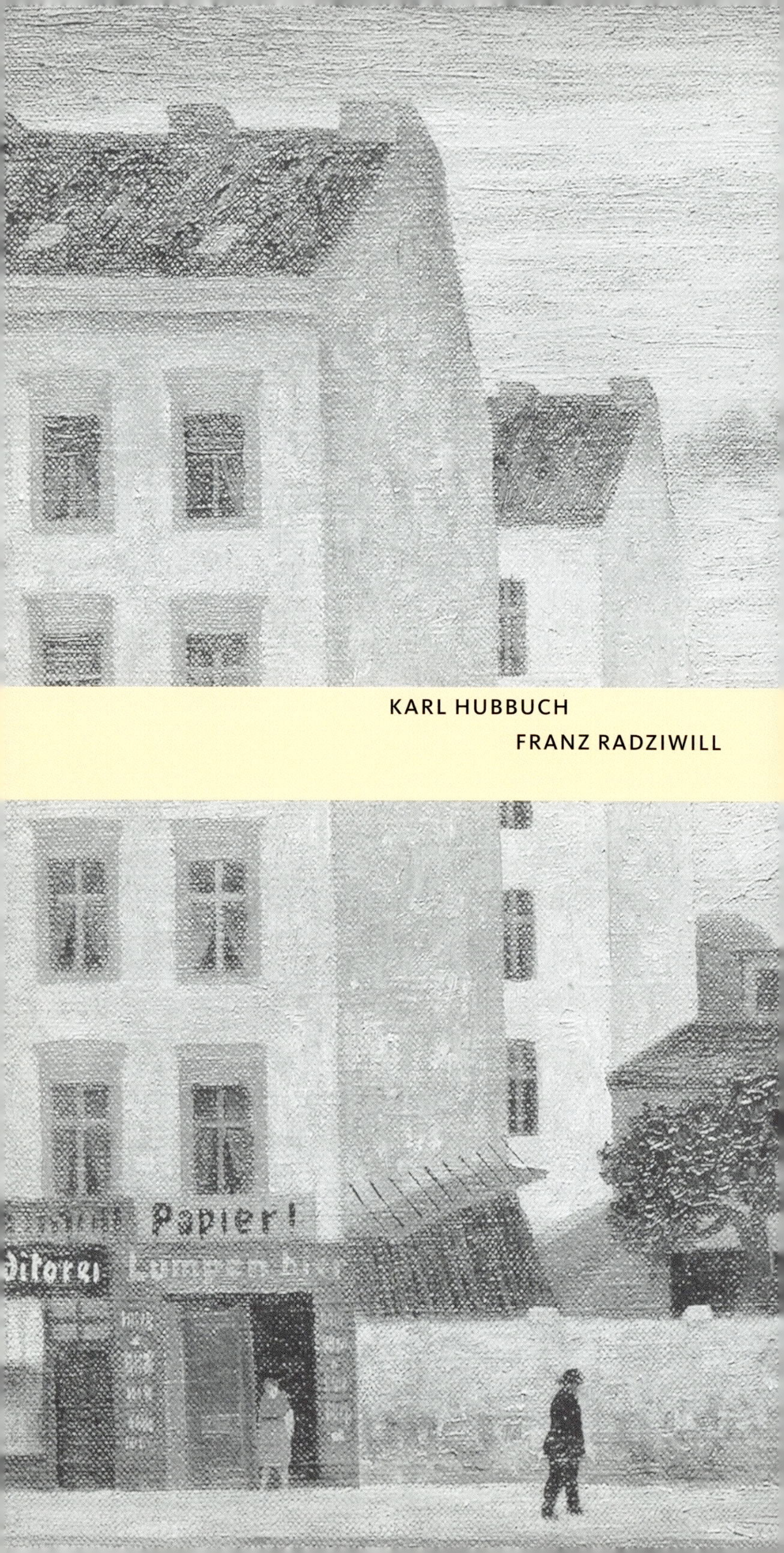

KARL HUBBUCH

FRANZ RADZIWILL

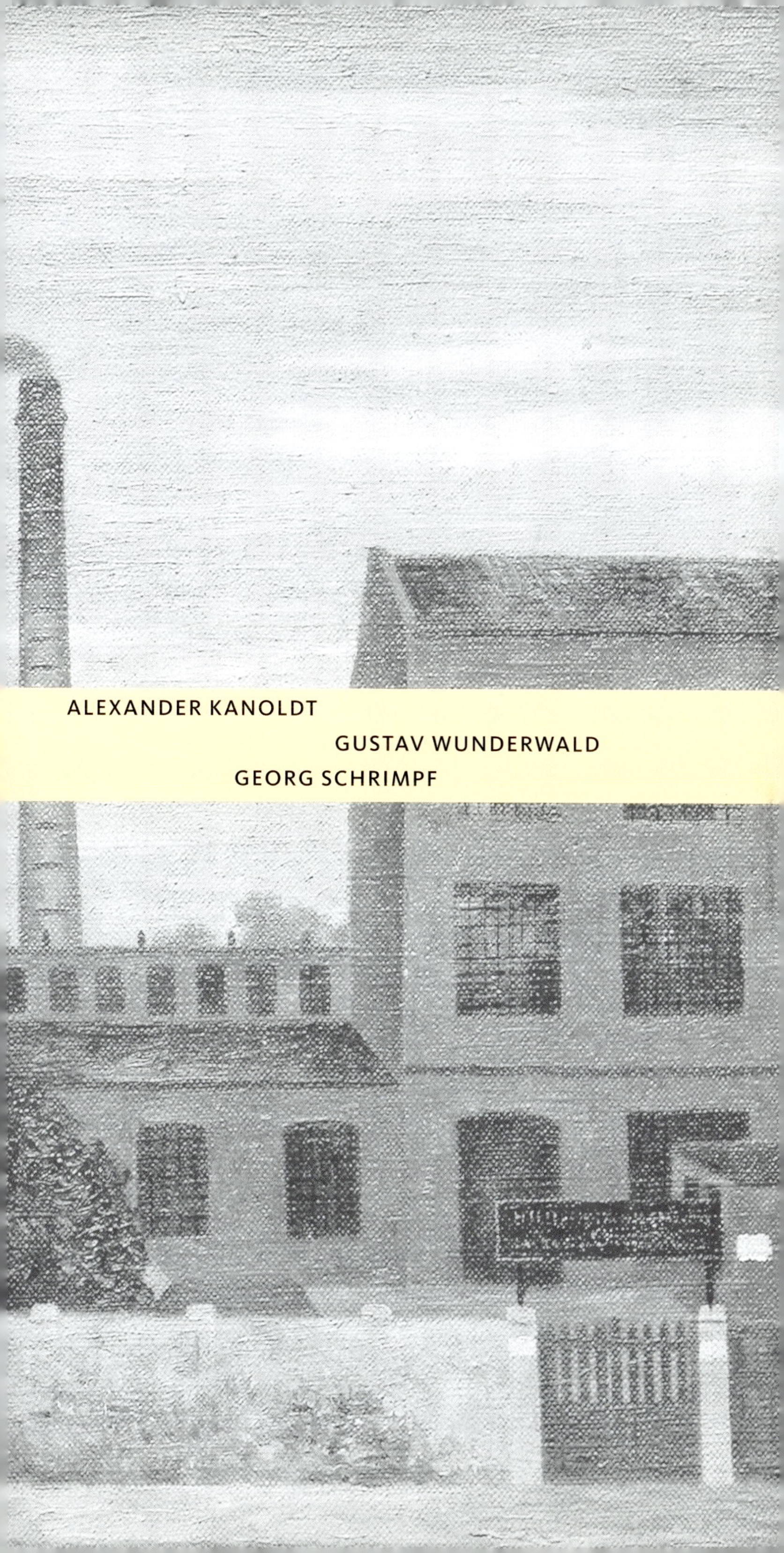

ALEXANDER KANOLDT

GUSTAV WUNDERWALD

GEORG SCHRIMPF

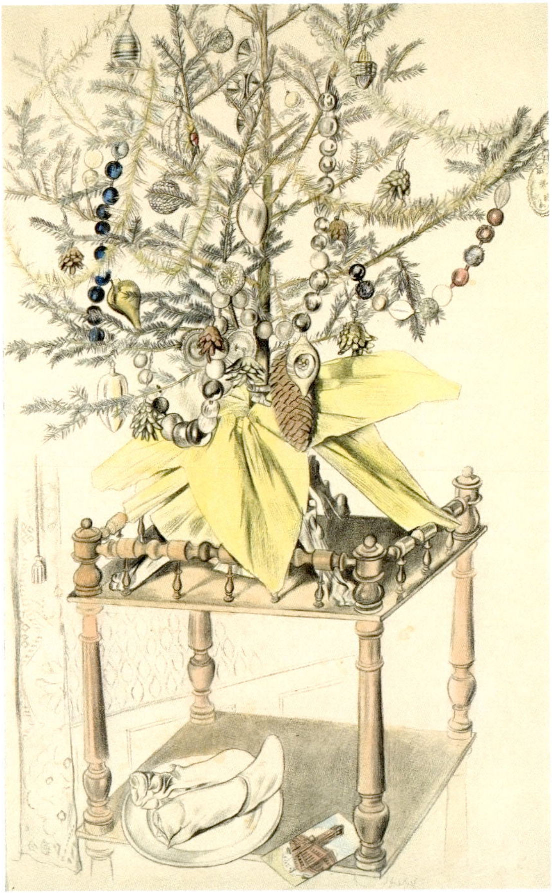

Christmas Tree, c. 1925

Pencil and Watercolour, 50 × 32.5 cm

Along with Otto Dix in Dresden, Karl Hubbuch in Karlsruhe is one of the important protagonists of Verism, a form of artistic expression within the New Objectivity. After studying at the Grossherzogliche Badische Akademie (Archducal Academy in Baden), Hubbuch's creative career began in the early 1920s with a wide-ranging series of drawings and prints. With an analytical gaze he documented in pencil the social conditions of his time; from the middle of the decade he produced large-format watercolour drawings with a pictorially powerful presence. Thus, for example, he used the most frugal stylistic means to record this meagre *Christmas Tree* standing on a table together with decorations and deliberately arranged objects, including the picture postcard with a view of the Red Town Hall in Berlin. After being appointed as director of a painting class in Karlsruhe in 1928, Hubbuch also turned his attention to oil painting. He started by creating large model studies on canvas, introducing into oil painting a softly modelled variation on the New Objectivity style. Initially Hubbuch concentrated on sketch-like *alla prima* painting, and then began to experiment with the style of the Old Masters in the so-called "Experimental Images". "Van Eyck technique" was his name for his paintings on wooden or hardboard panels over various priming coats. Around 1935 he focused on small pictures on a gold ground like this panel, *Engagement to be Announced*. The theme of two people meeting for the first time in a bar was used by Hubbuch several times; it is among the group of motifs caricaturing the subjects' physiognomy in an ironic manner and bearing witness to the artist's precise eye and gift for characterisation. During this time Hubbuch was already banned by the National Socialists from practising his profession and exhibiting his work. In 1933 he was dismissed from his post at the Karlsruhe Academy.

An Engagement is to be Announced, c. 1935
Gold ground and resin oil paint on hardboard, 30 × 32 cm

KARL HUBBUCH 1891–1979

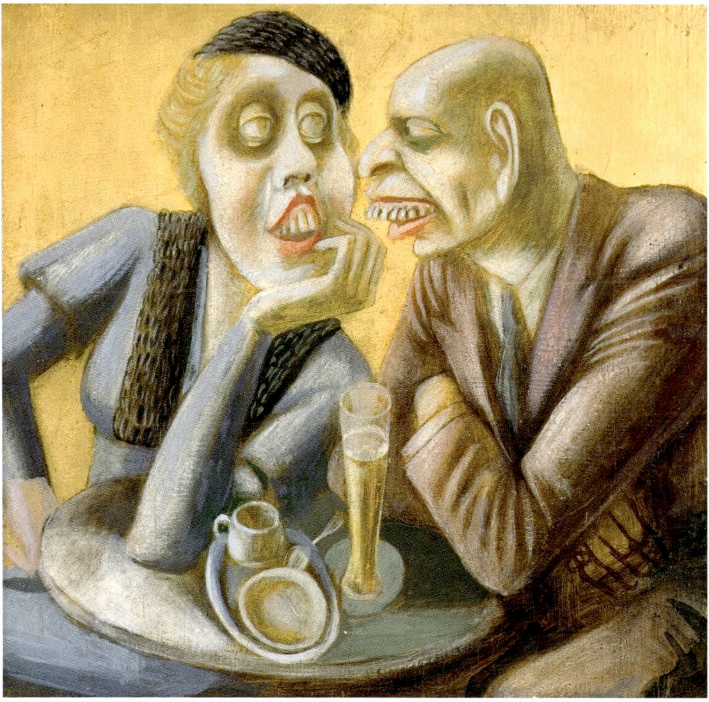

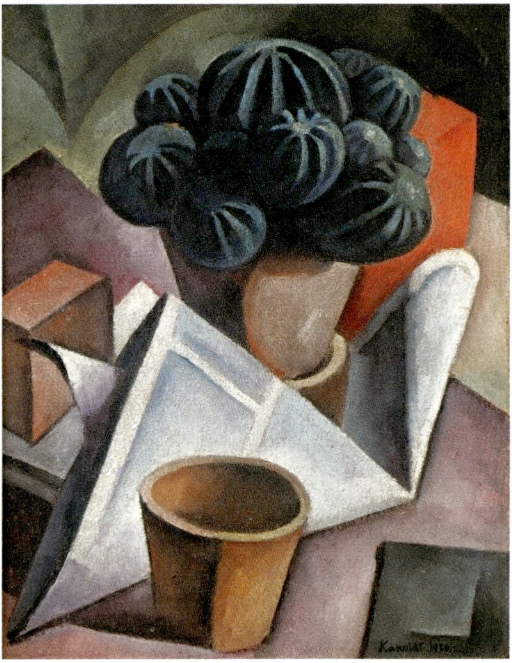

ALEXANDER KANOLDT 1881–1939

Still Life with Cactus (Still Life III), 1920

Oil on canvas, 41.3 × 33.5 cm

Alexander Kanoldt is one of the early protagonists of Modernism. In 1909 he was a founder member of the Neue Künstlervereinigung München (New Artists' Association of Munich), whose best-known representatives are Wassily Kandinsky and Alexej von Jawlensky. In 1911 the association was split as a result of Kandinsky's move towards abstraction. Later, after the First World War, artists such as Kanoldt developed their own contribution to the New Objectivity, within which the still life assumed a central position. Traditionally linked with the *vanitas* concept of a reminder of the transience of all earthly life, the genre was reinterpreted by the New Objectivity. It was precisely unchanging things such as evergreen plants and anonymous contemporary objects that determined the composition. Thus in his *Still Life with Cactus*, Kanoldt obliterates all reference to time, presenting a sculpturally folded paper which resembles a newspaper but without text or illustrations. Stylistically this work belongs to the artist's early New Objectivity works, in which the picture space is still two-dimensional and the motif is not yet executed with almost sterile precision.

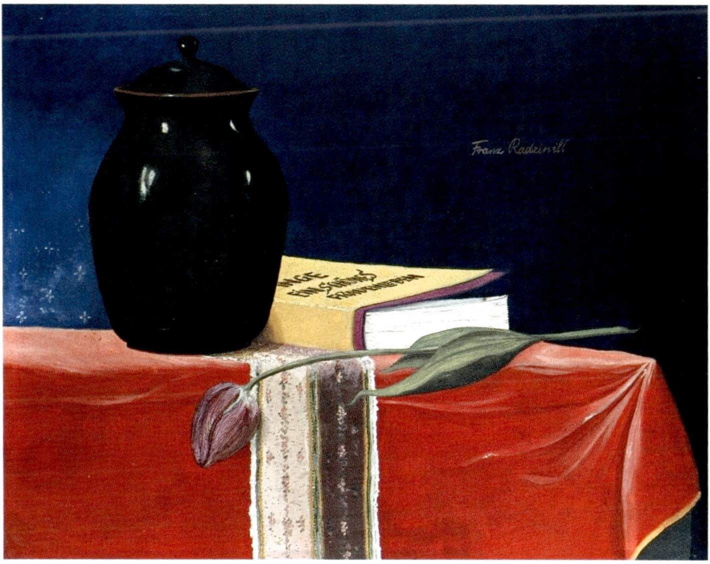

FRANZ RADZIWILL 1895–1983

Franz Radziwill is considered one of the typical representatives of the so-called Magic Realism within the art of New Objectivity. From 1915 he developed his own pictorial vocabulary, marked by imaginative and original compositions and colour schemes. Apart from landscapes which often seem menacing, the still life makes up a large part of his oeuvre. He continually varies arrangements of vases and jugs with plants or fruit as well as books on a table surface set horizontally across the lower half of the image. Generally these views are seen from a low angle or, as in this painting, frontally and slightly from above. While he often creates an oppressive rigidity and static calm by layering the objects in the image space, this ensemble gains in spatial depth through the diagonally placed tulip and the book. The book's title is shown as *Inge. Ein schönes Frauenleben* (Inge: A Beautiful Life of a Woman), which can be seen as a dedication to the painter's first wife, who had died only a few months previously. In terms of colour, this memorial still life is a brilliant harmony of primary and their respective complementary colours.

Still Life with Lidded Vase, Tulip and Yellow Book, 1943

Oil on canvas on wood,
32 × 42 cm
CR Schulze 523

Gustav Wunderwald, with his Berlin "vedute" of the 1920s, is an important representative of the New Objectivity. Although well-known, this area of his work does not, however, represent the main focus of his total oeuvre, for he was primarily active as a landscape painter. At first Wunderwald worked as a stage painter, in Stockholm, Düsseldorf and Berlin and elsewhere. His early artistic work consisted mainly of light-flooded landscapes painted in his free time. The *Three Larches in the Snow* were probably painted at the time of Wunderwald's work at the Stadttheater in Innsbruck. The composition resembles that of a stage set. Already typical of the painter's early work are his simplified forms, restricted to the essentials of the motif. Nevertheless, Wunderwald's particular fascination as an artist is clearly recognisable: like an anticipation of the still lifes of the New Objectivity, the sharply contoured, filigree branches of the bare conifers in front of a dark blue sky give an impression of a timeless moment of rigidity.

Three Larches in the Snow, 1909

Oil on canvas, 70 × 50 cm
CR Reinhardt 6

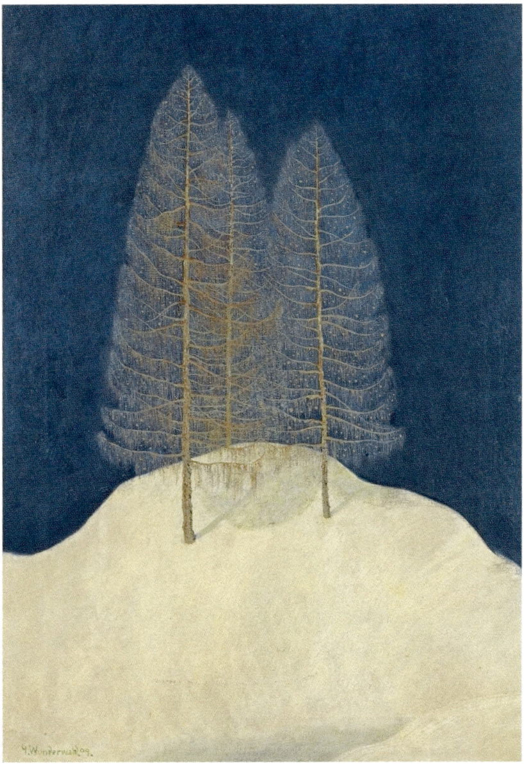

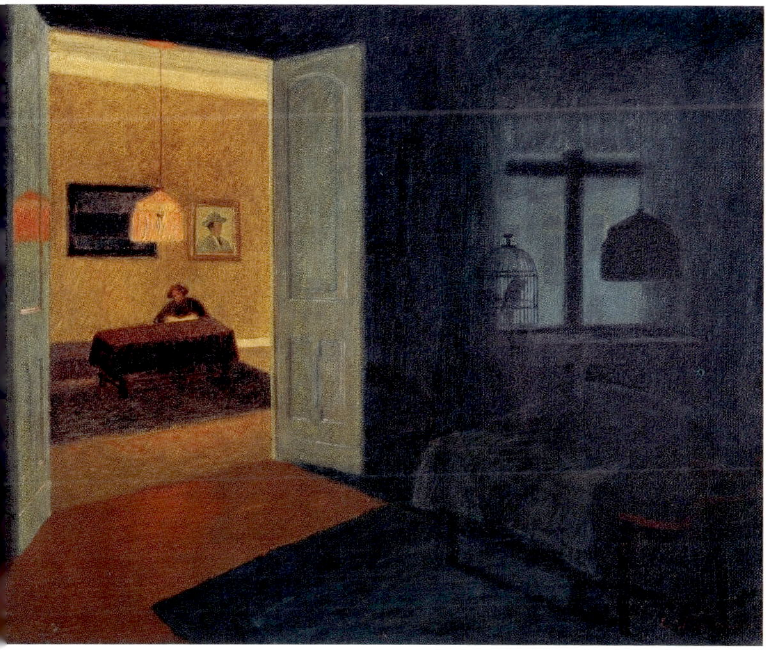

GUSTAV WUNDERWALD 1882–1945

From 1912 Wunderwald lived in Berlin. He first worked as a set designer at the Deutsche Oper, winning considerable international recognition. But Wunderwald's overriding desire was for free artistic creativity, so that he allowed his contract to expire in 1917. Wunderwald lived in an apartment in Charlottenburg, which served several times as the subject of his paintings in 1914. During this time he also created his first views of streets and buildings, which formed the prelude to his 'Berlin Portraits' of the 1920s. The *View of the Artist's Studio* astonishes above all with its light effects: from a darkened room in the foreground of the picture, one looks at the illuminated space beyond it, where the artist's wife sits reading at a table. Behind her hangs the self-portrait that Wunderwald created in the same year. The depth and tension of the painting are derived from the skilful composition of inner and outer rooms and the openings to interior and exterior.

View of the Artist's Studio, c. 1914

Oil on canvas, 52 × 66.5 cm
CR Reinhardt 26

Although he was born in Cologne, Gustav Wunderwald developed a particularly intense relationship with the German capital from the very beginning of his time in Berlin – so much so that, by his own account, he could hardly imagine living in the Rhineland again.

The artist was fascinated above all by the varied appearance of the industrial and working districts to the north and west of the city. Streets, houses, factories, courtyards and railway stations in Spandau, Moabit and Wedding are motifs that constantly recur in his paintings between 1924 and 1929. It was the "interesting sobriety and dreariness" that stimulated him in this work. With an unemotional, coolly observing gaze, untouched by any artificial accusations of social evils, Wunderwald documented entire series of streets. With these "Vedute" of the metropolis, typical of the New Objectivity, he created not only valuable works in terms of art history, but also documents of urban history and topography.

Factory in Moabit ("Hingabe"), 1926

Oil on canvas, 46 × 69.5 cm
CR Reinhardt 113

GUSTAV WUNDERWALD 1882–1945

On Lindower Strasse (Berlin N), 1927

Oil on canvas, 50 × 69.7 cm
CR Reinhardt 143

Greater Berlin, which was formed in 1920 through the union of eight towns (Berlin, Schöneberg, Charlottenburg, Neukölln and others), together with fifty-nine rural communities and twenty-seven private estates, became the painter's dominant theme and earned him the nickname of the "Utrillo of Berlin". His work was so precise that some views such as that seen in *On Lindower Strasse* in Wedding can still be clearly localised today. Its compositional pendant of 1926 is of interest particularly for its details. On the factory wall which runs parallel to the picture there are two scrawled graffiti in the centre. Apart from the swastika on the left, the word "Hingabe" (Devotion) is written in block capitals on the right. This is a reference to a right-wing conservative group of the 1920s which at that particular time was attracting attention throughout Germany. While for Wunderwald these were realistic details of the original scene at the time, for today's observer they serve as a reminder of the early beginnings of National Socialist subversive activities.

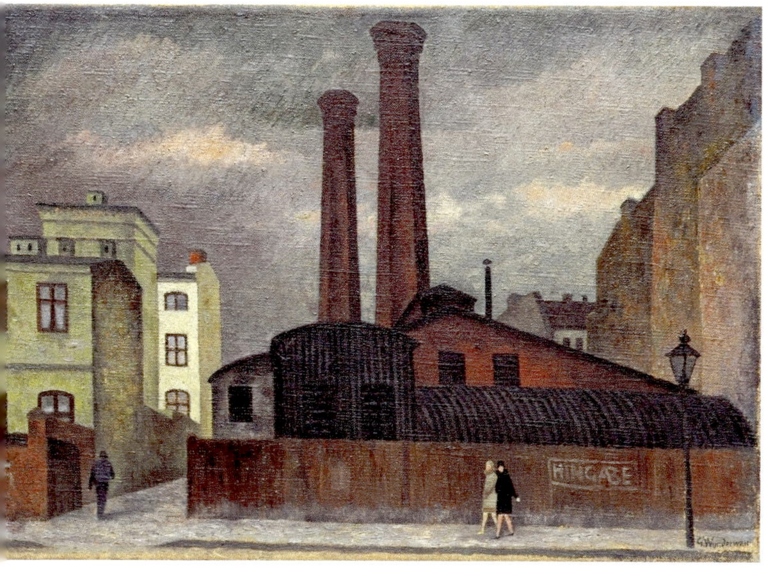

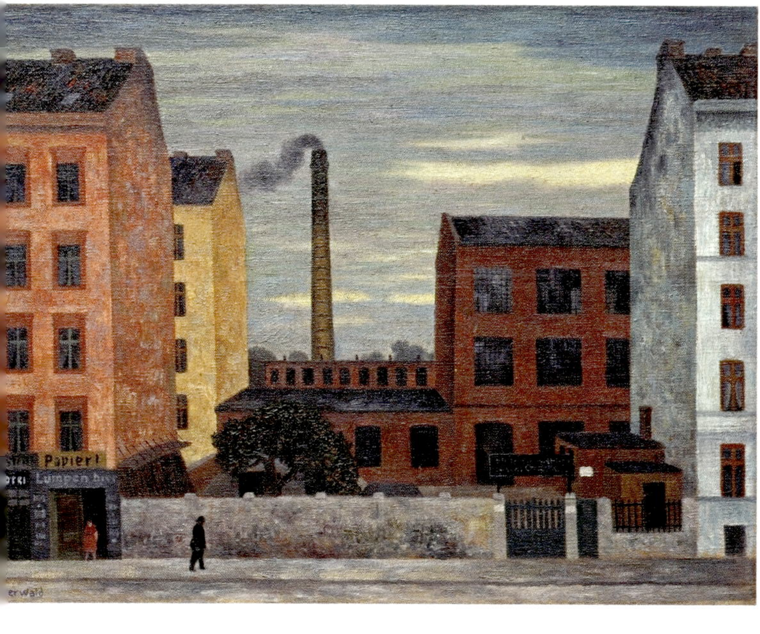
Papier

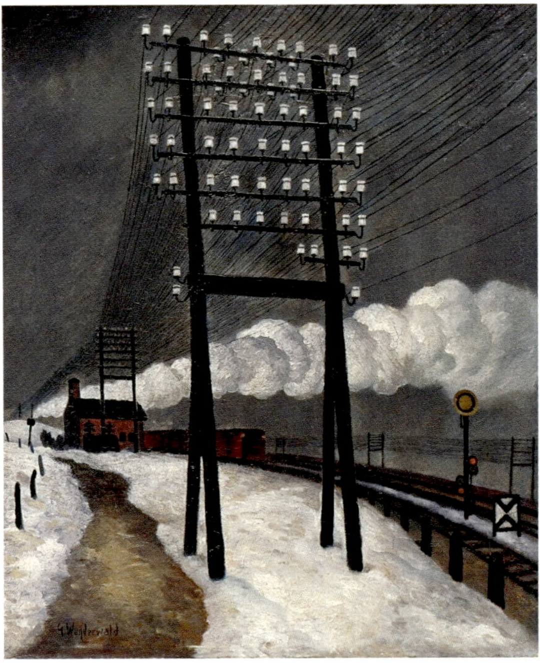

GUSTAV WUNDERWALD 1882–1945

Railway Embankment Berlin N, c. 1928

Oil on canvas, 71.5 × 61.5 cm
CR Reinhardt 149

The motif of the railway embankment forms an exception within the group of Wunderwald's urban views of Berlin. It shows a stretch from the northern edge of the city along the railway line towards Königs Wusterhausen. What primarily fascinates the painter is the strong perspective of the slipstream of the rails, which he additionally strengthens with the locomotive steam and the high-tension cables. All lines lead to a vanishing-point outside the left-hand edge of the picture. Apart from the compositional accentuations, Wunderwald skilfully guides the effect of the painting through his colour scheme, which shimmers in a handful of tones of blue, grey, ochre, yellow and red, loosened up and interrupted by the subdued white of the snow and the black of the towering high-tension masts.

From October 1924 to January 1925 Georg Schrimpf lived with his family in Sicily. For Schrimpf, Italy played an important part in the development of his artistic expression. Between 1909 and 1913 he spent much time in the reform groups on Monte Verità in Ascona in Switzerland, and up to 1930 travelled to Italy several times. He made an intensive study of early Italian art as well as the contemporary art of the *Valori Plastici* group and was particularly fascinated by the painting of Carlo Carrà. In response to these influences, after the First World War Schrimpf developed a style which tended towards the simplification of form, while nonetheless bringing out clearly the sculptural strengths of the figures and spaces. He departed from the originally strongly Expressionistic colour schemes of his paint-ings in favour of a delicate glazing painting style. At the "Neue Sachlichkeit" (New Objectivity) exhibition in Mannheim in 1925, which gave its name to the artistic movement, he was represented to a more than average extent by as many as twelve paintings.

Mondello near Palermo, 1925

Gouache on paper, 23 × 32 cm

GEORG SCHRIMPF 1889–1938

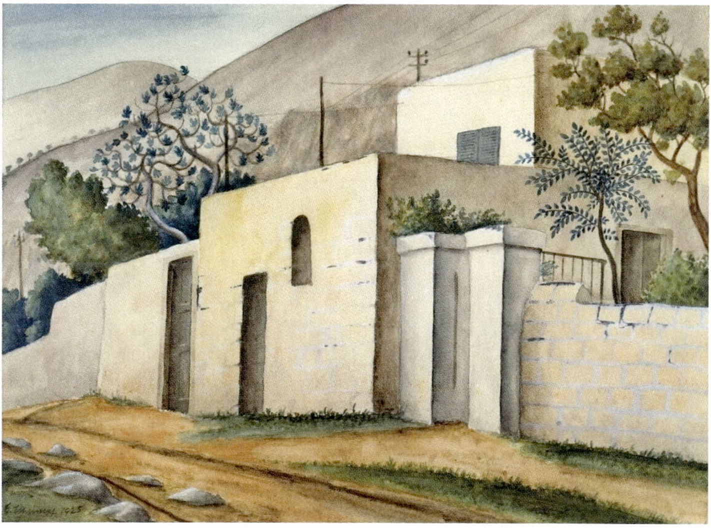

In terms of craftsmanship, the works of Georg Schrimpf, like those of the other artists of the New Objectivity, are marked by an excellent command of technique. In contrast to the Verists like Otto Dix, however, Schrimpf holds no critical mirror to his own age with his art. Rather, he uses comparable stylistic means to design works which present an alternative to the existing reality. After the death of his first wife, the painter Maria Uhden, in 1918, he developed his painterly oeuvre, in which the human figure and the landscape are decisive elements. Classical in physical volume, and for the most part spatially expansive, children and young women dominate the pictures, like these two children playing on the steps of a town house. While the presumably older girl is totally absorbed in playing with her doll, the boy's gaze travels past the viewer into a distant future. As with most of Schrimpf's works, a calm hangs over the image which almost amounts to rigidity, and lends a timeless aspect to the fleeting moment of a snapshot.

Children on the Steps, 1925

Oil on canvas, 58 × 53 cm
CR Hofmann/Praeger 1925/1

GEORG SCHRIMPF 1889–1938

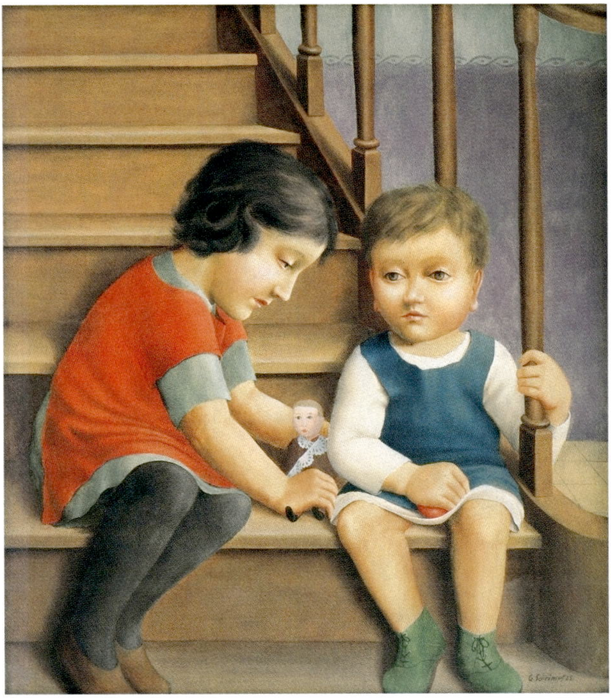

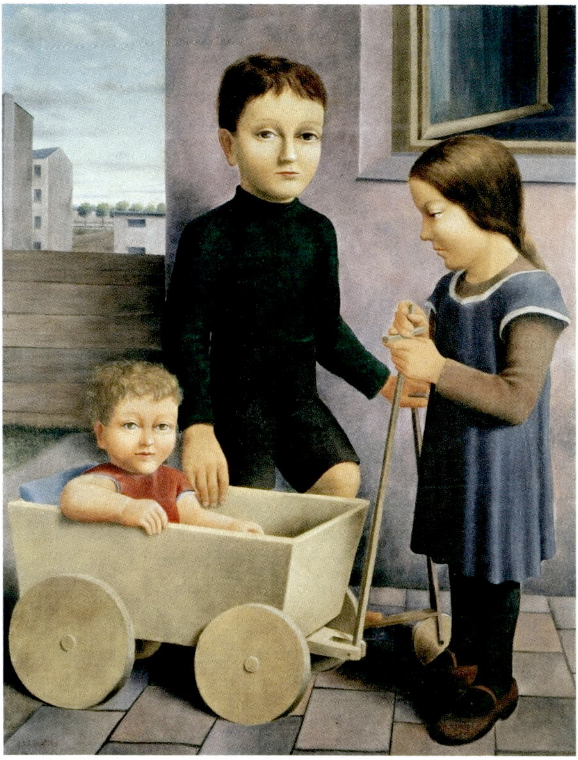

Three Children, 1926

Oil on canvas, 80.5 × 65.5 cm
CR Hofmann/Praeger 1926/3

Georg Schrimpf's artistic oeuvre is further marked by his preoccupation with art history, in particular the art of the Romantics. His pictures of children, for example, show clear parallels with the work of Philipp Otto Runge. In the painting *Three Children* he confronts, as though in a quotation, Runge's well-known painting of the *Hülsenbeck Children* (1805/06). Three children of different ages are playing on the street or in the paved inner courtyard of an apartment block. But Schrimpf, unlike Runge, does not show them actively in a moment of carefree play; instead, they linger in a strangely statuesque manner in front of the wall of the building. In this representation of a supposed childhood idyll, the viewer's eye is met by a small family marked by all the cares of a time of tribulation. While in Runge's painting the scene is set in natural surroundings, Schrimpf's children stand on a paved road, and the link with the landscape is obscured by a wooden fence and houses in the background. The depiction is characterised by a sense of determination.

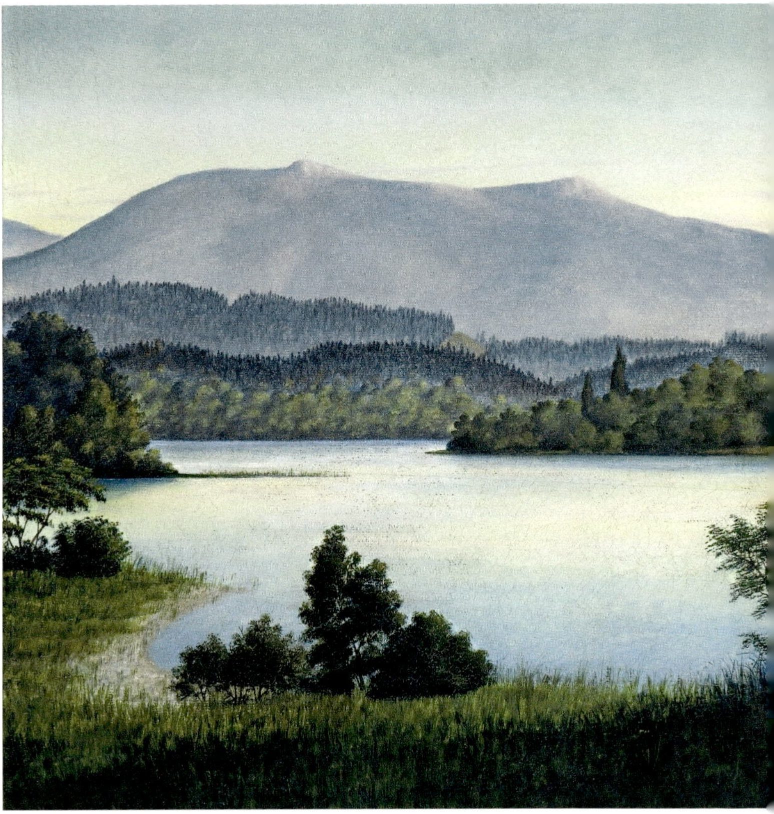

From 1926 the proportion of landscapes in Schrimpf's total output increases noticeably, until during the last years of his life they account exclusively for the motifs of his world. After he had found recognition from the mid-1920s as a painter of the New Objectivity, towards the end of the decade his political commitment declined markedly. At the same time, an artistic movement towards introspection began, and the artist's handwriting begins to change again. In the landscapes of this period above all it is the work of Caspar David Friedrich that shines through in the basic mood of nature, visibly expanded into the infinite. These depictions of the Staffelsee and Chiemsee lakes, flooded at first with a hard, strongly contouring light, gradually develop into wide views into the distance and compositions fading into the *sfumato* of the depth.

In spite of his post at the Staatliche Hochschule für Kunsterziehung (State College for Art Education) in

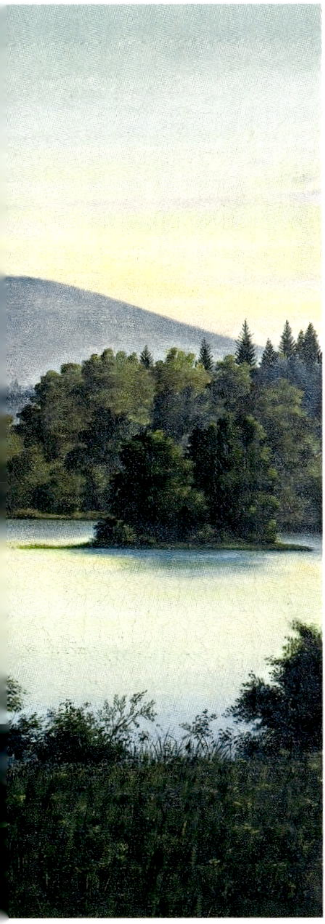

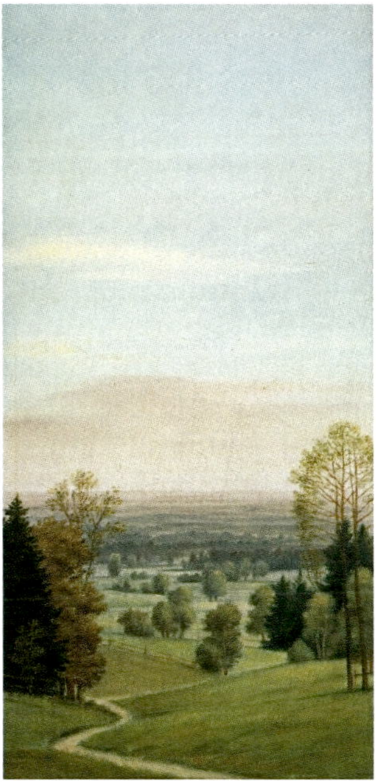

GEORG SCHRIMPF 1889–1938

Berlin, Schrimpf was exposed at the "Degenerate Art" exhibition of 1937 with a painting of 1915 from the former collection of Herwarth Walden, and at the end of the year he was dismissed from his teaching post because of his political activities before the First World War.

Staffelsee – East, 1926

Oil on canvas, 49 × 71 cm
CR Hofmann/Praeger 1926/10

View over Wide Landscape, 1937

Oil on cardboard, 36.5 × 17.5 cm
CR Hofmann/Praeger 1937/15

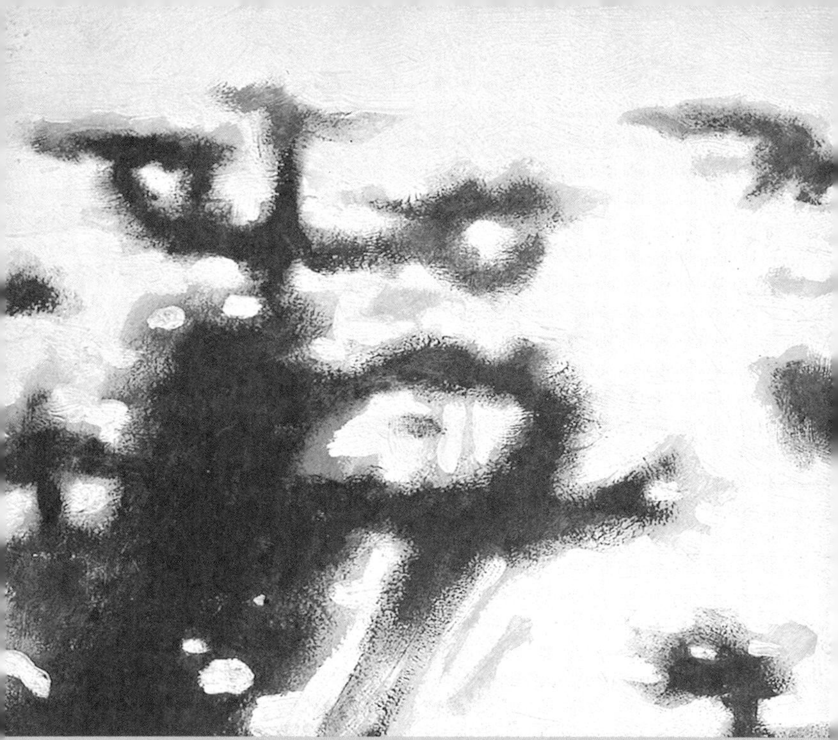

FRITZ STUCKENBERG

SERGE POLIAKOFF

EMIL SCHUMACHER

WILLI BAUMEISTER

FRITZ WINTER

ERNST WILHELM NAY

BERNARD SCHULTZE

Under the influence of the Impressionists, Fritz Stuckenberg achieved during his time in Paris a consolidation and simplification of forms as well as an Expressionist separation of colour from its link to the object at the beginning of the twentieth century. In the Berlin years between 1912 and 1919, during which he turned towards a non-representational mode of expression, Stuckenberg became one of the most important artists of Herwarth Walden's Sturm Gallery. In brilliant watercolours he composed mythological hues which presuppose an intensive dialogue with the Orphism of Delaunay and Kandinsky's "Improvisations". Over a basic accord of red-yellow-blue he varies the harmony of the tones and distributes graphic structures which give form to and dynamically enliven the surface. In the *Colour Drawings* Stuckenberg provides evidence in his free compositional handling of the paint as the logical development of abstraction out of the achievements of Expressionism.

Coloured Drawing
No. 12, 1918
Watercolour, 36.8 × 27.3 cm

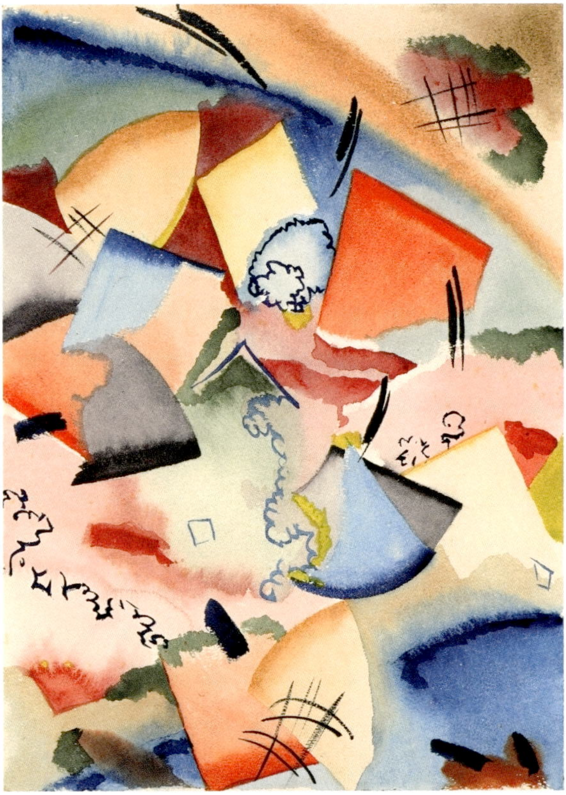

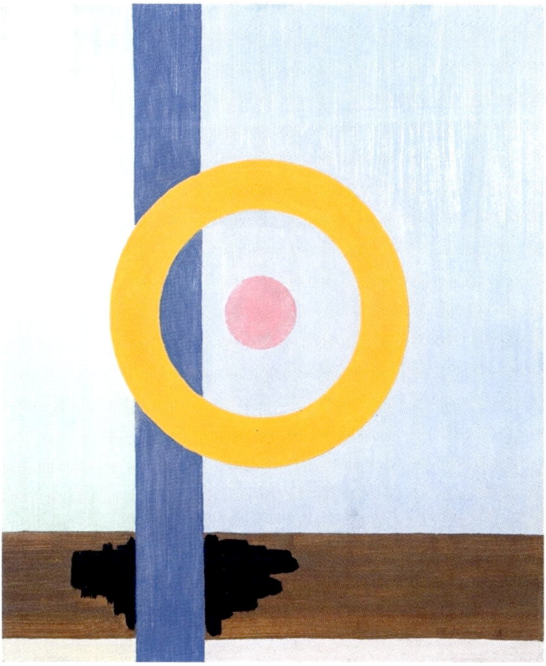

FRITZ STUCKENBERG 1881–1944

The Yellow Ring, 1928

Oil on card, 54 × 46 cm
CR Wandschneider 228

Stylistically, during the 1920s Stuckenberg developed further in the direction of geometric abstraction. Through contacts with artists of the Weimar Bauhaus he came to know the works of the Russian and Dutch Constructivists. In consequence he developed a certain manner of expression determined by geometric forms. *The Yellow Ring* is one of his central works of this period. "Circle (yellow ring) in front of dark rectangular bands running towards each other, placed in a delicately bright atmosphere", was Stuckenberg's description of this painting, which was shown in 1928 at the "Grosse Berliner Kunstausstellung" (Great Berlin Art Exhibition). While the watercolours suggest a dynamically abstract spatiality, the Constructivist works develop out of the clearly defined area, where by means of the juxtaposition of colours and details such as the black shadow on the brown band a third dimension is also created. With these paintings Stuckenberg diametrically opposes the National Socialist aesthetic, with the result that his works were removed from public possession and in 1937 were denounced as 'Degenerate Art'.

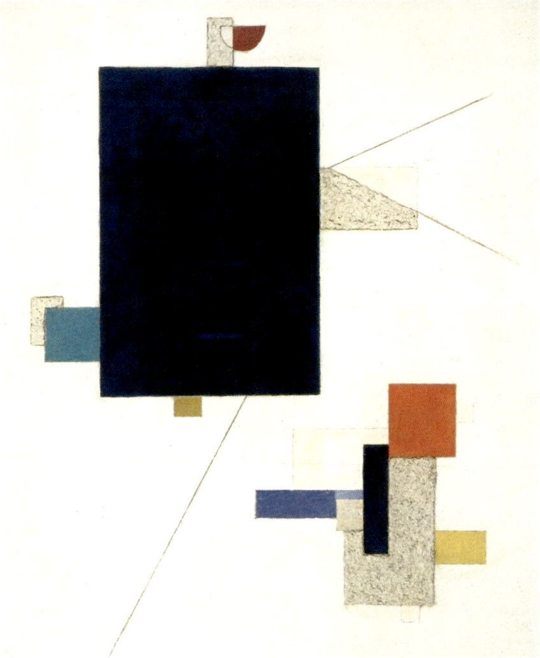

WILLI BAUMEISTER 1889–1955

Flächenkräfte, 1920

Oil, pencil, putty and sand on canvas on hardboard, 59.8 × 50 cm

CR Beye/Baumeister 230

Around 1920, Baumeister began to consolidate and simplify his composition, which was originally based on that of Cézanne. Without any knowledge of the work of the Russian Constructivists, he produced up to the middle of the decade groups of works comparable to theirs, the "Mauerbilder" and "Flächenkräfte". In the latter, Baumeister distances himself to the greatest extent from the object, exploring the structure of areas of different shapes and sizes, always in search of a harmonious tension between the individual components within the picture.

The most striking characteristic of his art from that time onwards is his serial work. He produces multiple variations of one and the same theme and sometimes takes it up again after lengthy pauses. At the same time as Dix was producing his great Verist paintings, Baumeister was marking out with these works the path of the international avant-garde in the milieu of the Bauhaus and the aesthetic of the Neues Bauen.

Around 1930, biomorphic formations began to appear in Baumeister's painting. In the years that followed he created the groups of works called "Flämchenbilder" and "Linienbilder", including the *Painting with Shell Form on Greyish-Purple*. For a time, the organically curving course of the line, taken from the outline of the human body, determined the composition of his pictures. As before, their structure remains true to the established principle of constructing the composition in relief form, forward from the surface of the image. Baumeister created variations on the present motif in four paintings, starting with a sketch from his journal. In the late 1930s he made some minor but decisive alterations to the present version. For example, he lightens the red line where it passes over the yellow area with white paint, and accentuates the circular form by overpainting it with a red that appears to push forward.

Painting with Shell Form on Greyish-Violet, 1932

Oil and sand on canvas, 80.5 × 64.5 cm
CR Beye/Baumeister 527

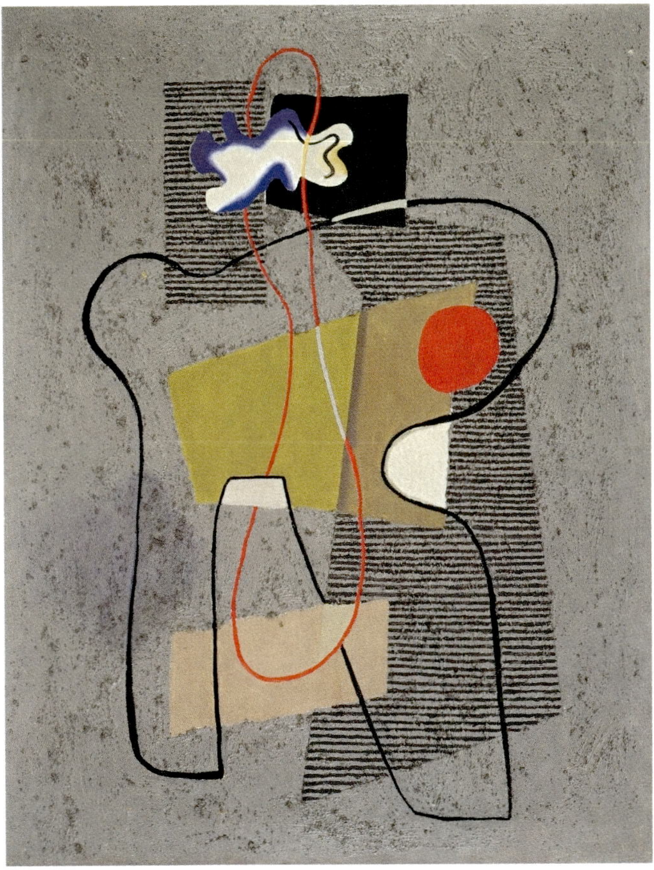

Immediately after the National Socialist seizure of power, on 31 March 1933 Willi Baumeister was dismissed from his teaching post at the Frankfurt Kunstgewerbeschule (School of Applied Arts). He returned to his home city of Stuttgart and survived the time of defamation by retreating into Inner Emigration. In particular, he began to devote himself to the history of prehistoric art and culture. Through reproductions he made the acquaintance of the rock paintings from the Valltorta caves in the Spanish province Castellón, which encouraged him considerably in the further development of his visual language. Up to 1935 he produced the sand reliefs named after this source, whose theme is the subject of the sportsman in motion. He applied to the canvas the typical "painting mush" that he had already developed in the 1920s, a mixture of oil paint, putty filler and sand. Within gaps in this surface he placed the amorphous forms of the moving runners, dancers and jumpers, which gain powerful pictorial monumentality from being embedded deeper within the picture.

Runner, 1934

Oil and sand on canvas,
54 × 65 cm
CR Beye/Baumeister 587

WILLI BAUMEISTER 1889–1955

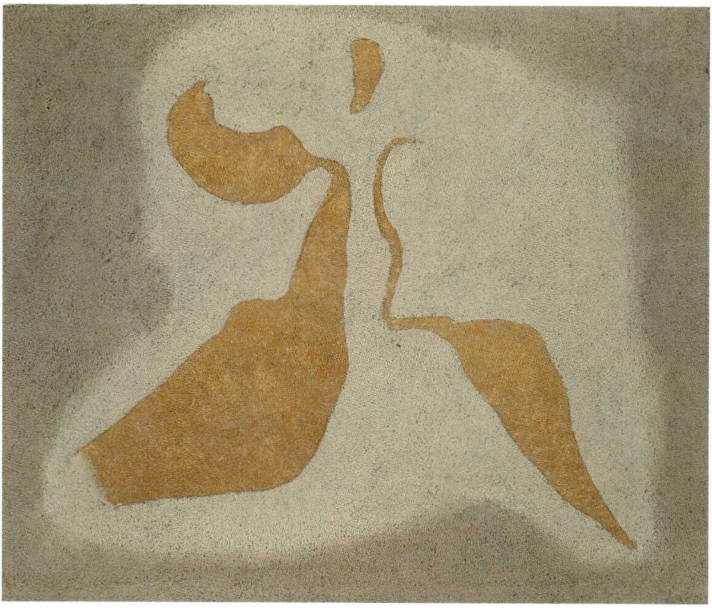

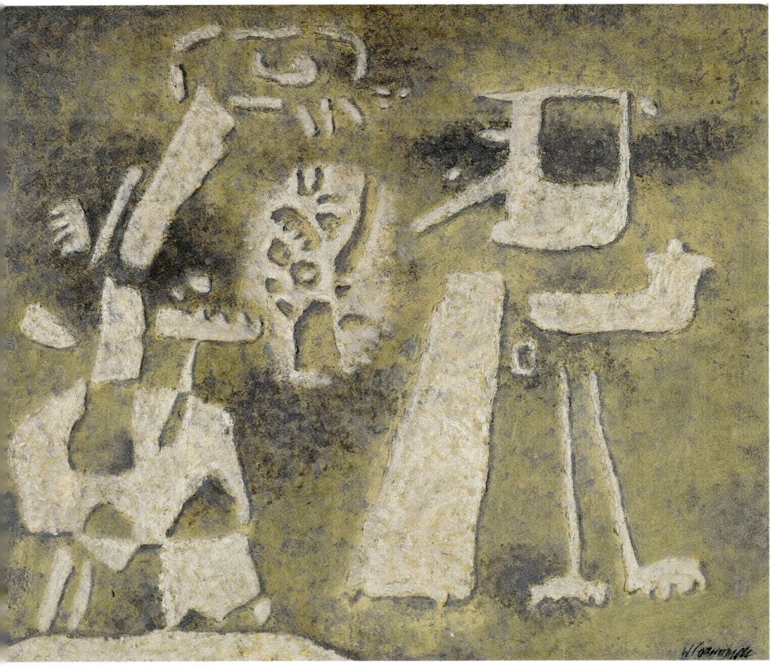

Siduri, the Question, 1951

Oil with synthetic resin and putty on hardboard, 65 × 81 cm
CR Beye/Baumeister 1209

"Presumably I will never again be able to show my pictures at exhibitions. So I will work exclusively for myself, alone," Baumeister noted on 10 March 1941 in his journal. Up to the end of World War II he was involved in research into materials for the Wuppertal paint manufacturer Kurt Herberts, who thus enabled him to survive financially during the time when he was banned from exhibiting and practising his profession. After the "Eidos" pictures of the late 1930s, from 1942 he became preoccupied with the Sumerian epic of *Gilgamesh*. Baumeister was interested in the dialogue between the main figures, which he translated into an abstract-amoebic form. "The figures acquire the significance of symbols. They have become signs. All that is inessential and unnecessary has fallen away." As "independent parallels" to the text, the depictions were intended to support the "motivating force on the viewer's part to create amplifying ideas". As he had done in the early 1930s, Baumeister once again varied his painting technique. The sign as a significant element is now formed from the mass of putty filler, while the picture base again functions clearly as an area.

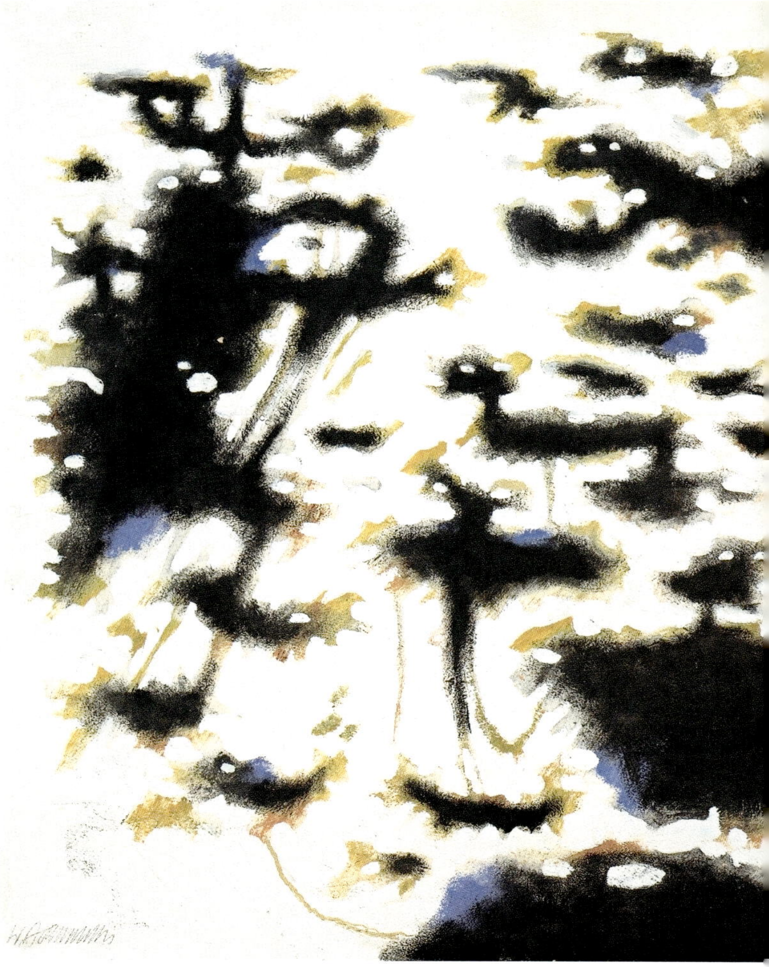

Parallel to the late "Gilgamesh" works, in the early 1950s Baumeister again took decisive steps to alter his vocabulary. True to his concept of the artist as the "witness of his time", he made an intensive study of current artistic tendencies, which led to Informal Painting. Influences from calligraphic art inspired him to a dynamic revival of his pictorial signs, which experienced the high point of their organoid variation in the "Wachstumskräfte". Once again Baumeister changed his painting method. His new pictures, which give the impression of spontaneous gestures, came into being through the layering of two painting levels.

WILLI BAUMEISTER 1889–1955

Wachstumskräfte,
1952/53

Oil with synthetic resin
and tempera on hardboard,
45.1 × 54 cm
CR Beye/Baumeister 1707

First, in "reverse painting", the artist applies the lower layer over the whole area, in a predominantly black tone, which releases the image-determining structures through the gaps left after overpainting in white.

In the last decade of his life, after his defamation and exclusion by the National Socialists, Baumeister received international recognition for his oeuvre following his participation – among other events – in the first "documenta" in 1955 in Kassel.

"The lone Klee student" was Hans Fischli's characterisation in 1968 of the young Fritz Winter, who studied at the Bauhaus in Dessau from 1927 to 1930. His time there served to form and enhance his skills. Less influenced by the idea of the school in total, he entered an intensive dialogue with his teachers Kandinsky and Klee. He used the *sgraffito* technique that he had borrowed from Klee to produce his paintings and drawings including the *Child in a Landscape.* Over a first, multicoloured layer of paint he layed a second, dark brown layer, most of which he scratched away again with the palette knife to form the motif. In this way, as well as by means of linear scratches, he worked out an abstract and two-dimensional motif of a child sitting in a summer meadow. After leaving the Bauhaus, Winter developed his own version of abstract painting. In dark-toned pictures, covered with black lines, he constructs a pantheistic image of nature in mainly large-format works.

Child in a Landscape
(Girl in a Village), 1928

Oil on plywood, 80 × 64.8 cm
CR Lohberg 13

FRITZ WINTER 1905–1976

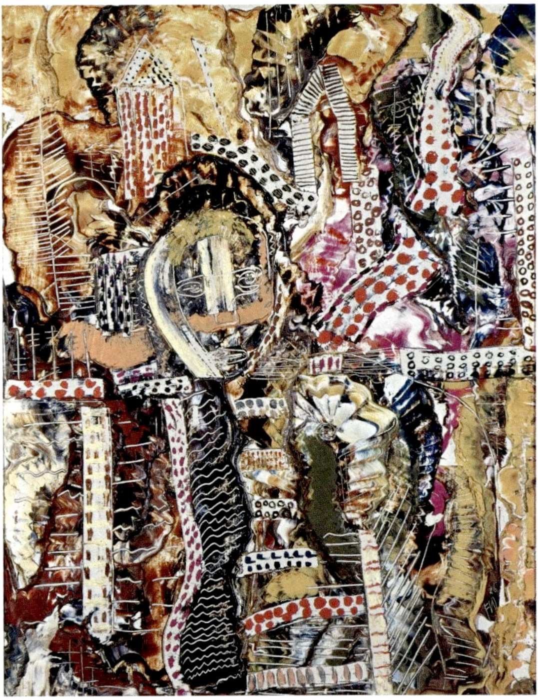

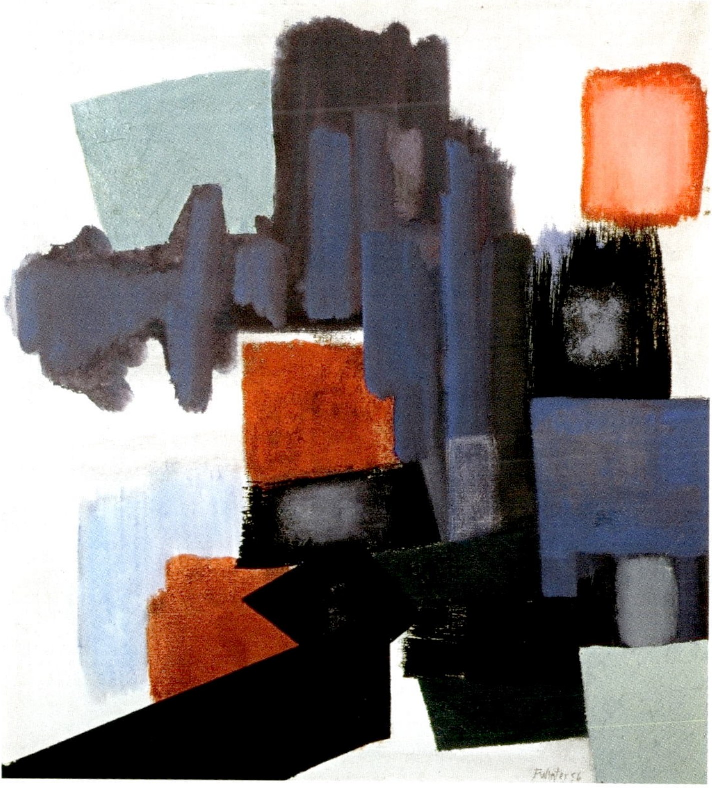

Foehn Wind in the Mountains, 1956

Oil on canvas, 145.4 × 135 cm
CR Lohberg 2092

After being denounced by the National Socialists and banned from painting and exhibiting his work, as well as his war service on the eastern front, from 1945 Fritz Winter became an important representative of non-representational art. As a founder member of the group *ZEN 49* he actively positioned himself in the artistic discourse of postwar West Germany. Following his work of the 1930s, he continually developed his vocabulary up to the end of his life. His predominantly gestural works of the early 1950s were followed by a phase during which he rigidified the forms, in which the motif, as in this painting, *Foehn Wind in the Mountains*, is determined by the application of colour with a thick brush or palette knife. The contrastive effect of the colour in the static forms as well as its arrangement within the space is later modified by the use of softer formations and a general primacy of colour.

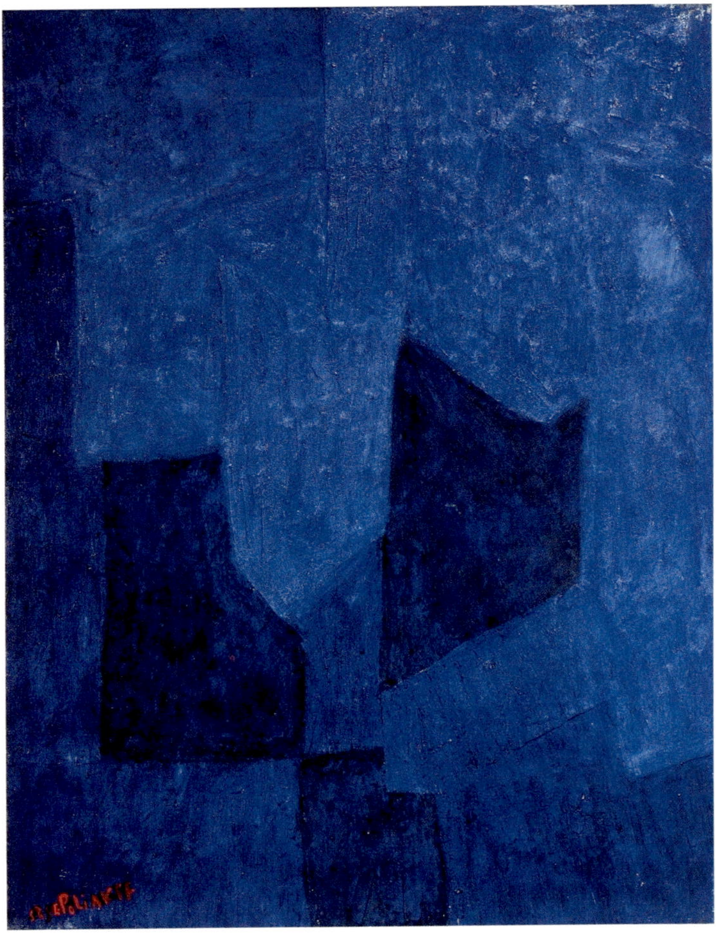

Composition abstrait bleu, 1961

Oil on canvas, 91 × 73 cm
Poliakoff Archive No. 961051

Born in Moscow in 1900, following the 1917 Revolution Serge Poliakoff first fled to Constantinople and then lived in Berlin from 1921 to 1923 before moving to Paris, where he died in 1969. There, as well as in 1936/37 in London, he studied painting.

Stimulated by his encounter with Kandinsky in 1937, he freed himself from narrow academic traditions and moved towards free handling of form and colour. After meeting Robert Delaunay and Otto Freundlich a year later, he achieved a synthesis of the theories of Classical Modernism and then developed his own contribution to a non-representational art. After the end of the war he became one of the most important international representatives of the *École de Paris* and in 1959 and 1964 exhibited at "documenta" in Kassel, as well as in 1962 in the French pavilion at the Venice Biennale.

His painting is determined by recurring geometrical formations, which are dovetailed with each other. From the 1950s he either created these areas in monochrome, in finely graduated values, or combined a few colours, carefully matched to each other. But they always possess an outstanding luminosity, which Poliakoff achieves through very fine, superimposed layers of complementary colours and combinations of various contrasting colours. Thereby he nevertheless works gesturally, leaving behind traces of his application of paint with the spatula, brush or knife.

Free from all links with traditional habits of seeing, his works stand in the context of contemporary existential philosophy and explore new aesthetic forms of perception, in which the 'motif' refers far beyond itself and is a modern emanation of the transcendent.

Composition, c. 1966

Oil and sand on canvas,
35 × 27 cm
Poliakoff Archive No. 966127

SERGE POLIAKOFF 1900–1969

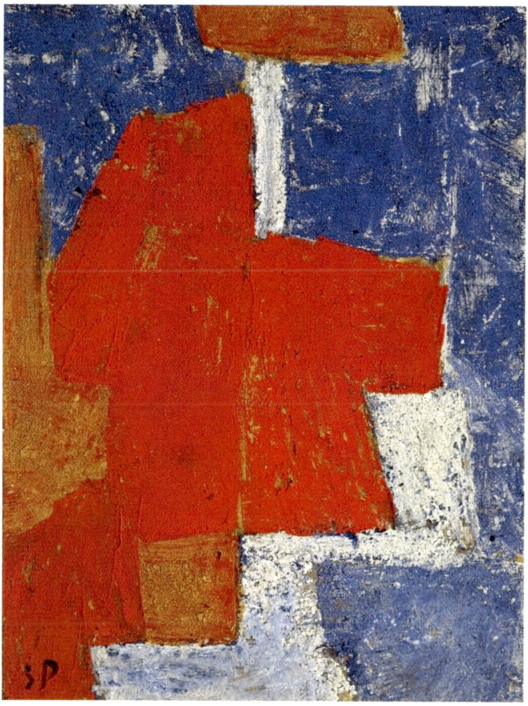

Ernst Wilhelm Nay is among those painters who made a decisive contribution to the developmental path of non-representational art in Germany after 1945. From 1925 up to the start of World War II, he adopted his own form of expressive painting. After being denounced and banned from working by the National Socialists, when the war ended Nay consistently continued to develop it. In the early 1950s, with his "Rhythmic Images", he found a mode of non-representational expression of his own, which was decisively determined by colour and rhythm. This group of works includes his *Rhythms in Blue and Orange*. With an 'all-over' technique Nay covers the surface of the painting with an abstract framework out of the triad of primary colours, structured and accentuated by white and black formations. At the same time as Poliakoff was experimenting in Paris with the transcendental appearance of his colour surfaces, Nay was taking an interest above all in the *Gestaltwert der Farbe* (Structural Value of Colour) – the title of his art-theoretical manifesto published in 1955.

Rhythms in Blue and Orange, 1953

Oil on canvas, 105 × 140.5 cm
CR Scheibler 677

ERNST WILHELM NAY 1902–1968

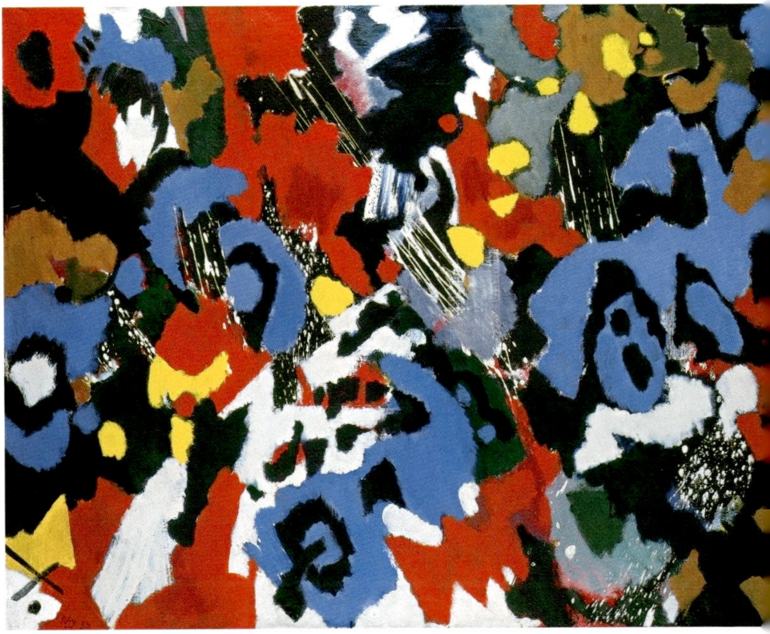

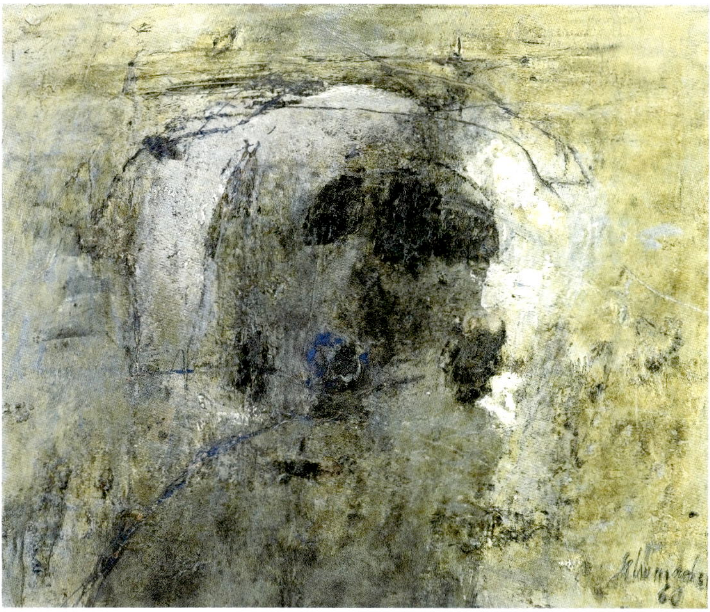

EMIL SCHUMACHER 1912–1999

Emil Schumacher is considered one of the most important German Informal painters. After beginnings in the mimetic representational sphere, within a few years after the end of the war he developed a non-representational pictorial language. In the early 1950s he produced his first abstract painting. "Colours draw forms towards themselves, signs demand colours – by allowing myself to be swept along, I attain my image," the artist commented in 1957. During this time he concentrated in his paintings primarily on one shade of colour, which he allows to take shape in its materiality on the image-bearer. From an accidentally discovered beginning, the painting process becomes a dialogue between the artist's subject and the art object resulting in the composition, which arises decisively from the interplay of colour and scriptorial textures. As in *Lalabo*, Schumacher often uses wooden media, since these hardly soak up the paint, so that he can build up the picture in haptic relief style. The singular materialisation of form and colour thus created opens up to the viewer a wide field of associative dialogue with what can be experienced.

Lalabo, 1960

Oil on wood, 96 × 116 cm

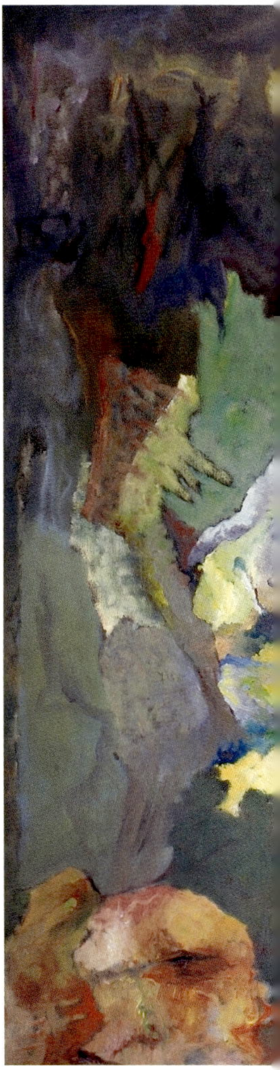

BERNARD SCHULTZE 1915–2005

Medea, 1996

Oil on canvas, 140 × 160 cm

Together with Emil Schumacher and Fred Thieler, Bernard Schultze is among the internationally significant representatives of *Art Informel* in Germany. Completing his education before World War II in Berlin and Düsseldorf, he lost all his early work in a fire at his studio in the spring of 1945. At the beginning of the new decade, however, as a member of the Frankfurt artists' group *Quadriga* he found his own mode of non-representational expression, strongly inspired by Wols and French Tachism. Freed from the political instrumentalising of representational art and driven by the longing to express himself independently and give form

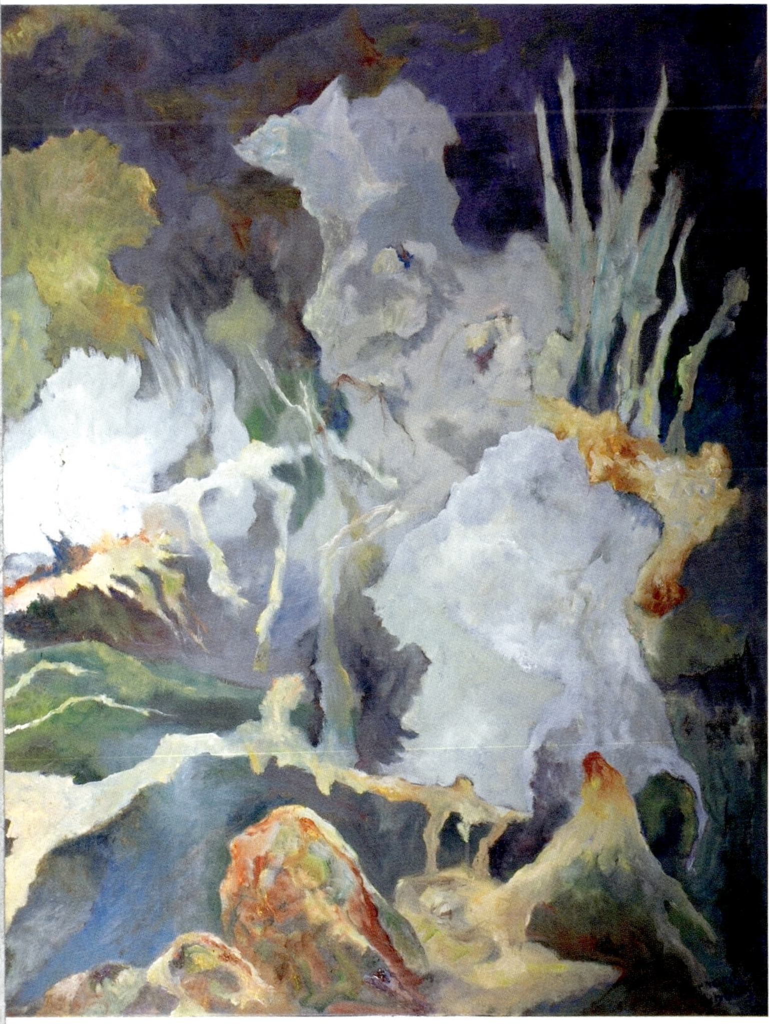

to the fantastic, in the decades that followed, Schultze designed colour-intensive, filigree works on the basis of Surrealist *écriture automatique*. In them the line acquires organically and naturally developed expressive value, and allows the unconscious to assume a shape in vegetative formations.

Medea belongs to the artist's late work, which began in the early 1980s and is characterised by bright, intense colouration as well as large formats, in which he allows his freely associated fantasy landscapes to pass over the canvas.

In 1900, the same year as the Worpswede painter Paula Modersohn-Becker, Hofer made his first trip to Paris. Like her, he was deeply impressed by the work of Paul Cézanne. Nonetheless, it was Hans von Marées whose work decisively affected Hofer's development as an artist. Under the influence of both painters, Hofer developed the carefully structured composition characteristic of his works, which are held together by coloured forms which give them a sense of classical balance. The *Two Girls Dressing* is held in the tension of a rigid arrangement of horizontal, vertical and diagonal lines. Even though the two figures are linked together within the composition, each occupies her own space, lending a static calm to the picture. Created in the early 1940s, the work belongs stylistically to the artist's mature works.

Although Hofer's creative works remain stricly representational and retain a broadly realistic form of expression, his symbolic compositions resulted in 1934 in his dismissal from his post at the Hochschule für Bildende

KARL HOFER 1878–1955

Künste (College of Fine Arts) in Berlin. The National Socialist doctrine denounced his work as "mask-like, empty, grimacing faces"; 313 of his works were removed from public collections as part of the "degenerate art" campaign. After World War II, Hofer was awarded numerous honours and prizes and was appointed Director of the Academy of Fine Arts, where, however, he became involved once more in political-artistic discussions. In the debate regarding the 'right' approach to art in a democratic Germany he proclaimed that he still had "the courage not to be modern". He thus came to represent an art bound up with the object, which since the 1970s has once again begun to assert itself.

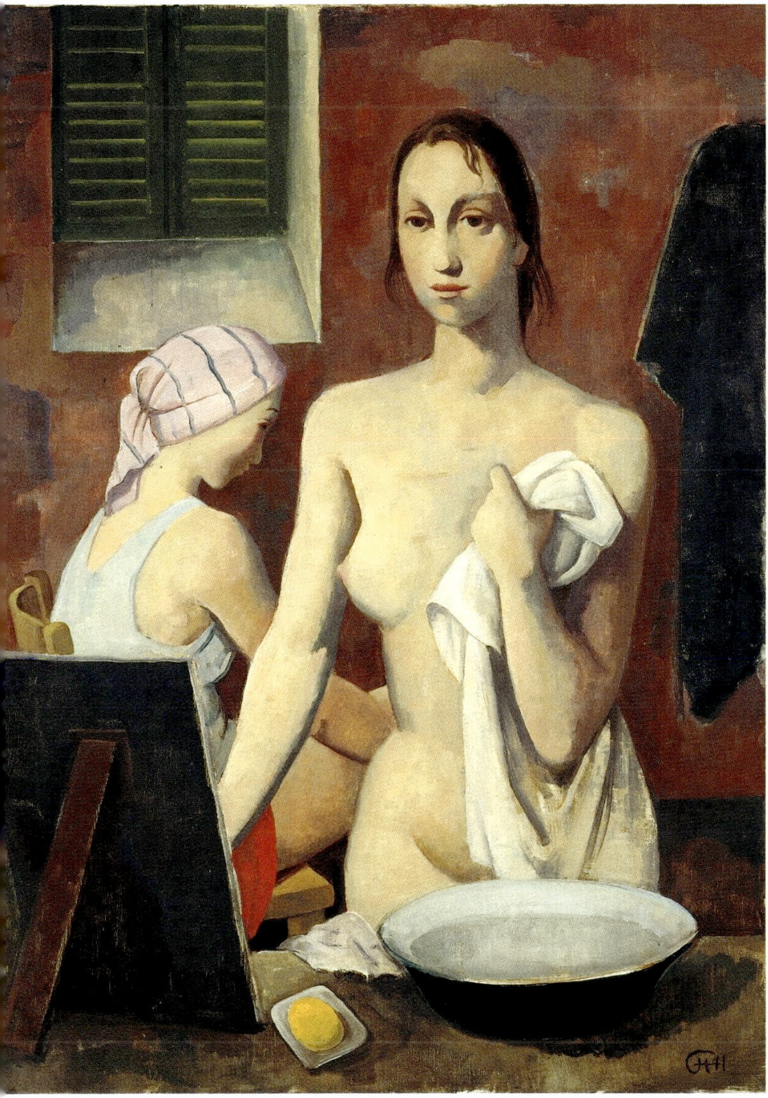

Two Girls Dressing, 1941

Oil on canvas, 98.5 × 75.5 cm
CR Wohlert 1545

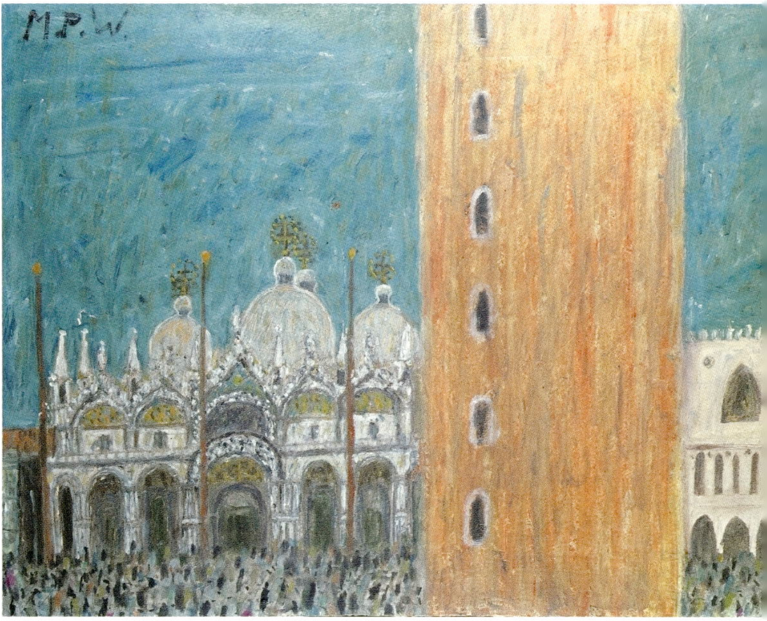

MAX PEIFFER WATENPHUL 1896–1976

Venice – S. Marco, 1947

Oil tempera on cloth-lined board, 52.3 × 70.5 cm
CR Pasqualucci G 373

Max Peiffer Watenphul came to the Bauhaus in Weimar in 1919 on the advice of Paul Klee, and it was there that he acquired his decisive artistic character. A graduate in ecclesiastical law, up to 1922 he concerned himself with the creative work of his teachers, above all that of Johannes Itten, and took a strong interest in the paintings of Jawlensky, whose personal acquaintance he made in 1921. From 1927 to 1931 he taught at the Folkwang Schule (Folkwang Art College) in Essen. After his defamation by the National Socialists he lived from 1946 in Venice; his well-known views align him with the long tradition of painters who have been preoccupied with the special charm of the city in the lagoon. In his paintings and watercolours Peiffer Watenphul records his own view of the city, often supplying unexpected vistas of famous buildings and squares. In this depiction of St Mark's Square the viewer is surprised by the unusual portrayal of the Campanile, which towers vertically through the image and divides it into two parts, with San Marco and the Doges' Palace to both sides.

While non-representational art and American Pop Art dominated national and international exhibitions of the 1950s and 1960s, artists such as Johannes Grützke consciously worked against the current of the time in a figurative, realistic manner. This *Chinese Self-Portrait* was created during his final year of study at the Hochschule für Bildende Künste (College of Fine Arts) in Berlin. Two years earlier, Grützke had been a pupil of Oskar Kokoschka in Salzburg.

In the manner of an expressive sketch, this portrait records the probing gaze with which the artist observes himself and his surroundings, in order to take as his theme the individual and social behaviour of mankind, both realistically and with touches of irony. Apart from the portrait, it is the human body that Grützke repeatedly records in his unusual compositions, often with complicated foreshortening and diagonal positioning of the bodies.

Chinese Self-Portrait, 1964

Oil on cardboard, 55 × 45 cm

JOHANNES GRÜTZKE *1937

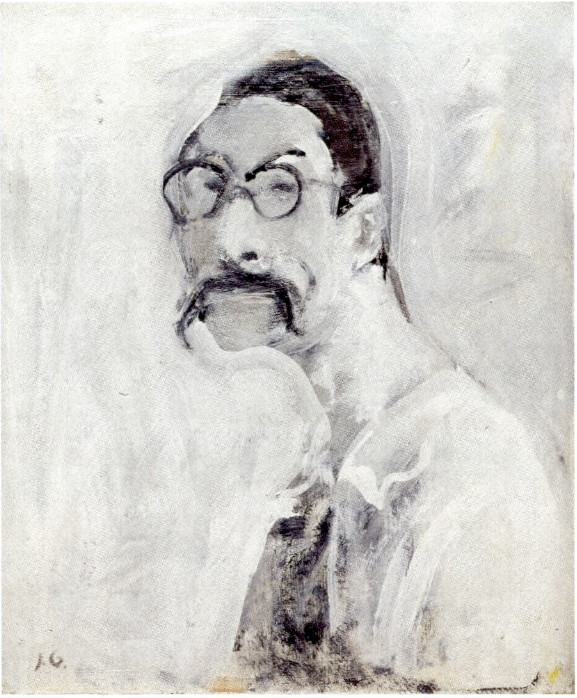

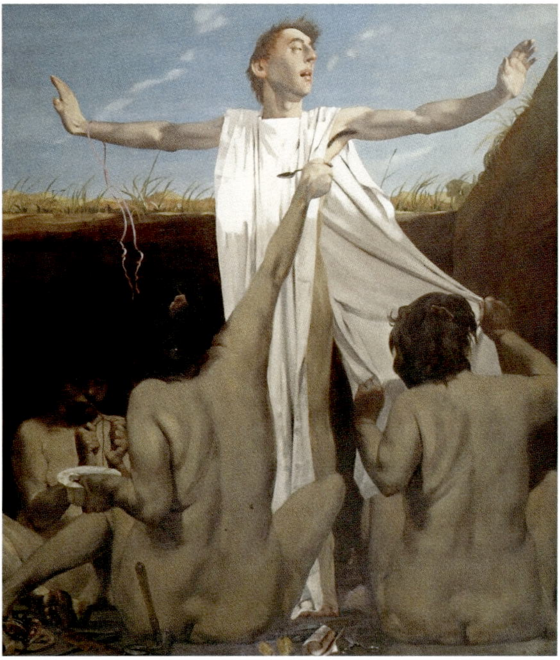

JOHANNES GRÜTZKE *1937

The Education of Alexander, 1978

Oil on canvas, 205 × 180 cm

In 1973 Johannes Grützke, together with three other painters, founded the '*Schule der Neuen Prächtigkeit*' (School of the New Splendour) in his Berlin studio. This loose association of artists was to last for five years. While Grützke's immediate theme is the condition of West German postwar society, which he depicts with touches of irony, in the 1970s he made intense use of allegory as a mode of artistic expression. In large-scale compositions alluding to traditional history painting, he tackles familiar episodes from Western cultural history, in order to stage them as modern allegories in his usual ironic language.

In *The Education of Alexander* he shows the great, world-changing Macedonian king as a young man trapped in a hole in the ground, from which he is being extracted by three women who never look out from the sphere. While they sew his garment and provide him with food, the hero stretches himself; with his outstretched arms and a dazzled look he measures the expanse of the world opening up before him.

During his studies, Grützke earned a living as a scene-shifter in the Theater des Westens in Berlin. During this time he developed an intense commitment to the theatre, which was reflected to a considerable extent in his artistic work. From 1979 he designed a number of stage sets, above all for Peter Zadek's productions at the Deutsches Schauspielhaus in Hamburg. On 2 January 1984 *Die Laube der Seligen* (The Arbour of the Blessed) by Max Hermann-Neisse was premiered at the Schiller-Theater in Berlin under the direction of Klaus Völker. Using the pastel technique of which he was a master, Grützke designed the poster for this one-act play by the Expressionist dramatist, which had already been written in 1907 and published in 1919. From a theatrical view from below, he shows almost life-size images of two of the main characters, as well as two central scenes of the play: the hanged man who gives rise to the plot, as well as the dead Joseph, strangling the young Babette.

Poster Design for 'The Arbour of the Blessed', 1983

Pastel, 150 × 100 cm

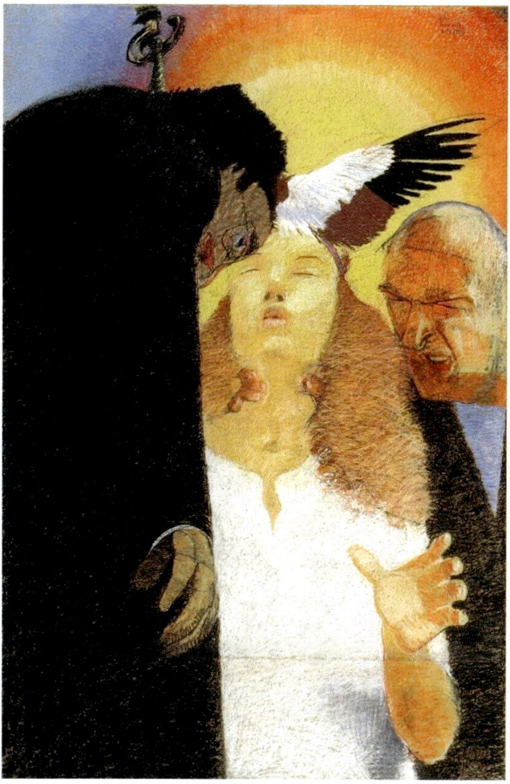

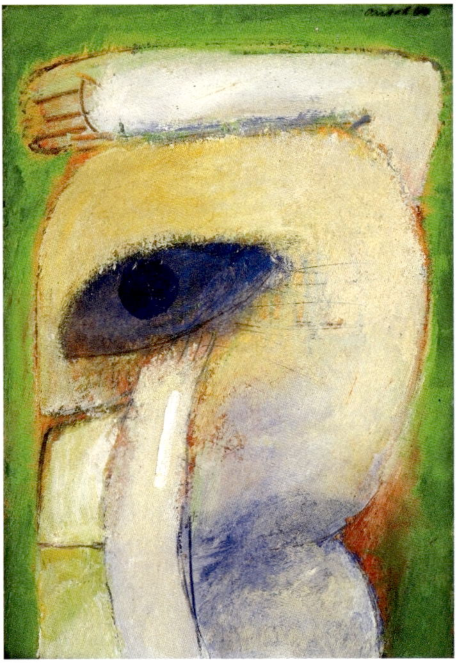

Small White Portrait, 1960/61

Oil on cardboard on wood, 31 × 23.5 cm

HORST ANTES *1936

In the 1960s, like Johannes Grützke, Horst Antes developed his own very individual contribution to representational art of postwar Germany. While the Informal painters were presented internationally as representatives of an intellectually free Germany, within a few years Antes adopted a recurring theme which is still associated with him today: the so-called 'Kopffüssler' or head-footers. As a pupil of HAP Grieshaber at the Kunstakademie Karlsruhe (Karlsruhe Academy of Art), the young painter moved from what were originally expressive formations based on colour to the "figuration" which preoccupied him for more than two decades, composed of individual, archaic-looking, oversize and image-dominating body parts. From an originally Informal colour basis, Antes lets the figure emerge, as in the *Small White Portrait*. The expressively layered application of colour later gives way to an opaque, two-dimensional style, in which Antes restricts himself to a repertoire of primary colours with the addition of green, orange and white. In the second half of the 1960s, he reached the final form of the 'Kopffüssler', which is reduced in its parts to the essential elements of the human body: the head as the seat of thought, and the limbs as the physical preconditions for the implementation of thought.

While the earlier "figurations" were still formed on the basis of Informal painting, the 'Kopffüssler' have acquired an organic firmness and their own space, in which they act in a similar way to human behaviour. They radiate a self-absorbed hieratic calm and arouse in the viewer a sense of "clumsy dignity" (Donald Kuspit). This becomes impressively clear with the *Yellow Figure with Animal*. The life-size yellow 'Kopffüssler', which bursts out of the format of the picture, stands in front of a neutral orange-coloured base, holding in its hands a lifeless white animal. Childishly naïve, natural and different, Antes' 'Kopffüssler' can be perceived as a critique of the mechanistic industrial society of the 1960s.

Yellow Figure with Animal (Orange), 1986

Aquatec on canvas, 179.4 × 130 cm

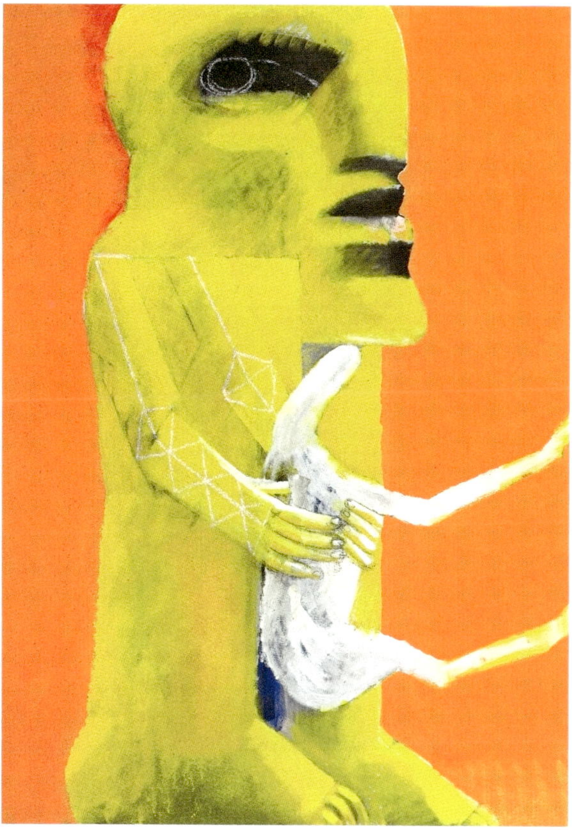

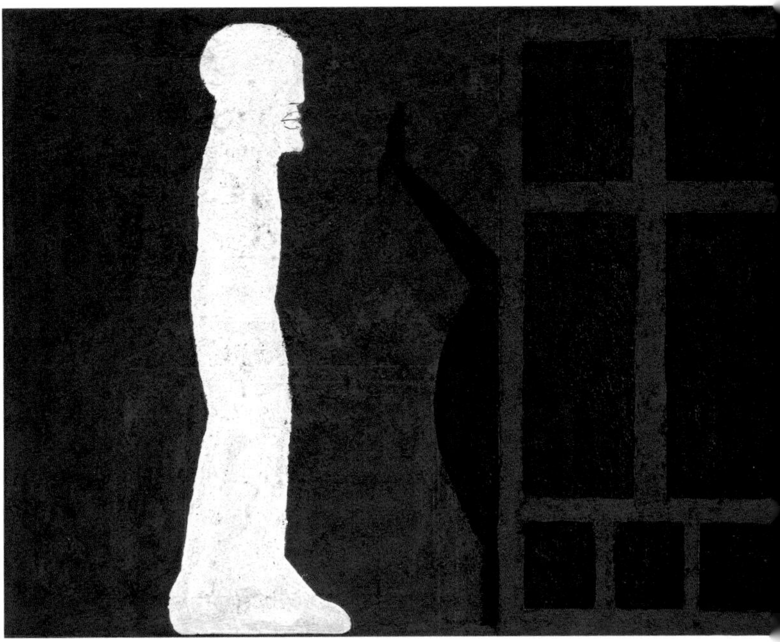

After more than two decades of intense preoccupation with the figure of the 'Kopffüssler', Horst Antes created his first painting of a house in 1986, thus establishing a new motif which he employed over a number of years in the form of serial works. The strangely homeless 'Kopffüssler', apparently always in search of something, has acquired a dwelling that could offer protection and seclusion to the vulnerable-looking creature. In a transition of motifs around 1987/88, the artist showed the successors to the 'Kopffüssler', the so-called 'pattern figures' linked with houses. Outside or indoors, they appear in a new environment.
A totally altered colouration is evident: it is no longer the brilliant, intense tones of the 'Kopffüssler' period that dominate, but dark, muted colours, mainly grey tones with black or blue. At the core of the series, the house emerges in almost anthropomorphic form, acquiring figurative human qualities while apparently developing its own individuality, and arousing emotional reactions in the viewer in its compositional structure, just as the 'Kopffüssler' does. These house paintings achieve their special effect through a radical reduction of the apparatus of forms and a strictly harmonised composition. Moreover, the roof, unexpectedly, is most often coloured blue; a fact attributed to Antes' intensive preoccupation with the culture of the Navajo Indians, for whom the roof does not hermetically seal off the human habitation, but rather, through its colour, opens it heavenward into the transcendental. Thus the house becomes a metaphor; houses become "images of meditation and contemplation" (Eberhard Roters).

White Standing Figure, Black Berlin Window, Bird, 1987

Aquatec and graphite on wood, 30 × 40 cm

HORST ANTES *1936

The House of the Marquesa de la Solana, 1989/90

Aquatec on wood, 30 × 40 cm

Klaus Fussmann is a painter of the same generation as Grützke and Antes. From the late 1960s he too has made his own independent contribution to postwar representational painting. Like his colleagues, he developed his pictorial language from initially *Art Informel* beginnings after studying at the Folkwang Schule (Folkwang Art College) in Essen and the Hochschule für Bildende Künste (College of Fine Arts) in Berlin. "Ragende Figuren" (Towering Figures) is his name for his attempts from 1963 on to create a new representational painting style. In memorable still-life arrangements he lends a remarkable presence to the object in his painting, which in its unpretentiousness describes the poetry of the mundane. Thus the artist is motivated by ensembles in his studio, by the appearance of painted walls or even the frozen moment of a garbage heap. As in this *Interior*, during the 1970s it is objects of his everyday working world as an artist to which he repeatedly gives shape in expressive directness.

Interior, 1979

Oil on canvas, 92 × 99 cm

KLAUS FUSSMANN *1938

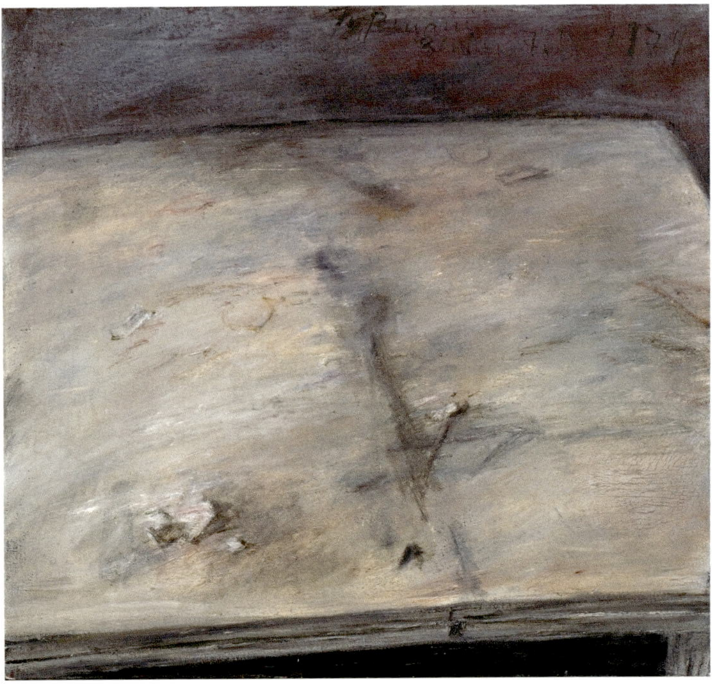

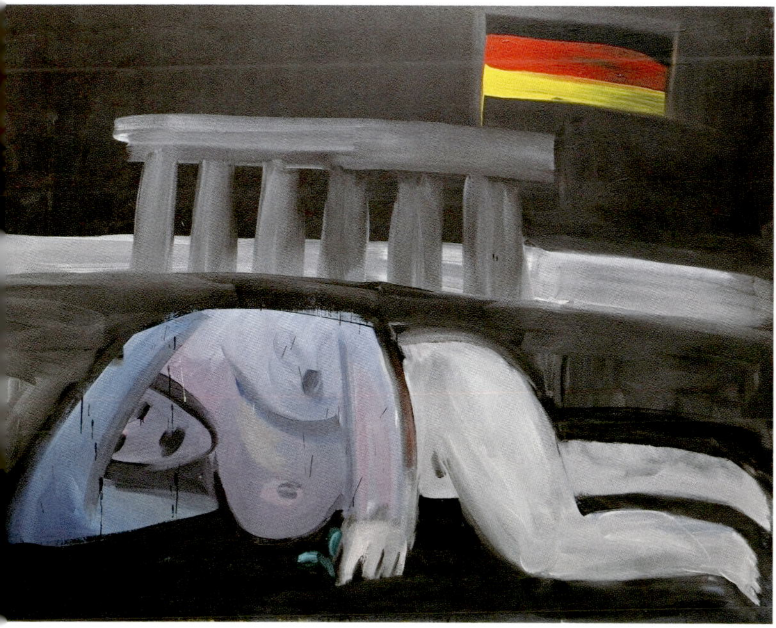

KARL HORST HÖDICKE *1938

A member of the same generation as Grützke and Antes, Karl Horst Hödicke also initially developed his painting from Informal beginnings as they did, as a clear counter-position to the abstraction dominating art. In 1964 he was a founder member of the producers' gallery at Grossgörschen 35 in Berlin, a disparate group of artists united by an explicit declaration of adherence to representational art. Hödicke lived in Berlin on completing his studies, and was active in a wide variety of artistic contexts. Nonetheless he returned time and again to painting, taking as his theme in expressive form "everyday myths", social conditions and the immediate German contemporary scene. In the mid-1980s he created the "Berliner Ring" works, which determinedly examine the division of Germany. In the quick painting technique characteristic of his work, with radically thinned paint, Hödicke created the *Sleep of Freedom* in 1986. A female figure rests in front of the Berlin Wall and the Brandenburg Gate with the German flag; protecting the (still) tender shoot of freedom.

Sleep II
(Sleep of Freedom),
1986

Synthetic resin on canvas,
170 × 230 cm

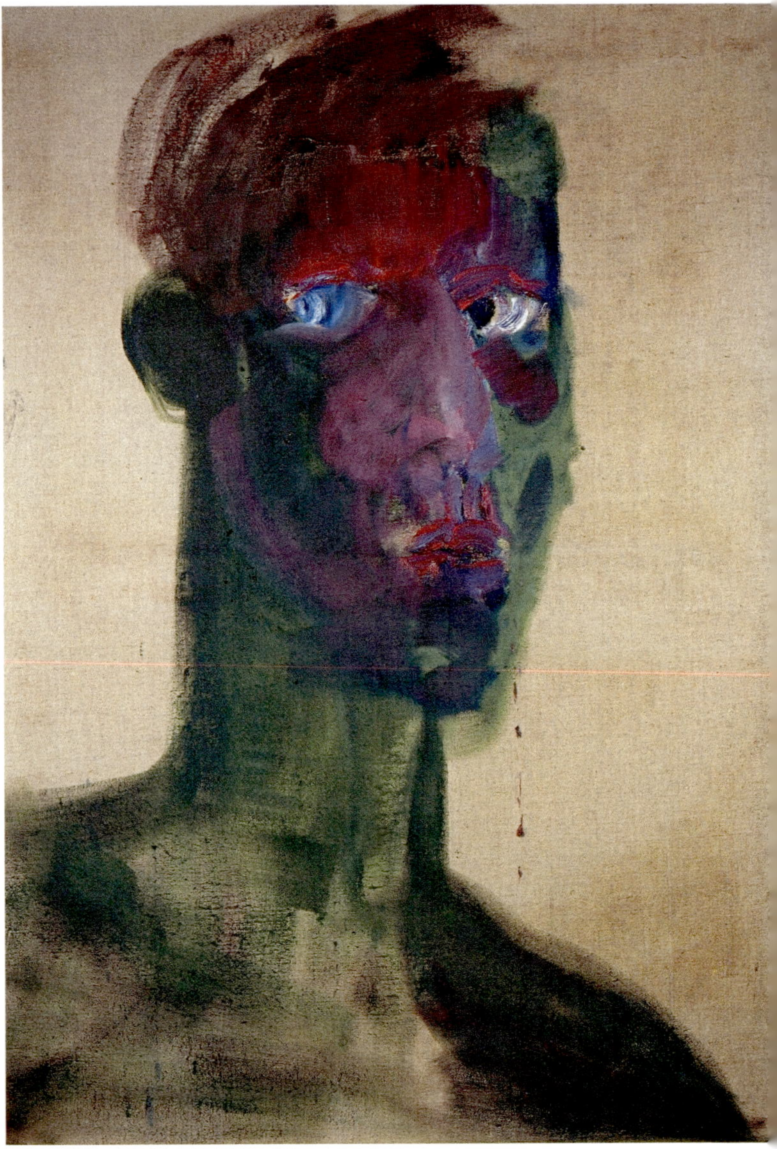

Self – Raw, 1989

Oil on canvas, 120 × 90 cm

Around 1980, in Berlin, Cologne and Düsseldorf, a young generation of artists came to public notice. They dedicated themselves with determination to painting, the medium that was continually declared dead. The 'Neue Wilde' (New Wild Ones) presented their work, which is marked by a directly expressive language, in the form of large-format canvases.
Rainer Fetting, a pupil of Hödicke, was one of these artists who broke with the bourgeois conventions of postwar society. Today he still works representationally, choosing as his themes human figures as well as the urban landscapes of Berlin and New York, where he lived between 1982 and 1994. Yet it is his confrontation with his own ego that runs through his work.
The title of the present painting is programmatic: *Self – Raw* shows the sceptically questioning gaze of the painter as he looks at himself. On a raw canvas he applies a minimum of paint to display with fierce expressiveness his head-and-shoulders portrait, worked out in detail only in the areas of the organs of the

RAINER FETTING *1949

senses, eyes, nose and mouth. What remains is the shifting impression of a modern existence, which had become questionable by the end of the twentieth century.

APPENDIX

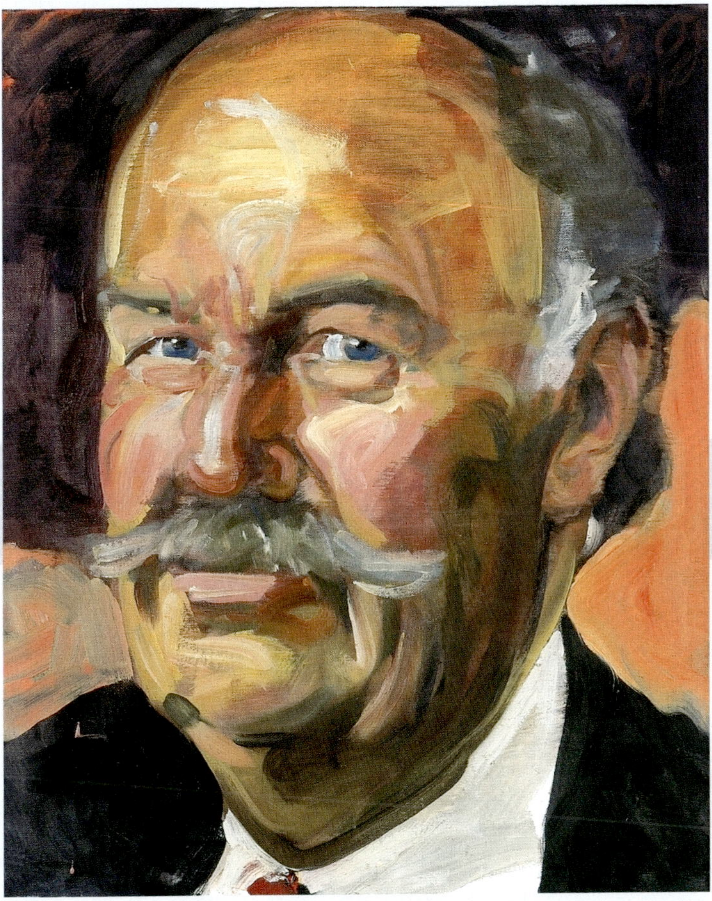

Johannes Grützke,
Portrait of
Dr Alfred Gunzenhauser,
12. 10. 1991, oil on canvas,
60 × 40 cm

LIST OF ARTISTS

The names in **bold type** refer to artists discussed in the museum guide.

Alt, Otmar
Altenbourg, Gerhard (i.e. Gerhard Ströch)
Antes, Horst
Arnold, Karl
Auriol, Georges
Averbuch, Ilan

Bachem, Bele
Baj, Enrico
Balet, Jan
Baluschek, Hans
Bargheer, Eduard
Baudrexel, Eduard
Bauer, Friedrich Franz
Baumeister, Willi
Becher, Bernd and Hilla
Bechtold, Erwin
Beckmann, Max
Behmer, Marcus
Bellmer, Hans
Berke, Hubert
Berrocal, Miguel
Blomberg, Hugo von
Bluth, Manfred
Bonnard, Pierre
Brummack, Heinrich
Bubenik, Gernot
Buchheister, Carl

Campendonk, Heinrich
Cavael, Rolf
Chadwick, Lynn Russell
Chillida, Eduardo
Christiansen, Hans
Christo, Javacheff
Corinth, Lovis
Czeschka, Carl Otto

Dahmen, Karl-Fred
Dalí, Salvador
Deimling, Rolf
Denis, Maurice
Diener, Christian
Diez, Julius
Dittrich, Simon
Dix, Otto
Döring, Adam Lude
Dollhausen, Jack

Ebert, Albert
Ehmsen, Heinrich
Ehrich, Otto
Eichler, Reinhold Max
Erbslöh, Adolf
Erler, Fritz
Erté (i.e. Romain de Tirtoff)
Evenepoel, Henri Jacques Edouard

Fani, Mario
Fassianos, Alecos
Feininger, Lyonel
Feješ, Emerik
Felixmüller, Conrad
Fetting, Rainer
Fife, Scott
Filonov, Pavel Nikolaevich
Francis, Sam
Francois, André
Fußmann, Klaus

Geiger, Rupprecht
Geiger, Willi
Georgi, Walter
Geyling, Remigius
Gill, Madge
Gontscharova, Natalia
Grabmayr, Franz
Grethe, Carlos
Griebel, Otto
Grieshaber, HAP
Grossmann, Rudolf
Grosz, George
Grützke, Johannes
Guimard, Hector
Gulbransson, Olaf

Haas, Michael
Habermann, Hugo von
Hain, Erhard
Heckel, Erich
Heckelmann, Ernst
Heine, Thomas Theodor
Heldt, Werner
Hilsing, Werner
Hockney, David
Hödicke, Karl Horst
Hoehme, Gerhard
Hölzel, Adolf
Hofer, Karl
Hofmann, Ludwig von
Hohenlohe-Oehringen, Feodora zu
Holtz, Karl
Hoppe, Emil
Hrdlicka, Alfred
Hubbuch, Karl
Hussel, Horst

Itten, Johannes

Jäger, Bernhard
Janssen, Horst
Jawlensky, Alexej von
Jurak, Drago

Kaletsch, Clemens
Kalinowski, Horst Egon
Kampehl, Peter
Kampmann, Gustav
Kandinsky, Wassily
Kanoldt, Alexander
Kaus, Max
Kirchner, Ernst Ludwig
Kirchner, Eugen
Klauke, Jürgen
Kley, Heinrich
Klimt, Gustav
Klose, Walter
Kobell, Ferdinand
Kogan, Moissey
Kohlem, Horst
Kokoschka, Oskar
Kolář, Jiři
Kolbe, Carl Wilhelm
Kolle, Helmut
Koller, Oskar
Kollwitz, Käthe
Krain, Willibald
Kramm, Willibald
Krenek, Carl
Krieg, Dieter
Kubin, Alfred
Küchenmeister, Rainer

Lablais, Michael
Lange, Otto
Lasserre, Juliette
Lausen, Uwe
Lebisch, Franz
Lemmen, Georges
Lenk, Franz
Likarz-Strauss, Maria

Macke, August
Mangold, Joseph
Mapplethorpe, Robert
Marquet, Albert
Marschand, Gerd
Matisse, Henri
Mayrshofer, Max
Meidner, Ludwig
Melzer, Moritz
Menzel, Adolf von
Metzinger, Jean
Meunier, Constantin Emile
Meyer-Amden, Otto
Minne, George
Modersohn-Becker, Paula
Moll, Oskar
Morgner, Wilhelm
Moser, Koloman
Mühlbeck, Joseph
Müller, Bettina
Münter, Gabriele
Münzer, Adolf
Muche, Georg
Munch, Edvard

Nägele, Reinhold
Nagel, Bill
Naujoks, Heino
Nay, Ernst Wilhelm
Neher, Caspar
Neubrand, Otto
Neuhaus, Uwe
Neumann, Max
Niemeyer, Adelbert
Nolde, Emil

Olbrich, Joseph Maria
Orlik, Emil

Pankok, Bernhard
Paul, Bruno
Pavlos (i.e. Pavlos Dionyssopoulos)
Pechstein, Hermann Max
Peiffer Watenphul, Max
Pichler, Walter
Poliakoff, Serge
Preetorius, Emil
Preiss, Karl
Preissig, Vojtěch
Prem, Heimrad
Profanter, Maria
Putz, Leo

Rabbow, Heinz
Rabuzin, Ivan
Räderscheidt, Anton
Radziwill, Franz
Raffler, Max
Rainer, Arnulf
Richter, Gerhard
Rickey, George
Rießbeck, Gerhard
Ringelnatz, Joachim
Rippl-Rónai, József
Ritschl, Otto
Rohlfs, Christian
Rysselberghe, Theo van

Sagert, Horst
Salzmann, Gottfried
Scheurich, Paul
Schiele, Egon
Schilling, Erich
Schlabitz, Adolf
Schlemmer, Oskar
Schmidt-Rottluff, Karl
Schmitz, Richard
Schmoll von Eisenwerth, Karl
Schneider, Herbert
Schöellhorn, Hans
Schrimpf, Georg
Schröder-Sonnenstern, Friedrich
Schultze, Bernard
Schultze-Bluhm, Ursula
Schulz, Wilhelm
Schulz-Rumpold, Volkmar
Schumacher, Emil
Schwitters, Kurt
Searle, Roland
Serra, Richard
Sintenis, Renée
Skarbina, Franz
Skurjeni, Mato
Sonderborg, K. R. H.
Steinlen, Theophile
Steinmeyer, Gottfried
Stepan, Bogomir
Stöckl, Rupert
Stöcklin, Nikolaus
Stöver, Dieter
Strathmann, Carl
Strawalde (i.e. Jürgen Böttcher)
Stuck, Franz von
Stuckenberg, Fritz

Taschner, Ignatius
Taschner, Maja
Tatafiore, Ernesto
Thieler, Fred
Thöny, Eduard
Toorop, Jan
Toulouse-Lautrec, Henri de

Uhlig, Max
Unger, Hans
Vallatton, Felix
Vennekampf, Johannes
Vogeler, Heinrich

Wagner, Reiner
Walser, Karl
Warhol, Andy
Wasserburger, C. A. (i.e. Alexander Hatzl)
Weinhold, Felix
Weiss, Emil Rudolf
Westpfahl, Conrad
Wilke, Erich
Winter, Fritz
Wischeropp, Elisabeth
Wunderwald, Gustav

Zille, Heinrich
Zimmer, Hans Peter
Zimmermann, Mac
Zush (i.e. Alberto Porta)

BIBLIOGRAPHY

Deutsche Malerei des 20. Jahrhunderts. Ansichten eines Privatsammlers, exhib. cat., Herwig Guratzsch and Ulf Küster (eds.), Museum der bildenden Künste, Leipzig, 1. 10. 1998–3. 1. 1999, Ostfildern-Ruit 1998.

Halbwelt auf Papier. Otto Dix und Conrad Felixmüller aus einer deutschen Privatsammlung, exhib. cat., Herwig Guratzsch and Thomas Gädeke (eds.), Stiftung Schleswig-Holsteinische Landesmuseen Schloss Gottorf, 4. 6.–13. 8. 2000, Museum der Bildenden Künste Leipzig, 6. 9.–5. 11. 2000, Ostfildern-Ruit 2000.

Kunstsammlungen Chemnitz – Museum Gunzenhauser, Christiane Borgelt, Regina Jost (text), Werner Huthmacher (photos). Berlin 2007 (= Neue Architekturführer, vol. 117).

Berend-Corinth, Charlotte: *Lovis Corinth. Die Gemälde. Neu bearbeitet von Béatrice Hernad*, 2nd revised edition, Munich 1992.

Beye, Peter and Felicitas Baumeister: *Willi Baumeister. Werkkatalog der Gemälde*, publ. by Archiv Baumeister. 2 vols, Ostfildern-Ruit 2002.

Chabert, Philippe: *Helmut Kolle 1899–1931. Catalogue raisonné de l'œuvre peint*, phil. diss. Paris I, Sorbonne, 2 vols., Paris 1981.

Felixmüller, Titus: *Conrad Felixmüller. Monographie und Werkverzeichnis der Gemälde*, Heinz Spielmann (ed.), Cologne 1996.

Göpel, Barbara and Erhard: *Max Beckmann. Katalog der Gemälde*, commissioned by the Max-Beckmann-Gesellschaft, Hans Martin von Erffa (ed), 2 vols., Berne 1976.

Gordon, Donald E.: *Ernst Ludwig Kirchner. Mit einem kritischen Katalog sämtlicher Gemälde*, Munich 1968.

Grohmann, Will: *Karl Schmidt-Rottluff*, Stuttgart 1965.

Hofmann, Karl-Ludwig and Christmut Praeger: *Georg Schrimpf und Maria Uhden. Leben und Werk*, Berlin 1985.

Alexej von Jawlensky. Catalogue Raisonné of the Oil Paintings. Maria Jawlensky, Lucia Pieroni-Jawlensky and Angelica Jawlensky Bianconi (eds.), 3 vols., Munich 1991–93.

Karsch, Florian: *Otto Dix. Das graphische Werk*, Hannover 1970.

Köcke, Ulrike: *Christian Rohlfs. Œuvre-Katalog der Gemälde*, Paul Vogt (ed.), Recklinghausen 1978.

Löffler, Fritz: *Otto Dix 1891–1969. Œuvre der Gemälde*, Recklinghausen 1981.

Lohberg, Gabriele: *Fritz Winter – Leben und Werk. Mit einem Werkverzeichnis der Gemälde*, Munich 1986.

Lorenz, Ulrike: *Otto Dix. Das Werkverzeichnis der Zeichnungen und Pastelle*, publ. by the Otto-Dix-Stiftung, Vaduz. 8 vols., Weimar 2003.

Paula Modersohn-Becker 1876–1907. Werkverzeichnis der Gemälde, publ. by the Paula Modersohn-Becker-Stiftung, Günter Busch and Wolfgang Werner (eds.), 2 vols., Munich 1998.

Pfäffle, Suse: *Otto Dix. Werkverzeichnis der Aquarelle und Gouachen*, Stuttgart 1991.

Reinhardt, Hildegard: *Gustav Wunderwald (1882–1945). Untersuchungen zum bildkünstlerischen Gesamtwerk*, Hildesheim, Zürich, New York 1988.

Scheibler, Aurel: *Ernst Wilhelm Nay. Werkverzeichnis der Ölgemälde*, publ. by the Museum Ludwig, Cologne, Cologne 1990.

Schulze, Rainer W.: *Franz Radziwill 1895–1983. Monographie und Werkverzeichnis*, Andrea Firmenich (ed.), Cologne 1995.

Söhn, Gerhart: *Conrad Felixmüller. Das graphische Werk 1912–1977*, 2nd improved edition, Düsseldorf 1987.

Vogt, Paul: *Erich Heckel*, Recklinghausen 1965.

Wandschneider, Andrea and Barbara Alms (eds.): *Fritz Stuckenberg 1881–1944*. exhib. cat. Delmenhorst, Berlin, Neuss with an index of the paintings, Berlin 1993.

Watenphul Pasqualucci, Grace and Alessandra Pasqualucci: *Max Peiffer Watenphul. Werkverzeichnis*. vol. 1: paintings, watercolours, Cologne 1989.

Wohlert, Karl Bernhard: *Karl Hofer. Werkverzeichnis*. vol. 1: paintings. Cologne 2007 [in preparation].

IMPRINT

Published by
Kunstsammlungen Chemnitz
MUSEUM GUNZENHAUSER

Idea and concept: Ingrid Mössinger, Thomas Friedrich

Texts: Thomas Friedrich

Photograph credits:
p. 23f., 80, 87, 95, 120f.,142, 187: PUNCTUM/Bertram Kober; p. 48: Rosmarie Nohr, Munich; p. 19: László Tóth, Chemnitz; p. 27: Thomas Friedrich, Chemnitz;
all other illustrations: Archive Stiftung Gunzenhauser, Chemnitz.

The publisher and Prestel Verlag have made every effort to trace all copyright owners. If there are any omissions, please contact Prestel Verlag or the Museum Gunzenhauser.

Library of Congress Control Number: 2007940038

British Library Cataloguing-in-Publication Data

A catalogue record for this book is available from the British Library; Deutsche Nationalbibliothek holds a record of this publication in the Deutschen National-bibliografie; detailed biblio-graphical data can be found under http://dnb.ddb.de.

Cover illustration:
Otto Dix: Self-Portrait with Walker's Hat, 1912
(see p. 78).

Prestel Verlag
Königinstrasse 9
D-80539 Munich
Tel.: +49 (89) 24 29 08-300
Fax.: +49 (89) 24 29 08-335
www.prestel.de

Prestel Publishing Ltd.
4, Bloomsbury Place
London, WC1A 2Qa
Tel.: +44 (020) 7323 5004
Fax.: +44 (020) 7636 8004

Prestel Publishing
900 Broadway, Suite 603
New York, NY 10003
Tel.: +1 (212) 995 2720
Fax.: ++1 (212) 995 2733
www.prestel.com

Copy-edited by:
Jane Michael, Munich

Translated from the German by:
Christine Shuttleworth, London

Cover design:
SOFAROBOTNIK, Augsburg & Munich

Design, layout and typesetting by:
a.visus, Michael Hempel, Munich

Production:
Sebastian Runow

Lithography:
Reproline Mediateam, Munich

Printing and binding:
Passavia, Passau

Printed in Germany on acid-free paper

ISBN 978-3-7913-3841-5
(German edition)

ISBN 978-3-7913-3842-2
(English edition)

MUSEUM INFORMATION

Opening hours

Tuesday – Friday
12.00 – 7.00 p.m.

Saturday, Sunday, Public holidays
11.00 a.m. – 7.00 p.m.

Closed:
24 and 31 December

How to reach us

The Museum Gunzenhauser is five minutes' walk from the centre of Chemnitz.

Rail:
Hauptbahnhof
(Chemnitz main station)

Bahnhof Chemnitz-Mitte
(Chemnitz central station)

Tram:
Tram stop Falkeplatz
Tram no. 2, 4

Bus:
Bus stop Falkeplatz
Bus no. 31

City-centre tram stop five minutes' walk from the museum

Service

Entry tickets and audio guides to the museum are available in the foyer of the Falkeplatz entrance, as well as a variety of publications about the Kunstsammlungen Chemnitz and the Museum Gunzenhauser. There is also a small cafeteria serving refreshments.

The building is accessible to visitors with restricted mobility. The exhibition floors can be reached via the main staircase and lift.

Kunstsammlungen Chemnitz
MUSEUM GUNZENHAUSER

Falkeplatz | Chemnitz
Germany

Postal address and access for wheelchair users:
Stollberger Straße 2 | 09119 Chemnitz

Kunstsammlungen Chemnitz

General Director: Ingrid Mössinger
Secretary/Assistance: Margit Mothes, Anja Richter
Theaterplatz 1 | 09111 Chemnitz
Germany
Tel.: +49 (371) 488 44 - 01/02
Fax: +49 (371) 488 44 - 99
kunstsammlungen@stadt-chemnitz.de

MUSEUM GUNZENHAUSER

Curator: Thomas Friedrich
Secretary: Beatrice Groh
Tel.: +49 (371) 488 70 - 01
Fax: +49 (371) 488 70 - 99
gunzenhauser@stadt-chemnitz.de

www.kunstsammlungen-chemnitz.de

Press contact/Marketing:
Silke Röhling
Tel.: +49 (371) 488 44 - 74
Fax: +49 (371) 488 44 - 99

Public relations/Events: Jörg Ivandic
Tel.: +49 (371) 488 44 - 23
Fax: +49 (371) 488 44 - 98

General information:

Museum Gunzenhauser (Ticket office)
Tel.: +49 (371) 488 70 - 24

Kunstsammlungen Chemnitz (Ticket office)
Tel.: +49 (371) 488 44 - 24